FROM THE **G**RADUATE **M**ANAGEMENT **A**DMISSION **C**OUNCIL®

W9-DEC-091

THE **OFFICIAL** GUIDE FOR

GMAT®

2015

QUANTITATIVE
REVIEW

NEW! Create your own practice sets online

NEW! Exclusive online videos with study tips and test-taking strategies

300 Problem Solving and Data Sufficiency questions and answer explanations

THE OFFICIAL GUIDE FOR GMAT® QUANTITATIVE REVIEW 2015

For general information on our other products and services or to obtain technical support please contact our Customer Care Department within the U.S. at (877) 762-2974, outside the U.S. at (317) 572-3993 or fax (317) 572-4002.

Wiley also publishes its books in a variety of electronic formats. Some content that appears in print may not be available in electronic books. For more information about Wiley products, please visit our Web site at www.wiley.com.

ISBN: 978-1-118-91414-4 (pbk); ISBN 978-1-118-91416-8 (ePDF); ISBN 978-1-118-91415-1 (ePub)

Printed in the United States of America

10 9 8 7 6 5 4 3 2 1

Updates to this book are available on the Downloads tab at this site: http://www.wiley.com/go/gmat2015updates.

Table of Contents

Visit gmat.wiley.com to access web-based supplemental features available in the print book as well. There you can access a question bank with customizable practice sets and answer explanations using 300 Problem Solving and Data Sufficiency questions and review topics like Arithmetic, Algebra, Geometry, and Word Problems. Watch exclusive videos stressing the importance of big data skills in the real world and offering insight into math skills necessary to be successful on the Quantitative section of the exam.

1.0   What Is the GMAT®?

1.0 What Is the GMAT®?

The Graduate Management Admission Test® (GMAT®) is a standardized, three-part test delivered in English. The test was designed to help admissions officers evaluate how suitable individual applicants are for their graduate business and management programs. It measures basic verbal, mathematical, and analytical writing skills that a test taker has developed over a long period of time through education and work.

The GMAT test does not measure a person's knowledge of specific fields of study. Graduate business and management programs enroll people from many different undergraduate and work backgrounds, so rather than test your mastery of any particular subject area, the GMAT test will assess your acquired skills. Your GMAT score will give admissions officers a statistically reliable measure of how well you are likely to perform academically in the core curriculum of a graduate business program.

Of course, there are many other qualifications that can help people succeed in business school and in their careers—for instance, job experience, leadership ability, motivation, and interpersonal skills. The GMAT test does not gauge these qualities. That is why your GMAT score is intended to be used as one standard admissions criterion among other, more subjective, criteria, such as admissions essays and interviews.

1.1 Why Take the GMAT® Test?

GMAT scores are used by admissions officers in roughly 1,800 graduate business and management programs worldwide. Schools that require prospective students to submit GMAT scores in the application process are generally interested in admitting the best-qualified applicants for their programs, which means that you may find a more beneficial learning environment at schools that require GMAT scores as part of your application.

Because the GMAT test gauges skills that are important to successful study of business and management at the graduate level, your scores will give you a good indication of how well prepared you are to succeed academically in a graduate management program; how well you do on the test may also help you choose the business schools to which you apply. Furthermore, the percentile table you receive with your scores will tell you how your performance on the test compares to the performance of other test takers, giving you one way to gauge your competition for admission to business school.

> ## *Myth* -vs- **FACT**
>
> *M* – **If I don't score in the 90th percentile, I won't get into any school I choose.**
>
> F – **Very few people get very high scores.**
>
> Fewer than 50 of the more than 200,000 people taking the GMAT test each year get a perfect score of 800. Thus, while you may be exceptionally capable, the odds are against your achieving a perfect score. Also, the GMAT test is just one piece of your application packet. Admissions officers use GMAT scores in conjunction with undergraduate records, application essays, interviews, letters of recommendation, and other information when deciding whom to accept into their programs.

Schools consider many different aspects of an application before making an admissions decision, so even if you score well on the GMAT test, you should contact the schools that interest you to learn more about them and to ask about how they use GMAT scores and other admissions criteria (such as your undergraduate grades, essays, and letters of recommendation) to evaluate candidates for admission. School admissions offices, school Web sites, and materials published by the school are the best sources for you to tap when you are doing research about where you might want to go to business school.

For more information about how schools should use GMAT scores in admissions decisions, please read Appendix A of this book. For more information on the GMAT, registering to take the test, sending your scores to schools, and applying to business school, please visit our Web site at www.mba.com.

1.2 GMAT® Test Format

The GMAT test consists of four separately timed sections (see the table on the next page). You start the test with two 30-minute Analytical Writing Assessment (AWA) questions that require you to type your responses using the computer keyboard. The writing section is followed by two 75-minute, multiple-choice sections: the Quantitative and Verbal sections of the test.

Myth -vs- **FACT**

M – **Getting an easier question means I answered the last one wrong.**

F – **Getting an easier question does not necessarily mean you got the previous question wrong.**

To ensure that everyone receives the same content, the test selects a specific number of questions of each type. The test may call for your next question to be a relatively hard problem-solving item involving arithmetic operations. But, if there are no more relatively difficult problem-solving items involving arithmetic, you might be given an easier item.

Most people are not skilled at estimating item difficulty, so don't worry when taking the test or waste valuable time trying to determine the difficulty of the questions you are answering.

The GMAT is a computer-adaptive test (CAT), which means that in the multiple-choice sections of the test, the computer constantly gauges how well you are doing on the test and presents you with questions that are appropriate to your ability level. These questions are drawn from a huge pool of possible test questions. So, although we talk about the GMAT as one test, the GMAT test you take may be completely different from the test of the person sitting next to you.

Here's how it works. At the start of each GMAT multiple-choice section (Verbal and Quantitative), you will be presented with a question of moderate difficulty. The computer uses your response to that first question to determine which question to present next. If you respond correctly, the test usually will give you questions of increasing difficulty. If you respond incorrectly, the next question you see usually will be easier than the one you answered incorrectly. As you continue to respond to the questions presented, the computer will narrow your score to the number that best characterizes your ability. When you complete each section, the computer will have an accurate assessment of your ability.

Because each question is presented on the basis of your answers to all previous questions, you must answer each question as it appears. You may not skip, return to, or change your responses to previous questions. Random guessing can significantly lower your scores. If you do not know the answer to a question, you should try to eliminate as many choices as possible, then select the answer you think is best. If you answer a question incorrectly by mistake—or correctly by lucky guess— your answers to subsequent questions will lead you back to questions that are at the appropriate level of difficulty for you.

Each multiple-choice question used in the GMAT test has been thoroughly reviewed by professional test developers. New multiple-choice questions are tested each time the test is administered. Answers to trial questions are not counted in the scoring of your test, but the trial questions are not identified and could appear anywhere in the test. Therefore, you should try to do your best on every question.

The test includes the types of questions found in this guide, but the format and presentation of the questions are different on the computer. When you take the test:

- Only one question at a time is presented on the computer screen.

- The answer choices for the multiple-choice questions will be preceded by circles, rather than by letters.

- Different question types appear in random order in the multiple-choice sections of the test.

- You must select your answer using the computer.

- You must choose an answer and confirm your choice before moving on to the next question.

- You may not go back to change answers to previous questions.

Format of the GMAT® Exam		
	Questions	Timing
Analytical Writing Analysis of an Argument	1	30 min.

Integrated Reasoning
    Multi-Source Reasoning
    Table Analysis
    Graphics Interpretation
    Two-Part Analysis
	12	30 min.

Optional break		

Quantitative
    Problem Solving
    Data Sufficiency
	37	75 min.

Optional break		

Verbal
    Reading Comprehension
    Critical Reasoning
    Sentence Correction
	41	75 min.

	Total Time:	210 min.

1.3 What Is the Content of the Test Like?

It is important to recognize that the GMAT test evaluates skills and abilities developed over a relatively long period of time. Although the sections contain questions that are basically verbal and mathematical, the complete test provides one method of measuring overall ability.

Keep in mind that although the questions in this guide are arranged by question type and ordered from easy to difficult, the test is organized differently. When you take the test, you may see different types of questions in any order.

1.4 Quantitative Section

The GMAT Quantitative section measures your ability to reason quantitatively, solve quantitative problems, and interpret graphic data.

Two types of multiple-choice questions are used in the Quantitative section:

- Problem solving
- Data sufficiency

Problem solving and data sufficiency questions are intermingled throughout the Quantitative section. Both types of questions require basic knowledge of:

- Arithmetic
- Elementary algebra
- Commonly known concepts of geometry

To review the basic mathematical concepts that will be tested in the GMAT Quantitative questions, see the math review in chapter 3. For test-taking tips specific to the question types in the Quantitative section of the GMAT test, sample questions, and answer explanations, see chapters 4 and 5.

1.5 Verbal Section

The GMAT Verbal section measures your ability to read and comprehend written material, to reason and evaluate arguments, and to correct written material to conform to standard written English. Because the Verbal section includes reading sections from several different content areas, you may be generally familiar with some of the material; however, neither the reading passages nor the questions assume detailed knowledge of the topics discussed.

Three types of multiple-choice questions are used in the Verbal section:

- Reading comprehension
- Critical reasoning
- Sentence correction

These question types are intermingled throughout the Verbal section.

For test-taking tips specific to each question type in the Verbal section, sample questions, and answer explanations, see *The Official Guide for GMAT Review*, 12th Edition, or *The Official Guide for GMAT Verbal Review*, 2nd Edition; both are available for purchase at www.mba.com.

1.6 What Computer Skills Will I Need?

You only need minimal computer skills to take the GMAT Computer-Adaptive Test (CAT). You will be required to type your essays on the computer keyboard using standard word-processing keystrokes. In the multiple-choice sections, you will select your responses using either your mouse or the keyboard.

To learn more about the specific skills required to take the GMAT CAT, download the free test-preparation software available at www.mba.com.

1.7 What Are the Test Centers Like?

The GMAT test is administered at a test center providing the quiet and privacy of individual computer workstations. You will have the opportunity to take two optional breaks—one after completing the essays and another between the Quantitative and Verbal sections. An erasable notepad will be provided for your use during the test.

1.8 How Are Scores Calculated?

Your GMAT scores are determined by:

- The number of questions you answer
- Whether you answer correctly or incorrectly
- The level of difficulty and other statistical characteristics of each question

Your Verbal, Quantitative, and Total GMAT scores are determined by a complex mathematical procedure that takes into account the difficulty of the questions that were presented to you and how you answered them. When you answer the easier questions correctly, you get a chance to answer harder questions—making it possible to earn a higher score. After you have completed all the questions on the test—or when your time is up—the computer will calculate your scores. Your scores on the Verbal and Quantitative sections are combined to produce your Total score. If you have not responded to all the questions in a section (37 Quantitative questions or 41 Verbal questions), your score is adjusted, using the proportion of questions answered.

Appendix A contains the 2007 percentile ranking tables that explain how your GMAT scores compare with scores of other 2007 GMAT test takers.

1.9 Analytical Writing Assessment Scores

The Analytical Writing Assessment consists of two writing tasks: Analysis of an Issue and Analysis of an Argument. The responses to each of these tasks are scored on a 6-point scale, with 6 being the highest score and 1, the lowest. A score of zero (0) is given to responses that are off-topic, are in a foreign language, merely attempt to copy the topic, consist only of keystroke characters, or are blank.

The readers who evaluate the responses are college and university faculty members from various subject matter areas, including management education. These readers read holistically—that is, they respond to the overall quality of your critical thinking and writing. (For details on how readers are qualified, visit www.mba.com.) In addition, responses may be scored by an automated scoring program designed to reflect the judgment of expert readers.

Each response is given two independent ratings. If the ratings differ by more than a point, a third reader adjudicates. (Because of ongoing training and monitoring, discrepant ratings are rare.)

Your final score is the average (rounded to the nearest half point) of the four scores independently assigned to your responses—two scores for the Analysis of an Issue and two for the Analysis of an Argument. For example, if you earned scores of 6 and 5 on the Analysis of an Issue and 4 and 4 on the Analysis of an Argument, your final score would be 5: $(6 + 5 + 4 + 4) \div 4 = 4.75$, which rounds up to 5.

Your Analytical Writing Assessment scores are computed and reported separately from the multiple-choice sections of the test and have no effect on your Verbal, Quantitative, or Total scores. The schools that you have designated to receive your scores may receive your responses to the Analytical Writing Assessment with your score report. Your own copy of your score report will not include copies of your responses.

1.10 Test Development Process

The GMAT test is developed by experts who use standardized procedures to ensure high-quality, widely appropriate test material. All questions are subjected to independent reviews and are revised or discarded as necessary. Multiple-choice questions are tested during GMAT test administrations. Analytical Writing Assessment tasks are tried out on first-year business school students and then assessed for their fairness and reliability. For more information on test development, see www.mba.com.

2.0   How to Prepare

2.0 How to Prepare

2.1 How Can I Best Prepare to Take the Test?

We at the Graduate Management Admission Council® (GMAC®) firmly believe that the test-taking skills you can develop by using this guide—and *The Official Guide for GMAT® Review*, 12th Edition, and *The Official Guide for GMAT® Verbal Review*, 2nd Edition, if you want additional practice—are all you need to perform your best when you take the GMAT® test. By answering questions that have appeared on the GMAT test before, you will gain experience with the types of questions you may see on the test when you take it. As you practice with this guide, you will develop confidence in your ability to reason through the test questions. No additional techniques or strategies are needed to do well on the standardized test if you develop a practical familiarity with the abilities it requires. Simply by practicing and understanding the concepts that are assessed on the test, you will learn what you need to know to answer the questions correctly.

2.2 What About Practice Tests?

Because a computer-adaptive test cannot be presented in paper form, we have created GMATPrep® software to help you prepare for the test. The software is available for download at no charge for those who have created a user profile on www. mba.com. It is also provided on a disk, by request, to anyone who has registered for the GMAT test. The software includes two practice GMAT tests plus additional practice questions, information about the test, and tutorials to help you become familiar with how the GMAT test will appear on the computer screen at the test center.

We recommend that you download the software as you start to prepare for the test. Take one practice test to familiarize yourself with the test and to get an idea of how you might score. After you have studied using this book, and as your test date approaches, take the second practice test to determine whether you need to shift your focus to other areas you need to strengthen.

> ## *Myth* -vs- **FACT**
>
> *M* – **You may need very advanced math skills to get a high GMAT score.**
>
> F – **The math skills test on the GMAT test are quite basic.**
>
> The GMAT test only requires basic quantitative analytic skills. You should review the math skills (algebra, geometry, basic arithmetic) presented both in this book (chapter 3) and in *The Official Guide for GMAT® Review*, 12th Edition, but the required skill level is low. The difficulty of GMAT Quantitative questions stems from the logic and analysis used to solve the problems and not the underlying math skills.

2.3 Where Can I Get Additional Practice?

If you complete all the questions in this guide and think you would like additional practice, you may purchase *The Official Guide for GMAT® Review*, 12th Edition, or *The Official Guide for GMAT® Verbal Review*, 2nd Edition, at www.mba.com.

Note: There may be some overlap between this book and the review sections of the GMATPrep® software.

2.4 General Test-Taking Suggestions

Specific test-taking strategies for individual question types are presented later in this book. The following are general suggestions to help you perform your best on the test.

1. Use your time wisely.

Although the GMAT test stresses accuracy more than speed, it is important to use your time wisely. On average, you will have about 1¾ minutes for each verbal question and about 2 minutes for each quantitative question. Once you start the test, an onscreen clock will continuously count the time you have left. You can hide this display if you want, but it is a good idea to check the clock periodically to monitor your progress. The clock will automatically alert you when 5 minutes remain in the allotted time for the section you are working on.

2. Answer practice questions ahead of time.

After you become generally familiar with all question types, use the sample questions in this book to prepare for the actual test. It may be useful to time yourself as you answer the practice questions to get an idea of how long you will have for each question during the actual GMAT test as well as to determine whether you are answering quickly enough to complete the test in the time allotted.

3. Read all test directions carefully.

The directions explain exactly what is required to answer each question type. If you read hastily, you may miss important instructions and lower your scores. To review directions during the test, click on the Help icon. But be aware that the time you spend reviewing directions will count against the time allotted for that section of the test.

4. Read each question carefully and thoroughly.

Before you answer a multiple-choice question, determine exactly what is being asked, then eliminate the wrong answers and select the best choice. Never skim a question or the possible answers; skimming may cause you to miss important information or nuances.

5. Do not spend too much time on any one question.

If you do not know the correct answer, or if the question is too time-consuming, try to eliminate choices you know are wrong, select the best of the remaining answer choices, and move on to the next question. Try not to worry about the impact on your score—guessing may lower your score, but not finishing the section will lower your score more.

Bear in mind that if you do not finish a section in the allotted time, you will still receive a score.

6. Confirm your answers ONLY when you are ready to move on.

Once you have selected your answer to a multiple-choice question, you will be asked to confirm it. Once you confirm your response, you cannot go back and change it. You may not skip questions, because the computer selects each question on the basis of your responses to preceding questions.

7. Plan your essay answers before you begin to write.

The best way to approach the two writing tasks that comprise the Analytical Writing Assessment is to read the directions carefully, take a few minutes to think about the question, and plan a response before you begin writing. Take care to organize your ideas and develop them fully, but leave time to reread your response and make any revisions that you think would improve it.

Myth -vs- FACT

M – It is more important to respond correctly to the test questions than it is to finish the test.

F – There is a severe penalty for not completing the GMAT test.

If you are stumped by a question, give it your best guess and move on. If you guess incorrectly, the computer program will likely give you an easier question, which you are likely to answer correctly, and the computer will rapidly return to giving you questions matched to your ability. If you don't finish the test, your score will be reduced greatly. Failing to answer five verbal questions, for example, could reduce your score from the 91st percentile to the 77th percentile. Pacing is important.

Myth -vs- FACT

M – The first 10 questions are critical and you should invest the most time on those.

F – All questions count.

It is true that the computer-adaptive testing algorithm uses the first 10 questions to obtain an initial estimate of your ability; however, that is only an *initial* estimate. As you continue to answer questions, the algorithm self-corrects by computing an updated estimate on the basis of all the questions you have answered, and then administers items that are closely matched to this new estimate of your ability. Your final score is based on all your responses and considers the difficulty of all the questions you answered. Taking additional time on the first 10 questions will not game the system and can hurt your ability to finish the test.

3.0 Math Review

3.0 Math Review

Although this chapter provides a review of some of the mathematical concepts of arithmetic, algebra, and geometry, it is not intended to be a textbook. You should use this chapter to familiarize yourself with the kinds of topics that are tested in the GMAT® test. You may wish to consult an arithmetic, algebra, or geometry book for a more detailed discussion of some of the topics.

Section 3.1, "Arithmetic," includes the following topics:

1. Properties of Integers
2. Fractions
3. Decimals
4. Real Numbers
5. Ratio and Proportion
6. Percents

7. Powers and Roots of Numbers
8. Descriptive Statistics
9. Sets
10. Counting Methods
11. Discrete Probability

Section 3.2, "Algebra," does not extend beyond what is usually covered in a first-year high school algebra course. The topics included are as follows:

1. Simplifying Algebraic Expressions
2. Equations
3. Solving Linear Equations with One Unknown
4. Solving Two Linear Equations with Two Unknowns
5. Solving Equations by Factoring
6. Solving Quadratic Equations

7. Exponents
8. Inequalities
9. Absolute Value
10. Functions

Section 3.3, "Geometry," is limited primarily to measurement and intuitive geometry or spatial visualization. Extensive knowledge of theorems and the ability to construct proofs, skills that are usually developed in a formal geometry course, are not tested. The topics included in this section are the following:

1. Lines
2. Intersecting Lines and Angles
3. Perpendicular Lines
4. Parallel Lines
5. Polygons (Convex)

6. Triangles
7. Quadrilaterals
8. Circles
9. Rectangular Solids and Cylinders
10. Coordinate Geometry

Section 3.4, "Word Problems," presents examples of and solutions to the following types of word problems:

1. Rate Problems
2. Work Problems
3. Mixture Problems
4. Interest Problems
5. Discount

6. Profit
7. Sets
8. Geometry Problems
9. Measurement Problems
10. Data Interpretation

3.1 Arithmetic

1. Properties of Integers

An *integer* is any number in the set $\{\ldots -3, -2, -1, 0, 1, 2, 3, \ldots\}$. If x and y are integers and $x \neq 0$, then x is a *divisor* (*factor*) of y provided that $y = xn$ for some integer n. In this case, y is also said to be *divisible* by x or to be a *multiple* of x. For example, 7 is a divisor or factor of 28 since $28 = (7)(4)$, but 8 is not a divisor of 28 since there is no integer n such that $28 = 8n$.

If x and y are positive integers, there exist unique integers q and r, called the *quotient* and *remainder*, respectively, such that $y = xq + r$ and $0 \leq r < x$. For example, when 28 is divided by 8, the quotient is 3 and the remainder is 4 since $28 = (8)(3) + 4$. Note that y is divisible by x if and only if the remainder r is 0; for example, 32 has a remainder of 0 when divided by 8 because 32 is divisible by 8. Also, note that when a smaller integer is divided by a larger integer, the quotient is 0 and the remainder is the smaller integer. For example, 5 divided by 7 has the quotient 0 and the remainder 5 since $5 = (7)(0) + 5$.

Any integer that is divisible by 2 is an *even integer*; the set of even integers is $\{\ldots -4, -2, 0, 2, 4, 6, 8, \ldots\}$. Integers that are not divisible by 2 are *odd integers*; $\{\ldots -3, -1, 1, 3, 5, \ldots\}$ is the set of odd integers.

If at least one factor of a product of integers is even, then the product is even; otherwise the product is odd. If two integers are both even or both odd, then their sum and their difference are even. Otherwise, their sum and their difference are odd.

A *prime* number is a positive integer that has exactly two different positive divisors, 1 and itself. For example, 2, 3, 5, 7, 11, and 13 are prime numbers, but 15 is not, since 15 has four different positive divisors, 1, 3, 5, and 15. The number 1 is not a prime number since it has only one positive divisor. Every integer greater than 1 either is prime or can be uniquely expressed as a product of prime factors. For example, $14 = (2)(7)$, $81 = (3)(3)(3)(3)$, and $484 = (2)(2)(11)(11)$.

The numbers $-2, -1, 0, 1, 2, 3, 4, 5$ are *consecutive integers*. Consecutive integers can be represented by $n, n + 1, n + 2, n + 3, \ldots$, where n is an integer. The numbers 0, 2, 4, 6, 8 are *consecutive even integers*, and 1, 3, 5, 7, 9 are *consecutive odd integers*. Consecutive even integers can be represented by $2n, 2n + 2, 2n + 4, \ldots$, and consecutive odd integers can be represented by $2n + 1, 2n + 3, 2n + 5, \ldots$, where n is an integer.

Properties of the integer 1. If n is any number, then $1 \cdot n = n$, and for any number $n \neq 0$, $n \cdot \frac{1}{n} = 1$.

The number 1 can be expressed in many ways; for example, $\frac{n}{n} = 1$ for any number $n \neq 0$.

Multiplying or dividing an expression by 1, in any form, does not change the value of that expression.

Properties of the integer 0. The integer 0 is neither positive nor negative. If n is any number, then $n + 0 = n$ and $n \cdot 0 = 0$. Division by 0 is not defined.

2. Fractions

In a fraction $\frac{n}{d}$, n is the *numerator* and d is the *denominator*. The denominator of a fraction can never be 0, because division by 0 is not defined.

Two fractions are said to be *equivalent* if they represent the same number. For example, $\frac{8}{36}$ and $\frac{14}{63}$ are equivalent since they both represent the number $\frac{2}{9}$. In each case, the fraction is reduced to lowest terms by dividing both numerator and denominator by their *greatest common divisor* (gcd). The gcd of 8 and 36 is 4 and the gcd of 14 and 63 is 7.

Addition and subtraction of fractions.

Two fractions with the same denominator can be added or subtracted by performing the required operation with the numerators, leaving the denominators the same. For example, $\frac{3}{5}+\frac{4}{5}=\frac{3+4}{5}=\frac{7}{5}$ and $\frac{5}{7}-\frac{2}{7}=\frac{5-2}{7}=\frac{3}{7}$. If two fractions do not have the same denominator, express them as equivalent fractions with the same denominator. For example, to add $\frac{3}{5}$ and $\frac{4}{7}$, multiply the numerator and denominator of the first fraction by 7 and the numerator and denominator of the second fraction by 5, obtaining $\frac{21}{35}$ and $\frac{20}{35}$, respectively; $\frac{21}{35}+\frac{20}{35}=\frac{41}{35}$.

For the new denominator, choosing the *least common multiple* (lcm) of the denominators usually lessens the work. For $\frac{2}{3}+\frac{1}{6}$, the lcm of 3 and 6 is 6 (not $3\times6=18$), so

$$\frac{2}{3}+\frac{1}{6}=\frac{2}{3}\times\frac{2}{2}+\frac{1}{6}=\frac{4}{6}+\frac{1}{6}=\frac{5}{6}.$$

Multiplication and division of fractions.

To multiply two fractions, simply multiply the two numerators and multiply the two denominators.

For example, $\frac{2}{3}\times\frac{4}{7}=\frac{2\times4}{3\times7}=\frac{8}{21}$.

To divide by a fraction, invert the divisor (that is, find its *reciprocal*) and multiply. For example,

$\frac{2}{3}\div\frac{4}{7}=\frac{2}{3}\times\frac{7}{4}=\frac{14}{12}=\frac{7}{6}$.

In the problem above, the reciprocal of $\frac{4}{7}$ is $\frac{7}{4}$. In general, the reciprocal of a fraction $\frac{n}{d}$ is $\frac{d}{n}$, where n and d are not zero.

Mixed numbers.

A number that consists of a whole number and a fraction, for example, $7\frac{2}{3}$, is a mixed number: $7\frac{2}{3}$ means $7 + \frac{2}{3}$.

To change a mixed number into a fraction, multiply the whole number by the denominator of the fraction and add this number to the numerator of the fraction; then put the result over the denominator of the fraction. For example, $7\frac{2}{3} = \frac{(3 \times 7) + 2}{3} = \frac{23}{3}$.

3. Decimals

In the decimal system, the position of the period or *decimal point* determines the place value of the digits. For example, the digits in the number 7,654.321 have the following place values:

Thousands	Hundreds	Tens	Ones or units	Tenths	Hundredths	Thousandths
7 ,	6	5	4 .	3	2	1

Some examples of decimals follow.

$$0.321 = \frac{3}{10} + \frac{2}{100} + \frac{1}{1,000} = \frac{321}{1,000}$$

$$0.0321 = \frac{0}{10} + \frac{3}{100} + \frac{2}{1,000} + \frac{1}{10,000} = \frac{321}{10,000}$$

$$1.56 = 1 + \frac{5}{10} + \frac{6}{100} = \frac{156}{100}$$

Sometimes decimals are expressed as the product of a number with only one digit to the left of the decimal point and a power of 10. This is called *scientific notation*. For example, 231 can be written as 2.31×10^{2} and 0.0231 can be written as 2.31×10^{-2}. When a number is expressed in scientific notation, the exponent of the 10 indicates the number of places that the decimal point is to be moved in the number that is to be multiplied by a power of 10 in order to obtain the product. The decimal point is moved to the right if the exponent is positive and to the left if the exponent is negative. For example, 2.013×10^{4} is equal to 20,130 and 1.91×10^{-4} is equal to 0.000191.

Addition and subtraction of decimals.

To add or subtract two decimals, the decimal points of both numbers should be lined up. If one of the numbers has fewer digits to the right of the decimal point than the other, zeros may be inserted to the right of the last digit. For example, to add 17.6512 and 653.27, set up the numbers in a column and add:

$$\begin{array}{r} 17.6512 \\ +\ 653.2700 \\ \hline 670.9212 \end{array}$$

Likewise for 653.27 minus 17.6512:

$$\begin{array}{r} 653.2700 \\ -\ 17.6512 \\ \hline 635.6188 \end{array}$$

Multiplication of decimals.

To multiply decimals, multiply the numbers as if they were whole numbers and then insert the decimal point in the product so that the number of digits to the right of the decimal point is equal to the sum of the numbers of digits to the right of the decimal points in the numbers being multiplied. For example:

$$\begin{array}{r} 2.09 \quad \left(2 \text{ digits to the right}\right)\\ \times\ 1.3 \quad \left(1 \text{ digit to the right}\right)\\ \hline 627 \quad\quad\\ 2090 \quad\quad\\ \hline 2.717 \quad \left(2+1=3 \text{ digits to the right}\right) \end{array}$$

Division of decimals.

To divide a number (the dividend) by a decimal (the divisor), move the decimal point of the divisor to the right until the divisor is a whole number. Then move the decimal point of the dividend the same number of places to the right, and divide as you would by a whole number. The decimal point in the quotient will be directly above the decimal point in the new dividend. For example, to divide 698.12 by 12.4:

$$12.4\overline{)698.12}$$

will be replaced by:

$$124\overline{)6981.2}$$

and the division would proceed as follows:

$$\begin{array}{r} 56.3 \\ 124\overline{)6981.2} \\ \underline{620} \\ 781 \\ \underline{744} \\ 372 \\ \underline{372} \\ 0 \end{array}$$

4. Real Numbers

All *real* numbers correspond to points on the number line and all points on the number line correspond to real numbers. All real numbers except zero are either positive or negative.

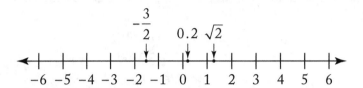

On a number line, numbers corresponding to points to the left of zero are negative and numbers corresponding to points to the right of zero are positive. For any two numbers on the number line, the number to the left is less than the number to the right; for example,

$$-4 < -3 < -\frac{3}{2} < -1, \text{ and } 1 < \sqrt{2} < 2.$$

To say that the number n is between 1 and 4 on the number line means that $n > 1$ and $n < 4$, that is, $1 < n < 4$. If n is "between 1 and 4, inclusive," then $1 \le n \le 4$.

The distance between a number and zero on the number line is called the *absolute value* of the number. Thus 3 and -3 have the same absolute value, 3, since they are both three units from zero. The absolute value of 3 is denoted $|3|$. Examples of absolute values of numbers are

$$|-5| = |5| = 5, \quad \left|-\frac{7}{2}\right| = \frac{7}{2}, \text{ and } |0| = 0.$$

Note that the absolute value of any nonzero number is positive.

Here are some properties of real numbers that are used frequently. If x, y, and z are real numbers, then

(1) $x + y = y + x$ and $xy = yx$.
    For example, $8 + 3 = 3 + 8 = 11$, and $(17)(5) = (5)(17) = 85$.

(2) $(x + y) + z = x + (y + z)$ and $(xy)z = x(yz)$.
    For example, $(7 + 5) + 2 = 7 + (5 + 2) = 7 + (7) = 14$, and $(5\sqrt{3})(\sqrt{3}) = (5)(\sqrt{3}\sqrt{3}) = (5)(3) = 15$.

(3) $xy + xz = x(y + z)$.
    For example, $718(36) + 718(64) = 718(36 + 64) = 718(100) = 71,800$.

(4)   If x and y are both positive, then $x + y$ and xy are positive.

(5)   If x and y are both negative, then $x + y$ is negative and xy is positive.

(6)   If x is positive and y is negative, then xy is negative.

(7)   If $xy = 0$, then $x = 0$ or $y = 0$. For example, $3y = 0$ implies $y = 0$.

(8) $|x + y| \le |x| + |y|$. For example, if $x = 10$ and $y = 2$, then $|x + y| = |12| = 12 = |x| + |y|$; and if $x = 10$ and $y = -2$, then $|x + y| = |8| = 8 < 12 = |x| + |y|$.

5. Ratio and Proportion

The *ratio* of the number a to the number b $\left(b \neq 0\right)$ is $\frac{a}{b}$.

A ratio may be expressed or represented in several ways. For example, the ratio of 2 to 3 can be written as 2 to 3, 2:3, or $\frac{2}{3}$. The order of the terms of a ratio is important. For example, the ratio of the number of months with exactly 30 days to the number with exactly 31 days is $\frac{4}{7}$, not $\frac{7}{4}$.

A *proportion* is a statement that two ratios are equal; for example, $\frac{2}{3} = \frac{8}{12}$ is a proportion. One way to solve a proportion involving an unknown is to cross multiply, obtaining a new equality. For example, to solve for n in the proportion $\frac{2}{3} = \frac{n}{12}$, cross multiply, obtaining $24 = 3n$; then divide both sides by 3, to get $n = 8$.

6. Percents

Percent means *per hundred* or *number out of 100*. A percent can be represented as a fraction with a denominator of 100, or as a decimal. For example:

$$37\% = \frac{37}{100} = 0.37.$$

To find a certain percent of a number, multiply the number by the percent expressed as a decimal or fraction. For example:

$$20\% \text{ of } 90 = 0.2 \times 90 = 18$$

or

$$20\% \text{ of } 90 = \frac{20}{100} \times 90 = \frac{1}{5} \times 90 = 18.$$

Percents greater than 100%.

Percents greater than 100% are represented by numbers greater than 1. For example:

$$300\% = \frac{300}{100} = 3$$

$$250\% \text{ of } 80 = 2.5 \times 80 = 200.$$

Percents less than 1%.

The percent 0.5% means $\frac{1}{2}$ of 1 percent. For example, 0.5% of 12 is equal to $0.005 \times 12 = 0.06$.

Percent change.

Often a problem will ask for the percent increase or decrease from one quantity to another quantity. For example, "If the price of an item increases from \$24 to \$30, what is the percent increase in price?" To find the percent increase, first find the amount of the increase; then divide this increase by the original amount, and express this quotient as a percent. In the example above, the percent increase would be found in the following way: the amount of the increase is $\left(30 - 24\right) = 6$. Therefore, the percent increase is $\frac{6}{24} = 0.25 = 25\%$.

Likewise, to find the percent decrease (for example, the price of an item is reduced from $30 to $24), first find the amount of the decrease; then divide this decrease by the original amount, and express this quotient as a percent. In the example above, the amount of decrease is $(30 - 24) = 6$.

Therefore, the percent decrease is $\frac{6}{30} = 0.20 = 20\%$.

Note that the percent increase from 24 to 30 is not the same as the percent decrease from 30 to 24.

In the following example, the increase is greater than 100 percent: If the cost of a certain house in 1983 was 300 percent of its cost in 1970, by what percent did the cost increase?

If n is the cost in 1970, then the percent increase is equal to $\frac{3n - n}{n} = \frac{2n}{n} = 2$, or 200%.

7. Powers and Roots of Numbers

When a number k is to be used n times as a factor in a product, it can be expressed as k^n, which means the nth power of k. For example, $2^2 = 2 \times 2 = 4$ and $2^3 = 2 \times 2 \times 2 = 8$ are powers of 2.

Squaring a number that is greater than 1, or raising it to a higher power, results in a larger number; squaring a number between 0 and 1 results in a smaller number. For example:

$$3^2 = 9 \qquad (9 > 3)$$
$$\left(\frac{1}{3}\right)^2 = \frac{1}{9} \qquad \left(\frac{1}{9} < \frac{1}{3}\right)$$
$$(0.1)^2 = 0.01 \qquad (0.01 < 0.1)$$

A *square root* of a number n is a number that, when squared, is equal to n. The square root of a negative number is not a real number. Every positive number n has two square roots, one positive and the other negative, but $\sqrt{n}$ denotes the positive number whose square is n. For example, $\sqrt{9}$ denotes 3. The two square roots of 9 are $\sqrt{9} = 3$ and $-\sqrt{9} = -3$.

Every real number r has exactly one real *cube root*, which is the number s such that $s^3 = r$. The real cube root of r is denoted by $\sqrt[3]{r}$. Since $2^3 = 8$, $\sqrt[3]{8} = 2$. Similarly, $\sqrt[3]{-8} = -2$, because $(-2)^3 = -8$.

8. Descriptive Statistics

A list of numbers, or numerical data, can be described by various statistical measures. One of the most common of these measures is the *average*, or *(arithmetic) mean*, which locates a type of "center" for the data. The average of n numbers is defined as the sum of the n numbers divided by n. For example, the average of 6, 4, 7, 10, and 4 is $\frac{6 + 4 + 7 + 10 + 4}{5} = \frac{31}{5} = 6.2$.

The *median* is another type of center for a list of numbers. To calculate the median of n numbers, first order the numbers from least to greatest; if n is odd, the median is defined as the middle number, whereas if n is even, the median is defined as the average of the two middle numbers. In the example above, the numbers, in order, are 4, 4, 6, 7, 10, and the median is 6, the middle number.

For the numbers 4, 6, 6, 8, 9, 12, the median is $\dfrac{6+8}{2}$ = 7. Note that the mean of these numbers is 7.5.

The median of a set of data can be less than, equal to, or greater than the mean. Note that for a large set of data (for example, the salaries of 800 company employees), it is often true that about half of the data is less than the median and about half of the data is greater than the median; but this is not always the case, as the following data show.

3, 5, 7, 7, 7, 7, 7, 7, 8, 9, 9, 9, 9, 10, 10

Here the median is 7, but only $\dfrac{2}{15}$ of the data is less than the median.

The *mode* of a list of numbers is the number that occurs most frequently in the list. For example, the mode of 1, 3, 6, 4, 3, 5 is 3. A list of numbers may have more than one mode. For example, the list 1, 2, 3, 3, 3, 5, 7, 10, 10, 10, 20 has two modes, 3 and 10.

The degree to which numerical data are spread out or dispersed can be measured in many ways. The simplest measure of dispersion is the *range*, which is defined as the greatest value in the numerical data minus the least value. For example, the range of 11, 10, 5, 13, 21 is 21 – 5 = 16. Note how the range depends on only two values in the data.

One of the most common measures of dispersion is the *standard deviation*. Generally speaking, the more the data are spread away from the mean, the greater the standard deviation. The standard deviation of *n* numbers can be calculated as follows: (1) find the arithmetic mean, (2) find the differences between the mean and each of the *n* numbers, (3) square each of the differences, (4) find the average of the squared differences, and (5) take the nonnegative square root of this average. Shown below is this calculation for the data 0, 7, 8, 10, 10, which have arithmetic mean 7.

x	$x-7$	$(x-7)^2$
0	–7	49
7	0	0
8	1	1
10	3	9
10	3	9
	Total	68

Standard deviation $\sqrt{\dfrac{68}{5}} \approx 3.7$

Notice that the standard deviation depends on every data value, although it depends most on values that are farthest from the mean. This is why a distribution with data grouped closely around the mean will have a smaller standard deviation than will data spread far from the mean. To illustrate this, compare the data 6, 6, 6.5, 7.5, 9, which also have mean 7. Note that the numbers in the second set of data seem to be grouped more closely around the mean of 7 than the numbers in the first set. This is reflected in the standard deviation, which is less for the second set (approximately 1.1) than for the first set (approximately 3.7).

There are many ways to display numerical data that show how the data are distributed. One simple way is with a *frequency distribution*, which is useful for data that have values occurring with varying frequencies. For example, the 20 numbers

$$-4 \quad 0 \quad 0 \quad -3 \quad -2 \quad -1 \quad -1 \quad 0 \quad -1 \quad -4$$
$$-1 \quad -5 \quad 0 \quad -2 \quad 0 \quad -5 \quad -2 \quad 0 \quad 0 \quad -1$$

are displayed on the next page in a frequency distribution by listing each different value *x* and the frequency *f* with which *x* occurs.

Data Value x	Frequency f
–5	2
–4	2
–3	1
–2	3
–1	5
0	7
Total	20

From the frequency distribution, one can readily compute descriptive statistics:

$$\text{Mean:} = \frac{(-5)(2)+(-4)(2)+(-3)(1)+(-2)(3)+(-1)(5)+(0)(7)}{20} = -1.6$$

Median: –1 (the average of the 10th and 11th numbers)
Mode: 0 (the number that occurs most frequently)
Range: $0 - (-5) = 5$

$$\text{Standard deviation:} \sqrt{\frac{(-5+1.6)^2(2)+(-4+1.6)^2(2)+...+(0+1.6)^2(7)}{20}} \approx 1.7$$

9. Sets

In mathematics a *set* is a collection of numbers or other objects. The objects are called the *elements* of the set. If S is a set having a finite number of elements, then the number of elements is denoted by $|S|$. Such a set is often defined by listing its elements; for example, $S = \{-5, 0, 1\}$ is a set with $|S| = 3$.
The order in which the elements are listed in a set does not matter; thus $\{-5, 0, 1\} = \{0, 1, -5\}$.

If all the elements of a set S are also elements of a set T, then S is a *subset* of T; for example, $S = \{-5, 0, 1\}$ is a subset of $T = \{-5, 0, 1, 4, 10\}$.

For any two sets A and B, the *union* of A and B is the set of all elements that are in A or in B or in both. The *intersection* of A and B is the set of all elements that are both in A and in B. The union is denoted by $A \cup B$ and the intersection is denoted by $A \cap B$. As an example, if $A = \{3, 4\}$ and $B = \{4, 5, 6\}$, then $A \cup B = \{3, 4, 5, 6\}$ and $A \cap B = \{4\}$. Two sets that have no elements in common are said to be *disjoint* or *mutually exclusive*.

The relationship between sets is often illustrated with a *Venn diagram* in which sets are represented by regions in a plane. For two sets S and T that are not disjoint and neither is a subset of the other, the intersection $S \cap T$ is represented by the shaded region of the diagram below.

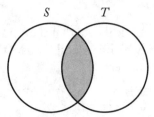

This diagram illustrates a fact about any two finite sets S and T: the number of elements in their union equals the sum of their individual numbers of elements minus the number of elements in their intersection (because the latter are counted twice in the sum); more concisely,

$$|S \cup T| = |S| + |T| - |S \cap T|.$$

This counting method is called the general addition rule for two sets. As a special case, if S and T are disjoint, then

$$|S \cup T| = |S| + |T|$$

since $|S \cap T| = 0$.

10. Counting Methods

There are some useful methods for counting objects and sets of objects without actually listing the elements to be counted. The following principle of multiplication is fundamental to these methods.

If an object is to be chosen from a set of m objects and a second object is to be chosen from a different set of n objects, then there are mn ways of choosing both objects simultaneously.

As an example, suppose the objects are items on a menu. If a meal consists of one entree and one dessert and there are 5 entrees and 3 desserts on the menu, then there are $5 \times 3 = 15$ different meals that can be ordered from the menu. As another example, each time a coin is flipped, there are two possible outcomes, heads and tails. If an experiment consists of 8 consecutive coin flips, then the experiment has 2^8 possible outcomes, where each of these outcomes is a list of heads and tails in some order.

A symbol that is often used with the multiplication principle is the *factorial*. If n is an integer greater than 1, then n factorial, denoted by the symbol $n!$, is defined as the product of all the integers from 1 to n. Therefore,

$$2! = (1)(2) = 2,$$
$$3! = (1)(2)(3) = 6,$$
$$4! = (1)(2)(3)(4) = 24, \text{ etc.}$$

Also, by definition, $0! = 1! = 1$.

The factorial is useful for counting the number of ways that a set of objects can be ordered. If a set of n objects is to be ordered from 1st to nth, then there are n choices for the 1st object, $n - 1$ choices for the 2nd object, $n - 2$ choices for the 3rd object, and so on, until there is only 1 choice for the nth object. Thus, by the multiplication principle, the number of ways of ordering the n objects is

$$n(n - 1)(n - 2) \cdots (3)(2)(1) = n!.$$

For example, the number of ways of ordering the letters A, B, and C is 3!, or 6:

ABC, ACB, BAC, BCA, CAB, and CBA.

These orderings are called the *permutations* of the letters A, B, and C.

A permutation can be thought of as a selection process in which objects are selected one by one in a certain order. If the order of selection is not relevant and only k objects are to be selected from a larger set of n objects, a different counting method is employed.

Specifically, consider a set of n objects from which a complete selection of k objects is to be made without regard to order, where $0 \le k \le n$. Then the number of possible complete selections of k objects is called the number of *combinations* of n objects taken k at a time and is denoted by $\binom{n}{k}$.

The value of $\binom{n}{k}$ is given by $\binom{n}{k} = \dfrac{n!}{k!(n-k)!}$.

Note that $\binom{n}{k}$ is the number of k-element subsets of a set with n elements. For example, if $S = \{A, B, C, D, E\}$, then the number of 2-element subsets of S, or the number of combinations of 5 letters taken 2 at a time, is $\binom{5}{2} = \dfrac{5!}{2!3!} = \dfrac{120}{(2)(6)} = 10$.

The subsets are $\{A, B\}$, $\{A, C\}$, $\{A, D\}$, $\{A, E\}$, $\{B, C\}$, $\{B, D\}$, $\{B, E\}$, $\{C, D\}$, $\{C, E\}$, and $\{D, E\}$.

Note that $\binom{5}{2} = 10 = \binom{5}{3}$ because every 2-element subset chosen from a set of 5 elements corresponds to a unique 3-element subset consisting of the elements *not* chosen. In general, $\binom{n}{k} = \binom{n}{n-k}$.

11. Discrete Probability

Many of the ideas discussed in the preceding three topics are important to the study of discrete probability. Discrete probability is concerned with *experiments* that have a finite number of *outcomes*. Given such an experiment, an *event* is a particular set of outcomes. For example, rolling a number cube with faces numbered 1 to 6 (similar to a 6-sided die) is an experiment with 6 possible outcomes: 1, 2, 3, 4, 5, or 6. One event in this experiment is that the outcome is 4, denoted $\{4\}$; another event is that the outcome is an odd number: $\{1, 3, 5\}$.

The probability that an event E occurs, denoted by $P(E)$, is a number between 0 and 1, inclusive. If E has no outcomes, then E is *impossible* and $P(E) = 0$; if E is the set of all possible outcomes of the experiment, then E is *certain* to occur and $P(E) = 1$. Otherwise, E is possible but uncertain, and $0 < P(E) < 1$. If F is a subset of E, then $P(F) \le P(E)$. In the example above, if the probability of each of the 6 outcomes is the same, then the probability of each outcome is $\dfrac{1}{6}$, and the outcomes are said to be *equally likely*. For experiments in which all the individual outcomes are equally likely, the probability of an event E is

$$P(E) = \frac{\text{The number of outcomes in } E}{\text{The total number of possible outcomes}}.$$

In the example, the probability that the outcome is an odd number is

$$P(\{1, 3, 5\}) = \frac{|\{1, 3, 5\}|}{6} = \frac{3}{6} = \frac{1}{2}.$$

Given an experiment with events E and F, the following events are defined:
"*not E*" is the set of outcomes that are not outcomes in E;
"*E or F*" is the set of outcomes in E or F or both, that is, $E \cup F$;
"*E and F*" is the set of outcomes in both E and F, that is, $E \cap F$.

The probability that E does not occur is $P(\text{not } E) = 1 - P(E)$. The probability that "$E$ or F" occurs is $P(E \text{ or } F) = P(E) + P(F) - P(E \text{ and } F)$, using the general addition rule at the end of section 3.1.9 ("Sets"). For the number cube, if E is the event that the outcome is an odd number, $\{1, 3, 5\}$, and F is the event that the outcome is a prime number, $\{2, 3, 5\}$, then $P(E \text{ and } F) = P(\{3, 5\}) = \dfrac{2}{6} = \dfrac{1}{3}$ and so $P(E \text{ or } F) = P(E) + P(F) - P(E \text{ and } F) = \dfrac{3}{6} + \dfrac{3}{6} - \dfrac{2}{6} = \dfrac{4}{6} = \dfrac{2}{3}$.

Note that the event "E or F" is $E \cup F = \{1, 2, 3, 5\}$, and hence $P(E \text{ or } F) = \dfrac{|\{1, 2, 3, 5\}|}{6} = \dfrac{4}{6} = \dfrac{2}{3}$.

If the event "E and F" is impossible (that is, $E \cap F$ has no outcomes), then E and F are said to be *mutually exclusive* events, and $P(E \text{ and } F) = 0$. Then the general addition rule is reduced to $P(E \text{ or } F) = P(E) + P(F)$.

This is the special addition rule for the probability of two mutually exclusive events.

Two events A and B are said to be *independent* if the occurrence of either event does not alter the probability that the other event occurs. For one roll of the number cube, let $A = \{2, 4, 6\}$ and let $B = \{5, 6\}$. Then the probability that A occurs is $P(A) = \dfrac{|A|}{6} = \dfrac{3}{6} = \dfrac{1}{2}$, while, *presuming B occurs*, the probability that A occurs is

$$\dfrac{|A \cap B|}{|B|} = \dfrac{|\{6\}|}{|\{5, 6\}|} = \dfrac{1}{2}.$$

Similarly, the probability that B occurs is $P(B) = \dfrac{|B|}{6} = \dfrac{2}{6} = \dfrac{1}{3}$, while, *presuming A occurs*, the probability that B occurs is

$$\dfrac{|B \cap A|}{|A|} = \dfrac{|\{6\}|}{|\{2, 4, 6\}|} = \dfrac{1}{3}.$$

Thus, the occurrence of either event does not affect the probability that the other event occurs. Therefore, A and B are independent.

The following multiplication rule holds for any independent events E and F:
$P(E \text{ and } F) = P(E)P(F)$.

For the independent events A and B above, $P(A \text{ and } B) = P(A)P(B) = \left(\dfrac{1}{2}\right)\left(\dfrac{1}{3}\right) = \left(\dfrac{1}{6}\right)$.

Note that the event "A and B" is $A \cap B = \{6\}$, and hence $P(A \text{ and } B) = P(\{6\}) = \dfrac{1}{6}$. It follows from the general addition rule and the multiplication rule above that if E and F are independent, then

$$P(E \text{ or } F) = P(E) + P(F) - P(E)P(F).$$

For a final example of some of these rules, consider an experiment with events A, B, and C for which $P(A) = 0.23$, $P(B) = 0.40$, and $P(C) = 0.85$. Also, suppose that events A and B are mutually exclusive and events B and C are independent. Then

$$P(A \text{ or } B) = P(A) + P(B) \quad \left(\text{since } A \text{ or } B \text{ are mutually exclusive}\right)$$

$$= 0.23 + 0.40$$

$$= 0.63$$

$$P(B \text{ or } C) = P(B) + P(C) - P(B)P(C) \quad \left(\text{by independence}\right)$$

$$= 0.40 + 0.85 - (0.40)(0.85)$$

$$= 0.91$$

Note that $P(A \text{ or } C)$ and $P(A \text{ and } C)$ cannot be determined using the information given. But it can be determined that A and C are *not* mutually exclusive since $P(A) + P(C) = 1.08$, which is greater than 1, and therefore cannot equal $P(A \text{ or } C)$; from this it follows that $P(A \text{ and } C) \geq 0.08$. One can also deduce that $P(A \text{ and } C) \leq P(A) = 0.23$, since $A \cap C$ is a subset of A, and that $P(A \text{ or } C) \geq P(C) = 0.85$ since C is a subset of $A \cup C$. Thus, one can conclude that $0.85 \leq P(A \text{ or } C) \leq 1$ and $0.08 \leq P(A \text{ and } C) \leq 0.23$.

3.2 Algebra

Algebra is based on the operations of arithmetic and on the concept of an *unknown quantity*, or *variable*. Letters such as x or n are used to represent unknown quantities. For example, suppose Pam has 5 more pencils than Fred. If F represents the number of pencils that Fred has, then the number of pencils that Pam has is $F + 5$. As another example, if Jim's present salary S is increased by 7%, then his new salary is $1.07S$. A combination of letters and arithmetic operations, such as

$F + 5$, $\dfrac{3x^2}{2x-5}$, and $19x^2 - 6x + 3$, is called an *algebraic expression*.

The expression $19x^2 - 6x + 3$ consists of the *terms* $19x^2$, $-6x$, and 3, where 19 is the *coefficient* of x^2, -6 is the coefficient of x^1, and 3 is a *constant term* (or coefficient of $x^0 = 1$). Such an expression is called a *second degree* (or *quadratic*) *polynomial in x* since the highest power of x is 2. The expression $F + 5$ is a *first degree* (or *linear*) *polynomial in F* since the highest power of F is 1. The expression $\dfrac{3x^2}{2x-5}$ is not a polynomial because it is not a sum of terms that are each powers of x multiplied by coefficients.

1. Simplifying Algebraic Expressions

Often when working with algebraic expressions, it is necessary to simplify them by factoring or combining *like* terms. For example, the expression $6x + 5x$ is equivalent to $(6 + 5)x$, or $11x$. In the expression $9x - 3y$, 3 is a factor common to both terms: $9x - 3y = 3(3x - y)$. In the expression $5x^2 + 6y$, there are no like terms and no common factors.

If there are common factors in the numerator and denominator of an expression, they can be divided out, provided that they are not equal to zero.

For example, if $x \neq 3$, then $\dfrac{x-3}{x-3}$ is equal to 1; therefore,

$$\frac{3xy - 9y}{x - 3} = \frac{3y(x - 3)}{x - 3}$$
$$= (3y)(1)$$
$$= 3y$$

To multiply two algebraic expressions, each term of one expression is multiplied by each term of the other expression. For example:

$$(3x - 4)(9y + x) = 3x(9y + x) - 4(9y + x)$$
$$= (3x)(9y) + (3x)(x) + (-4)(9y) + (-4)(x)$$
$$= 27xy + 3x^2 - 36y - 4x$$

An algebraic expression can be evaluated by substituting values of the unknowns in the expression. For example, if $x = 3$ and $y = -2$, then $3xy - x^2 + y$ can be evaluated as

$$3(3)(-2) - (3)^2 + (-2) = -18 - 9 - 2 = -29$$

2. Equations

A major focus of algebra is to solve equations involving algebraic expressions. Some examples of such equations are

$$5x - 2 = 9 - x \quad \left(\text{a linear equation with one unknown}\right)$$
$$3x + 1 = y - 2 \quad \left(\text{a linear equation with two unknowns}\right)$$
$$5x^2 + 3x - 2 = 7x \quad \left(\text{a quadratic equation with one unknown}\right)$$
$$\frac{x(x - 3)(x^2 + 5)}{x - 4} = 0 \quad \left(\text{an equation that is factored on one side with 0 on the other}\right)$$

The *solutions* of an equation with one or more unknowns are those values that make the equation true, or "satisfy the equation," when they are substituted for the unknowns of the equation. An equation may have no solution or one or more solutions. If two or more equations are to be solved together, the solutions must satisfy all the equations simultaneously.

Two equations having the same solution(s) are *equivalent equations*. For example, the equations

$$2 + x = 3$$
$$4 + 2x = 6$$

each have the unique solution $x = 1$. Note that the second equation is the first equation multiplied by 2. Similarly, the equations

$$3x - y = 6$$
$$6x - 2y = 12$$

have the same solutions, although in this case each equation has infinitely many solutions. If any value is assigned to x, then $3x - 6$ is a corresponding value for y that will satisfy both equations; for example, $x = 2$ and $y = 0$ is a solution to both equations, as is $x = 5$ and $y = 9$.

3. Solving Linear Equations with One Unknown

To solve a linear equation with one unknown (that is, to find the value of the unknown that satisfies the equation), the unknown should be isolated on one side of the equation. This can be done by performing the same mathematical operations on both sides of the equation. Remember that if the same number is added to or subtracted from both sides of the equation, this does not change the equality; likewise, multiplying or dividing both sides by the same nonzero number does not change the equality. For example, to solve the equation $\frac{5x-6}{3} = 4$ for x, the variable x can be isolated using the following steps:

$$5x - 6 = 12 \quad \left(\text{multiplying by } 3\right)$$
$$5x = 18 \quad \left(\text{adding } 6\right)$$
$$x = \frac{18}{5} \quad \left(\text{dividing by } 5\right)$$

The solution, $\frac{18}{5}$, can be checked by substituting it for x in the original equation to determine whether it satisfies that equation:

$$\frac{5\left(\frac{18}{5}\right) - 6}{3} = \frac{18 - 6}{3} = \frac{12}{3} = 4$$

Therefore, $x = \frac{18}{5}$ is the solution.

4. Solving Two Linear Equations with Two Unknowns

For two linear equations with two unknowns, if the equations are equivalent, then there are infinitely many solutions to the equations, as illustrated at the end of section 3.2.2 ("Equations"). If the equations are not equivalent, then they have either one unique solution or no solution. The latter case is illustrated by the two equations:

$$3x + 4y = 17$$
$$6x + 8y = 35$$

Note that $3x + 4y = 17$ implies $6x + 8y = 34$, which contradicts the second equation. Thus, no values of x and y can simultaneously satisfy both equations.

There are several methods of solving two linear equations with two unknowns. With any method, if a contradiction is reached, then the equations have no solution; if a trivial equation such as $0 = 0$ is reached, then the equations are equivalent and have infinitely many solutions. Otherwise, a unique solution can be found.

One way to solve for the two unknowns is to express one of the unknowns in terms of the other using one of the equations, and then substitute the expression into the remaining equation to obtain an equation with one unknown. This equation can be solved and the value of the unknown substituted into either of the original equations to find the value of the other unknown. For example, the following two equations can be solved for x and y.

$$\left(1\right)\ 3x + 2y = 11$$
$$\left(2\right)\ \ \ x - y = 2$$

In equation (2), $x = 2 + y$. Substitute $2 + y$ in equation (1) for x:

$$3\left(2 + y\right) + 2y = 11$$
$$6 + 3y + 2y = 11$$
$$6 + 5y = 11$$
$$5y = 5$$
$$y = 1$$

If $y = 1$, then $x - 1 = 2$ and $x = 2 + 1 = 3$.

There is another way to solve for x and y by eliminating one of the unknowns. This can be done by making the coefficients of one of the unknowns the same (disregarding the sign) in both equations and either adding the equations or subtracting one equation from the other. For example, to solve the equations

$$\left(1\right)\ 6x + 5y = 29$$
$$\left(2\right)\ 4x - 3y = -6$$

by this method, multiply equation (1) by 3 and equation (2) by 5 to get

$$18x + 15y = 87$$
$$20x - 15y = -30$$

Adding the two equations eliminates y, yielding $38x = 57$, or $x = \dfrac{3}{2}$. Finally, substituting $\dfrac{3}{2}$ for x in one of the equations gives $y = 4$. These answers can be checked by substituting both values into both of the original equations.

5. Solving Equations by Factoring

Some equations can be solved by factoring. To do this, first add or subtract expressions to bring all the expressions to one side of the equation, with 0 on the other side. Then try to factor the nonzero side into a product of expressions. If this is possible, then using property (7) in section 3.1.4 ("Real Numbers") each of the factors can be set equal to 0, yielding several simpler equations that possibly can be solved. The solutions of the simpler equations will be solutions of the factored equation. As an example, consider the equation $x^3 - 2x^2 + x = -5\left(x - 1\right)^2$:

$$x^3 - 2x^2 + x + 5\left(x - 1\right)^2 = 0$$
$$x\left(x^2 + 2x + 1\right) + 5\left(x - 1\right)^2 = 0$$
$$x\left(x - 1\right)^2 + 5\left(x - 1\right)^2 = 0$$
$$\left(x + 5\right)\left(x - 1\right)^2 = 0$$
$$x + 5 = 0 \text{ or } \left(x - 1\right)^2 = 0$$
$$x = -5 \text{ or } x = 1.$$

For another example, consider $\dfrac{x(x-3)(x^2+5)}{x-4} = 0$. A fraction equals 0 if and only if its numerator equals 0. Thus, $x(x-3)(x^2+5) = 0$:

$$x = 0 \text{ or } x - 3 = 0 \text{ or } x^2 + 5 = 0$$
$$x = 0 \text{ or } x = 3 \text{ or } x^2 + 5 = 0.$$

But $x^2 + 5 = 0$ has no real solution because $x^2 + 5 > 0$ for every real number. Thus, the solutions are 0 and 3.

The solutions of an equation are also called the *roots* of the equation. These roots can be checked by substituting them into the original equation to determine whether they satisfy the equation.

6. Solving Quadratic Equations

The standard form for a *quadratic equation* is

$$ax^2 + bx + c = 0,$$

where a, b, and c are real numbers and $a \neq 0$; for example:

$$x^2 + 6x + 5 = 0$$
$$3x^2 - 2x = 0, \text{ and}$$
$$x^2 + 4 = 0$$

Some quadratic equations can easily be solved by factoring. For example:

(1)
$$x^2 + 6x + 5 = 0$$
$$(x + 5)(x + 1) = 0$$
$$x + 5 = 0 \text{ or } x + 1 = 0$$
$$x = -5 \text{ or } x = -1$$

(2)
$$3x^2 - 3 = 8x$$
$$3x^2 - 8x - 3 = 0$$
$$(3x + 1)(x - 3) = 0$$
$$3x + 1 = 0 \text{ or } x - 3 = 0$$
$$x = -\frac{1}{3} \text{ or } x = 3$$

A quadratic equation has at most two real roots and may have just one or even no real root. For example, the equation $x^2 - 6x + 9 = 0$ can be expressed as $(x - 3)^2 = 0$, or $(x - 3)(x - 3) = 0$; thus the only root is 3. The equation $x^2 + 4 = 0$ has no real root; since the square of any real number is greater than or equal to zero, $x^2 + 4$ must be greater than zero.

An expression of the form $a^2 - b^2$ can be factored as $(a - b)(a + b)$.

For example, the quadratic equation $9x^2 - 25 = 0$ can be solved as follows.

$$(3x - 5)(3x + 5) = 0$$
$$3x - 5 = 0 \text{ or } 3x + 5 = 0$$
$$x = \frac{5}{3} \text{ or } x = -\frac{5}{3}$$

If a quadratic expression is not easily factored, then its roots can always be found using the *quadratic formula*: If $ax^2 + bx + c = 0 \left(a \neq 0\right)$, then the roots are

$$x = \frac{-b + \sqrt{b^2 - 4ac}}{2a} \text{ and } x = \frac{-b - \sqrt{b^2 - 4ac}}{2a}$$

These are two distinct real numbers unless $b^2 - 4ac \leq 0$. If $b^2 - 4ac = 0$, then these two expressions for x are equal to $-\frac{b}{2a}$, and the equation has only one root. If $b^2 - 4ac < 0$, then $\sqrt{b^2 - 4ac}$ is not a real number and the equation has no real roots.

7. Exponents

A positive integer exponent of a number or a variable indicates a product, and the positive integer is the number of times that the number or variable is a factor in the product. For example, x^5 means $(x)(x)(x)(x)(x)$; that is, x is a factor in the product 5 times.

Some rules about exponents follow.

Let x and y be any positive numbers, and let r and s be any positive integers.

(1) $\left(x^r\right)\left(x^s\right) = x^{(r + s)}$; for example, $\left(2^2\right)\left(2^3\right) = 2^{(2 + 3)} = 2^5 = 32$.

(2) $\dfrac{x^r}{x^s} = x^{(r - s)}$; for example, $\dfrac{4^5}{4^2} = 4^{5 - 2} = 4^3 = 64$.

(3) $\left(x^r\right)\left(y^r\right) = \left(xy\right)^r$; for example, $\left(3^3\right)\left(4^3\right) = 12^3 = 1,728$.

(4) $\left(\dfrac{x}{y}\right)^r = \dfrac{x^r}{y^r}$; for example, $\left(\dfrac{2}{3}\right)^3 = \dfrac{2^3}{3^3} = \dfrac{8}{27}$.

(5) $\left(x^r\right)^s = x^{rs} = \left(x^s\right)^r$; for example, $\left(x^3\right)^4 = x^{12} = \left(x^4\right)^3$.

(6) $x^{-r} = \dfrac{1}{x^r}$; for example, $3^{-2} = \dfrac{1}{3^2} = \dfrac{1}{9}$.

(7) $x^0 = 1$; for example, $6^0 = 1$.

(8) $x^{\frac{r}{s}} = \left(x^{\frac{1}{s}}\right)^r = \left(x^r\right)^{\frac{1}{s}} = \sqrt[s]{x^r}$; for example, $8^{\frac{2}{3}} = \left(8^{\frac{1}{3}}\right)^2 = \left(8^2\right)^{\frac{1}{3}} = \sqrt[3]{8^2} = \sqrt[3]{64} = 4$

and $9^{\frac{1}{2}} = \sqrt{9} = 3$.

It can be shown that rules 1–6 also apply when r and s are not integers and are not positive, that is, when r and s are any real numbers.

8. Inequalities

An *inequality* is a statement that uses one of the following symbols:

$\neq$ not equal to

$>$ greater than

$\geq$ greater than or equal to

$<$ less than

$\leq$ less than or equal to

Some examples of inequalities are $5x - 3 < 9$, $6x \geq y$, and $\frac{1}{2} < \frac{3}{4}$. Solving a linear inequality with one unknown is similar to solving an equation; the unknown is isolated on one side of the inequality. As in solving an equation, the same number can be added to or subtracted from both sides of the inequality, or both sides of an inequality can be multiplied or divided by a positive number without changing the truth of the inequality. However, multiplying or dividing an inequality by a negative number reverses the order of the inequality. For example, $6 > 2$, but $(-1)(6) < (-1)(2)$.

To solve the inequality $3x - 2 > 5$ for x, isolate x by using the following steps:

$$3x - 2 > 5$$
$$3x > 7 \quad \left(\text{adding 2 to both sides}\right)$$
$$x > \frac{7}{3} \quad \left(\text{dividing both sides by 3}\right)$$

To solve the inequality $\frac{5x - 1}{-2} < 3$ for x, isolate x by using the following steps:

$$\frac{5x - 1}{-2} < 3$$
$$5x - 1 > -6 \quad \left(\text{multiplying both sides by } -2\right)$$
$$5x > -5 \quad \left(\text{adding 1 to both sides}\right)$$
$$x > -1 \quad \left(\text{dividing both sides by 5}\right)$$

9. Absolute Value

The absolute value of x, denoted $|x|$, is defined to be x if $x \geq 0$ and $-x$ if $x < 0$. Note that $\sqrt{x^2}$ denotes the nonnegative square root of x^2, and so $\sqrt{x^2} = |x|$.

10. Functions

An algebraic expression in one variable can be used to define a *function* of that variable. A function is denoted by a letter such as f or g along with the variable in the expression. For example, the expression $x^3 - 5x^2 + 2$ defines a function f that can be denoted by

$$f(x) = x^3 - 5x^2 + 2.$$

The expression $\frac{2z + 7}{\sqrt{z + 1}}$ defines a function g that can be denoted by

$$g(z) = \frac{2z + 7}{\sqrt{z + 1}}.$$

The symbols "$f(x)$" or "$g(z)$" do not represent products; each is merely the symbol for an expression, and is read "f of x" or "g of z."

Function notation provides a short way of writing the result of substituting a value for a variable. If $x = 1$ is substituted in the first expression, the result can be written $f(1) = -2$, and $f(1)$ is called the "value of f at $x = 1$." Similarly, if $z = 0$ is substituted in the second expression, then the value of g at $z = 0$ is $g(0) = 7$.

Once a function $f(x)$ is defined, it is useful to think of the variable x as an input and $f(x)$ as the corresponding output. In any function there can be no more than one output for any given input. However, more than one input can give the same output; for example, if $h(x) = |x + 3|$, then $h(-4) = 1 = h(-2)$.

The set of all allowable inputs for a function is called the *domain* of the function. For f and g defined above, the domain of f is the set of all real numbers and the domain of g is the set of all numbers greater than −1. The domain of any function can be arbitrarily specified, as in the function defined by "$h(x) = 9x - 5$ for $0 \le x \le 10$." Without such a restriction, the domain is assumed to be all values of x that result in a real number when substituted into the function.

The domain of a function can consist of only the positive integers and possibly 0. For example,

$$a(n) = n^2 + \frac{n}{5} \text{ for } n = 0, 1, 2, 3, \ldots.$$

Such a function is called a *sequence* and $a(n)$ is denoted by a_n. The value of the sequence a_n at $n = 3$ is $a_3 = 3^2 + \frac{3}{5} = 9.60$. As another example, consider the sequence defined by $b_n = (-1)^n (n!)$ for $n = 1, 2, 3, \ldots$. A sequence like this is often indicated by listing its values in the order $b_1, b_2, b_3, \ldots, b_n, \ldots$ as follows:

$-1, 2, -6, \ldots, (-1)^n(n!), \ldots$, and $(-1)^n(n!)$ is called the nth term of the sequence.

3.3 Geometry

1. Lines

In geometry, the word "line" refers to a straight line that extends without end in both directions.

The line above can be referred to as line PQ or line ℓ. The part of the line from P to Q is called a *line segment*. P and Q are the *endpoints* of the segment. The notation $\overline{PQ}$ is used to denote line segment PQ and PQ is used to denote the length of the segment.

2. Intersecting Lines and Angles

If two lines intersect, the opposite angles are called *vertical angles* and have the same measure. In the figure

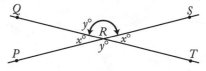

$\angle PRQ$ and $\angle SRT$ are vertical angles and $\angle QRS$ and $\angle PRT$ are vertical angles. Also, $x + y = 180°$ since PRS is a straight line.

3. Perpendicular Lines

An angle that has a measure of $90°$ is a *right angle*. If two lines intersect at right angles, the lines are *perpendicular*. For example:

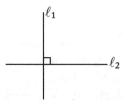

ℓ_1 and ℓ_2 above are perpendicular, denoted by $\ell_1 \perp \ell_2$. A right angle symbol in an angle of intersection indicates that the lines are perpendicular.

4. Parallel Lines

If two lines that are in the same plane do not intersect, the two lines are *parallel*. In the figure

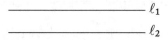

lines ℓ_1 and ℓ_2 are parallel, denoted by $\ell_1 \parallel \ell_2$. If two parallel lines are intersected by a third line, as shown below, then the angle measures are related as indicated, where $x + y = 180°$.

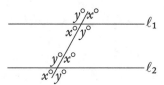

5. Polygons (Convex)

A *polygon* is a closed plane figure formed by three or more line segments, called the *sides* of the polygon. Each side intersects exactly two other sides at their endpoints. The points of intersection of the sides are *vertices*. The term "polygon" will be used to mean a convex polygon, that is, a polygon in which each interior angle has a measure of less than $180°$.

The following figures are polygons:

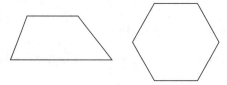

The following figures are not polygons:

A polygon with three sides is a *triangle*; with four sides, a *quadrilateral*; with five sides, a *pentagon*; and with six sides, a *hexagon*.

The sum of the interior angle measures of a triangle is $180°$. In general, the sum of the interior angle measures of a polygon with n sides is equal to $(n-2)180°$. For example, this sum for a pentagon is $(5-2)180° = (3)180° = 540°$.

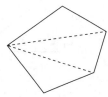

Note that a pentagon can be partitioned into three triangles and therefore the sum of the angle measures can be found by adding the sum of the angle measures of three triangles.

The *perimeter* of a polygon is the sum of the lengths of its sides.

The commonly used phrase "area of a triangle" (or any other plane figure) is used to mean the area of the region enclosed by that figure.

6. Triangles

There are several special types of triangles with important properties. But one property that all triangles share is that the sum of the lengths of any two of the sides is greater than the length of the third side, as illustrated below.

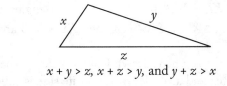

$x + y > z$, $x + z > y$, and $y + z > x$

An *equilateral* triangle has all sides of equal length. All angles of an equilateral triangle have equal measure. An *isosceles* triangle has at least two sides of the same length. If two sides of a triangle have the same length, then the two angles opposite those sides have the same measure. Conversely, if two angles of a triangle have the same measure, then the sides opposite those angles have the same length. In isosceles triangle *PQR* below, $x = y$ since $PQ = QR$.

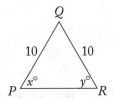

A triangle that has a right angle is a *right* triangle. In a right triangle, the side opposite the right angle is the *hypotenuse*, and the other two sides are the *legs*. An important theorem concerning right triangles is the *Pythagorean theorem*, which states: In a right triangle, the square of the length of the hypotenuse is equal to the sum of the squares of the lengths of the legs.

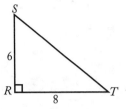

In the figure above, ΔRST is a right triangle, so $\left(RS\right)^2 + \left(RT\right)^2 = \left(ST\right)^2$. Here, $RS = 6$ and $RT = 8$, so $ST = 10$, since $6^2 + 8^2 = 36 + 64 = 100 = \left(ST\right)^2$ and $ST = \sqrt{100}$. Any triangle in which the lengths of the sides are in the ratio 3:4:5 is a right triangle. In general, if a, b, and c are the lengths of the sides of a triangle and $a^2 + b^2 = c^2$, then the triangle is a right triangle.

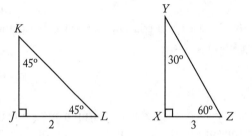

In $45° - 45° - 90°$ triangles, the lengths of the sides are in the ratio $1:1:\sqrt{2}$. For example, in ΔJKL, if $JL = 2$, then $JK = 2$ and $KL = 2\sqrt{2}$. In $30° - 60° - 90°$ triangles, the lengths of the sides are in the ratio $1:\sqrt{3}:2$. For example, in ΔXYZ, if $XZ = 3$, then $XY = 3\sqrt{3}$ and $YZ = 6$.

The *altitude* of a triangle is the segment drawn from a vertex perpendicular to the side opposite that vertex. Relative to that vertex and altitude, the opposite side is called the *base*.

The area of a triangle is equal to:

$$\frac{\left(\text{the length of the altitude}\right) \times \left(\text{the length of the base}\right)}{2}$$

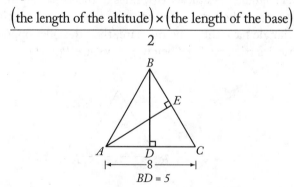

In ΔABC, $\overline{BD}$ is the altitude to base $\overline{AC}$ and $\overline{AE}$ is the altitude to base $\overline{BC}$. The area of ΔABC is equal to

$$\frac{BD \times AC}{2} = \frac{5 \times 8}{2} = 20.$$

The area is also equal to $\dfrac{AE \times BC}{2}$. If $\triangle ABC$ above is isosceles and $AB = BC$, then altitude $\overline{BD}$ bisects the base; that is, $AD = DC = 4$. Similarly, any altitude of an equilateral triangle bisects the side to which it is drawn.

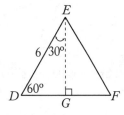

In equilateral triangle DEF, if $DE = 6$, then $DG = 3$ and $EG = 3\sqrt{3}$. The area of $\triangle DEF$ is equal to $\dfrac{3\sqrt{3} \times 6}{2} = 9\sqrt{3}$.

7. Quadrilaterals

A polygon with four sides is a *quadrilateral*. A quadrilateral in which both pairs of opposite sides are parallel is a *parallelogram*. The opposite sides of a parallelogram also have equal length.

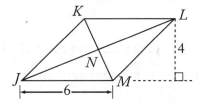

In parallelogram $JKLM$, $\overline{JK} \parallel \overline{LM}$ and $JK = LM$; $\overline{KL} \parallel \overline{JM}$ and $KL = JM$.

The diagonals of a parallelogram bisect each other (that is, $KN = NM$ and $JN = NL$).

The area of a parallelogram is equal to

$$(\text{the length of the altitude}) \times (\text{the length of the base}).$$

The area of $JKLM$ is equal to $4 \times 6 = 24$.

A parallelogram with right angles is a *rectangle*, and a rectangle with all sides of equal length is a *square*.

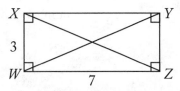

The perimeter of $WXYZ = 2(3) + 2(7) = 20$ and the area of $WXYZ$ is equal to $3 \times 7 = 21$.

The diagonals of a rectangle are equal; therefore $WY = XZ = \sqrt{9 + 49} = \sqrt{58}$.

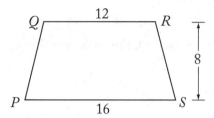

A quadrilateral with two sides that are parallel, as shown above, is a *trapezoid*. The area of trapezoid *PQRS* may be calculated as follows:

$$\frac{1}{2}(\text{the sum of the lengths of the bases})(\text{the height}) = \frac{1}{2}(QR + PS)(8) = \frac{1}{2}(28 \times 8) = 112.$$

8. Circles

A *circle* is a set of points in a plane that are all located the same distance from a fixed point (the *center* of the circle).

A *chord* of a circle is a line segment that has its endpoints on the circle. A chord that passes through the center of the circle is a *diameter* of the circle. A *radius* of a circle is a segment from the center of the circle to a point on the circle. The words "diameter" and "radius" are also used to refer to the lengths of these segments.

The *circumference* of a circle is the distance around the circle. If r is the radius of the circle, then the circumference is equal to $2\pi r$, where π is approximately $\frac{22}{7}$ or 3.14. The *area* of a circle of radius r is equal to πr^2.

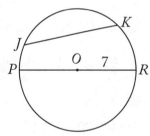

In the circle above, O is the center of the circle and $\overline{JK}$ and $\overline{PR}$ are chords. $\overline{PR}$ is a diameter and $\overline{OR}$ is a radius. If $OR = 7$, then the circumference of the circle is $2\pi(7) = 14\pi$ and the area of the circle is $\pi(7)^2 = 49\pi$.

The number of degrees of arc in a circle (or the number of degrees in a complete revolution) is 360.

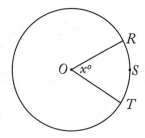

In the circle with center O above, the length of arc RST is $\dfrac{x}{360}$ of the circumference of the circle; for example, if $x = 60$, then arc RST has length $\dfrac{1}{6}$ of the circumference of the circle.

A line that has exactly one point in common with a circle is said to be *tangent* to the circle, and that common point is called the *point of tangency*. A radius or diameter with an endpoint at the point of tangency is perpendicular to the tangent line, and, conversely, a line that is perpendicular to a radius or diameter at one of its endpoints is tangent to the circle at that endpoint.

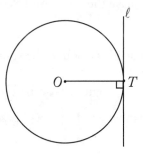

The line ℓ above is tangent to the circle and radius $\overline{OT}$ is perpendicular to ℓ.

If each vertex of a polygon lies on a circle, then the polygon is *inscribed* in the circle and the circle is *circumscribed* about the polygon. If each side of a polygon is tangent to a circle, then the polygon is *circumscribed* about the circle and the circle is *inscribed* in the polygon.

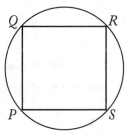 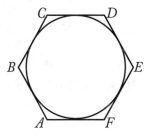

In the figure above, quadrilateral $PQRS$ is inscribed in a circle and hexagon $ABCDEF$ is circumscribed about a circle.

If a triangle is inscribed in a circle so that one of its sides is a diameter of the circle, then the triangle is a right triangle.

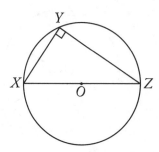

In the circle above, $\overline{XZ}$ is a diameter and the measure of $\angle XYZ$ is $90°$.

9. Rectangular Solids and Cylinders

A *rectangular solid* is a three-dimensional figure formed by 6 rectangular surfaces, as shown below. Each rectangular surface is a *face*. Each solid or dotted line segment is an *edge*, and each point at which the edges meet is a *vertex*. A rectangular solid has 6 faces, 12 edges, and 8 vertices. Opposite faces are parallel rectangles that have the same dimensions. A rectangular solid in which all edges are of equal length is a *cube*.

The *surface area* of a rectangular solid is equal to the sum of the areas of all the faces. The *volume* is equal to

$$(\text{length}) \times (\text{width}) \times (\text{height});$$

in other words, $(\text{area of base}) \times (\text{height})$.

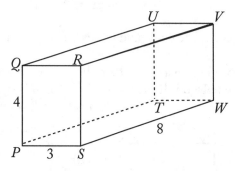

In the rectangular solid above, the dimensions are 3, 4, and 8. The surface area is equal to $2(3 \times 4) + 2(3 \times 8) + 2(4 \times 8) = 136$. The volume is equal to $3 \times 4 \times 8 = 96$.

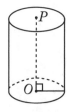

The figure above is a right circular *cylinder*. The two bases are circles of the same size with centers O and P, respectively, and altitude (height) $\overline{OP}$ is perpendicular to the bases. The surface area of a right circular cylinder with a base of radius r and height h is equal to $2(\pi r^2) + 2\pi rh$ (the sum of the areas of the two bases plus the area of the curved surface).

The volume of a cylinder is equal to $\pi r^2 h$, that is,

$$(\text{area of base}) \times (\text{height}).$$

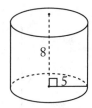

In the cylinder above, the surface area is equal to

$$2(25\pi) + 2\pi(5)(8) = 130\pi,$$

and the volume is equal to

$$25\pi(8) = 200\pi.$$

10. Coordinate Geometry

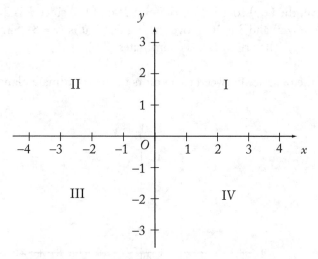

The figure above shows the (rectangular) *coordinate plane*. The horizontal line is called the *x-axis* and the perpendicular vertical line is called the *y-axis*. The point at which these two axes intersect, designated *O*, is called the *origin*. The axes divide the plane into four quadrants, I, II, III, and IV, as shown.

Each point in the plane has an *x-coordinate* and a *y-coordinate*. A point is identified by an ordered pair (*x*,*y*) of numbers in which the *x*-coordinate is the first number and the *y*-coordinate is the second number.

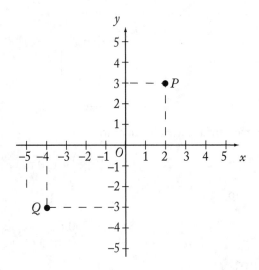

In the graph above, the (x,y) coordinates of point P are $(2,3)$ since P is 2 units to the right of the y-axis (that is, $x = 2$) and 3 units above the x-axis (that is, $y = 3$). Similarly, the (x,y) coordinates of point Q are $(-4,-3)$. The origin O has coordinates $(0,0)$.

One way to find the distance between two points in the coordinate plane is to use the Pythagorean theorem.

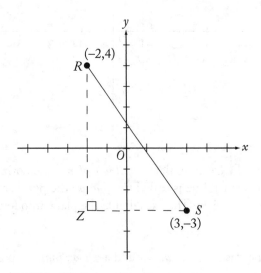

To find the distance between points R and S using the Pythagorean theorem, draw the triangle as shown. Note that Z has (x,y) coordinates $(-2,-3)$, $RZ = 7$, and $ZS = 5$. Therefore, the distance between R and S is equal to

$$\sqrt{7^2 + 5^2} = \sqrt{74}.$$

For a line in the coordinate plane, the coordinates of each point on the line satisfy a linear equation of the form $y = mx + b$ (or the form $x = a$ if the line is vertical). For example, each point on the line on the next page satisfies the equation $y = -\frac{1}{2}x + 1$. One can verify this for the points $(-2,2)$, $(2,0)$, and $(0,1)$ by substituting the respective coordinates for x and y in the equation.

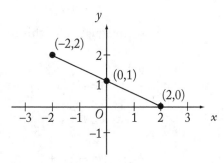

In the equation $y = mx + b$ of a line, the coefficient m is the *slope* of the line and the constant term b is the *y-intercept* of the line. For any two points on the line, the slope is defined to be the ratio of the difference in the y-coordinates to the difference in the x-coordinates. Using $(-2, 2)$ and $(2, 0)$ above, the slope is

$$\frac{\text{The difference in the } y\text{-coordinates}}{\text{The difference in the } x\text{-coordinates}} = \frac{0 - 2}{2 - (-2)} = \frac{-2}{4} = -\frac{1}{2}.$$

The y-intercept is the y-coordinate of the point at which the line intersects the y-axis. For the line above, the y-intercept is 1, and this is the resulting value of y when x is set equal to 0 in the equation $y = -\frac{1}{2}x + 1$. The *x-intercept* is the x-coordinate of the point at which the line intersects the x-axis. The x-intercept can be found by setting $y = 0$ and solving for x. For the line $y = -\frac{1}{2}x + 1$, this gives

$$-\frac{1}{2}x + 1 = 0$$

$$-\frac{1}{2}x = -1$$

$$x = 2.$$

Thus, the x-intercept is 2.

Given any two points (x_1, y_1) and (x_2, y_2) with $x_1 \neq x_2$, the equation of the line passing through these points can be found by applying the definition of slope. Since the slope is $m = \dfrac{y_2 - y_1}{x_2 - x_1}$, then using a point known to be on the line, say (x_1, y_1), any point (x, y) on the line must satisfy $\dfrac{y - y_1}{x - x_1} = m$, or $y - y_1 = m(x - x_1)$. (Using (x_2, y_2) as the known point would yield an equivalent equation.) For example, consider the points $(-2, 4)$ and $(3, -3)$ on the line below.

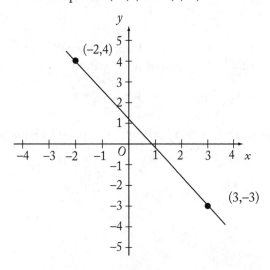

The slope of this line is $\dfrac{-3-4}{3-(-2)} = \dfrac{-7}{5}$, so an equation of this line can be found using the point (3,–3) as follows:

$$y - \left(-3\right) = -\frac{7}{5}\left(x - 3\right)$$

$$y + 3 = -\frac{7}{5}x + \frac{21}{5}$$

$$y = -\frac{7}{5}x + \frac{6}{5}$$

The y-intercept is $\dfrac{6}{5}$. The x-intercept can be found as follows:

$$0 = -\frac{7}{5}x + \frac{6}{5}$$

$$\frac{7}{5}x = \frac{6}{5}$$

$$x = \frac{6}{7}$$

Both of these intercepts can be seen on the graph.

If the slope of a line is negative, the line slants downward from left to right; if the slope is positive, the line slants upward. If the slope is 0, the line is horizontal; the equation of such a line is of the form $y = b$ since $m = 0$. For a vertical line, slope is not defined, and the equation is of the form $x = a$, where a is the x-intercept.

There is a connection between graphs of lines in the coordinate plane and solutions of two linear equations with two unknowns. If two linear equations with unknowns x and y have a unique solution, then the graphs of the equations are two lines that intersect in one point, which is the solution. If the equations are equivalent, then they represent the same line with infinitely many points or solutions. If the equations have no solution, then they represent parallel lines, which do not intersect.

There is also a connection between functions (see section 3.2.10) and the coordinate plane. If a function is graphed in the coordinate plane, the function can be understood in different and useful ways. Consider the function defined by

$$f\left(x\right) = -\frac{7}{5}x + \frac{6}{5}.$$

If the value of the function, $f(x)$, is equated with the variable y, then the graph of the function in the xy-coordinate plane is simply the graph of the equation

$$y = -\frac{7}{5}x + \frac{6}{5}$$

shown above. Similarly, any function $f(x)$ can be graphed by equating y with the value of the function:

$$y = f\left(x\right).$$

So for any x in the domain of the function f, the point with coordinates $(x, f(x))$ is on the graph of f, and the graph consists entirely of these points.

As another example, consider a quadratic polynomial function defined by $f(x) = x^2 - 1$. One can plot several points $(x, f(x))$ on the graph to understand the connection between a function and its graph:

x	$f(x)$
-2	3
-1	0
0	-1
1	0
2	3

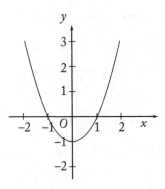

If all the points were graphed for $-2 \le x \le 2$, then the graph would appear as follows.

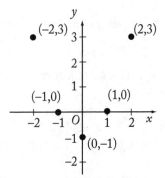

The graph of a quadratic function is called a *parabola* and always has the shape of the curve above, although it may be upside down or have a greater or lesser width. Note that the roots of the equation $f(x) = x^2 - 1 = 0$ are $x = 1$ and $x = -1$; these coincide with the x-intercepts since x-intercepts are found by setting $y = 0$ and solving for x. Also, the y-intercept is $f(0) = -1$ because this is the value of y corresponding to $x = 0$. For any function f, the x-intercepts are the solutions of the equation $f(x) = 0$ and the y-intercept is the value $f(0)$.

3.4 Word Problems

Many of the principles discussed in this chapter are used to solve word problems. The following discussion of word problems illustrates some of the techniques and concepts used in solving such problems.

1. Rate Problems

The distance that an object travels is equal to the product of the average speed at which it travels and the amount of time it takes to travel that distance, that is,

$$\text{Rate} \times \text{Time} = \text{Distance}.$$

Example 1: If a car travels at an average speed of 70 kilometers per hour for 4 hours, how many kilometers does it travel?

Solution: Since rate × time = distance, simply multiply 70 km/hour × 4 hours. Thus, the car travels 280 kilometers in 4 hours.

To determine the average rate at which an object travels, divide the total distance traveled by the total amount of traveling time.

Example 2: On a 400-mile trip, Car X traveled half the distance at 40 miles per hour (mph) and the other half at 50 mph. What was the average speed of Car X ?

Solution: First it is necessary to determine the amount of traveling time. During the first 200 miles, the car traveled at 40 mph; therefore, it took $\frac{200}{40} = 5$ hours to travel the first 200 miles.

During the second 200 miles, the car traveled at 50 mph; therefore, it took $\frac{200}{50} = 4$ hours to travel the second 200 miles. Thus, the average speed of Car X was $\frac{400}{9} = 44\frac{4}{9}$ mph. Note that the average speed is *not* $\frac{40+50}{2} = 45$.

Some rate problems can be solved by using ratios.

Example 3: If 5 shirts cost $44, then, at this rate, what is the cost of 8 shirts?

Solution: If c is the cost of the 8 shirts, then $\frac{5}{44} = \frac{8}{c}$. Cross multiplication results in the equation

$$5c = 8 \times 44 = 352$$

$$c = \frac{352}{5} = 70.40$$

The 8 shirts cost $70.40.

2. Work Problems

In a work problem, the rates at which certain persons or machines work alone are usually given, and it is necessary to compute the rate at which they work together (or vice versa).

The basic formula for solving work problems is $\frac{1}{r} + \frac{1}{s} = \frac{1}{h}$, where r and s are, for example, the number of hours it takes Rae and Sam, respectively, to complete a job when working alone, and h is the number of hours it takes Rae and Sam to do the job when working together. The reasoning is that in 1 hour Rae does $\frac{1}{r}$ of the job, Sam does $\frac{1}{s}$ of the job, and Rae and Sam together do $\frac{1}{h}$ of the job.

Example 1: If Machine X can produce 1,000 bolts in 4 hours and Machine Y can produce 1,000 bolts in 5 hours, in how many hours can Machines X and Y, working together at these constant rates, produce 1,000 bolts?

Solution:

$$\frac{1}{4} + \frac{1}{5} = \frac{1}{h}$$

$$\frac{5}{20} + \frac{4}{20} = \frac{1}{h}$$

$$\frac{9}{20} = \frac{1}{h}$$

$$9h = 20$$

$$h = \frac{20}{9} = 2\frac{2}{9}$$

Working together, Machines X and Y can produce 1,000 bolts in $2\frac{2}{9}$ hours.

Example 2: If Art and Rita can do a job in 4 hours when working together at their respective constant rates and Art can do the job alone in 6 hours, in how many hours can Rita do the job alone?

Solution:

$$\frac{1}{6} + \frac{1}{R} = \frac{1}{4}$$

$$\frac{R+6}{6R} = \frac{1}{4}$$

$$4R + 24 = 6R$$

$$24 = 2R$$

$$12 = R$$

Working alone, Rita can do the job in 12 hours.

3. Mixture Problems

In mixture problems, substances with different characteristics are combined, and it is necessary to determine the characteristics of the resulting mixture.

Example 1: If 6 pounds of nuts that cost $1.20 per pound are mixed with 2 pounds of nuts that cost $1.60 per pound, what is the cost per pound of the mixture?

Solution: The total cost of the 8 pounds of nuts is

$$6\left(\$1.20\right) + 2\left(\$1.60\right) = \$10.40.$$

The cost per pound is $\dfrac{\$10.40}{8} = \$1.30.$

Example 2: How many liters of a solution that is 15 percent salt must be added to 5 liters of a solution that is 8 percent salt so that the resulting solution is 10 percent salt?

Solution: Let n represent the number of liters of the 15% solution. The amount of salt in the 15% solution [0.15n] plus the amount of salt in the 8% solution [(0.08)(5)] must be equal to the amount of salt in the 10% mixture $\left[0.10\left(n + 5\right)\right]$. Therefore,

$$0.15n + 0.08\left(5\right) = 0.10\left(n + 5\right)$$
$$15n + 40 = 10n + 50$$
$$5n = 10$$
$$n = 2 \text{ liters}$$

Two liters of the 15% salt solution must be added to the 8% solution to obtain the 10% solution.

4. Interest Problems

Interest can be computed in two basic ways. With simple annual interest, the interest is computed on the principal only and is equal to $\left(\text{principal}\right) \times \left(\text{interest rate}\right) \times \left(\text{time}\right)$. If interest is compounded, then interest is computed on the principal as well as on any interest already earned.

Example 1: If $8,000 is invested at 6 percent simple annual interest, how much interest is earned after 3 months?

Solution: Since the annual interest rate is 6%, the interest for 1 year is

$$\left(0.06\right)\left(\$8,000\right) = \$480.$$

The interest earned in 3 months is $\dfrac{3}{12}\left(\$480\right) = \$120.$

Example 2: If $10,000 is invested at 10 percent annual interest, compounded semiannually, what is the balance after 1 year?

Solution: The balance after the first 6 months would be

$$10,000 + \left(10,000\right)\left(0.05\right) = \$10,500.$$

The balance after one year would be $10,500 + \left(10,500\right)\left(0.05\right) = \$11,025.$

Note that the interest rate for each 6-month period is 5%, which is half of the 10% annual rate. The balance after one year can also be expressed as

$$10,000\left(1 + \frac{0.10}{2}\right)^2 \text{ dollars.}$$

5. Discount

If a price is discounted by n percent, then the price becomes $(100 - n)$ percent of the original price.

Example 1: A certain customer paid $24 for a dress. If that price represented a 25 percent discount on the original price of the dress, what was the original price of the dress?

Solution: If p is the original price of the dress, then $0.75p$ is the discounted price and $0.75\,p = \$24$, or $p = \$32$. The original price of the dress was $32.

Example 2: The price of an item is discounted by 20 percent and then this reduced price is discounted by an additional 30 percent. These two discounts are equal to an overall discount of what percent?

Solution: If p is the original price of the item, then $0.8p$ is the price after the first discount. The price after the second discount is $(0.7)(0.8)\,p = 0.56\,p$. This represents an overall discount of 44 percent $(100\% - 56\%)$.

6. Profit

Gross profit is equal to revenues minus expenses, or selling price minus cost.

Example: A certain appliance costs a merchant $30. At what price should the merchant sell the appliance in order to make a gross profit of 50 percent of the cost of the appliance?

Solution: If s is the selling price of the appliance, then $s - 30 = (0.5)(30)$, or $s = \$45$. The merchant should sell the appliance for $45.

7. Sets

If S is the set of numbers 1, 2, 3, and 4, you can write $S = \{1, 2, 3, 4\}$. Sets can also be represented by Venn diagrams. That is, the relationship among the members of sets can be represented by circles.

Example 1: Each of 25 people is enrolled in history, mathematics, or both. If 20 are enrolled in history and 18 are enrolled in mathematics, how many are enrolled in both history and mathematics?

Solution: The 25 people can be divided into three sets: those who study history only, those who study mathematics only, and those who study history and mathematics. Thus a Venn diagram may be drawn as follows, where n is the number of people enrolled in both courses, $20 - n$ is the number enrolled in history only, and $18 - n$ is the number enrolled in mathematics only.

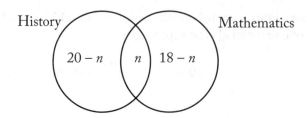

Since there is a total of 25 people, $(20 - n) + n + (18 - n) = 25$, or $n = 13$. Thirteen people are enrolled in both history and mathematics. Note that $20 + 18 - 13 = 25$, which is the general addition rule for two sets (see section 3.1.9).

Example 2: In a certain production lot, 40 percent of the toys are red and the remaining toys are green. Half of the toys are small and half are large. If 10 percent of the toys are red and small, and 40 toys are green and large, how many of the toys are red and large.

Solution: For this kind of problem, it is helpful to organize the information in a table:

	Red	Green	Total
Small	10%		50%
Large			50%
Total	40%	60%	100%

The numbers in the table are the percentages given. The following percentages can be computed on the basis of what is given:

	Red	Green	Total
Small	10%	40%	50%
Large	30%	20%	50%
Total	40%	60%	100%

Since 20% of the number of toys (n) are green and large, $0.20n = 40$ (40 toys are green and large), or $n = 200$. Therefore, 30% of the 200 toys, or $(0.3)(200) = 60$, are red and large.

8. Geometry Problems

The following is an example of a word problem involving geometry.
Example:

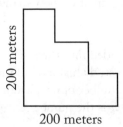

The figure above shows an aerial view of a piece of land. If all angles shown are right angles, what is the perimeter of the piece of land?

Solution: For reference, label the figure as

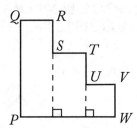

If all the angles are right angles, then $QR + ST + UV = PW$, and $RS + TU + VW = PQ$. Hence, the perimeter of the land is $2PW + 2PQ = 2 \times 200 + 2 \times 200 = 800$ meters.

9. Measurement Problems

Some questions on the GMAT involve metric units of measure, whereas others involve English units of measure. However, except for units of time, if a question requires conversion from one unit of measure to another, the relationship between those units will be given.

Example: A train travels at a constant rate of 25 meters per second. How many kilometers does it travel in 5 minutes? $\left(1 \text{ kilometer} = 1{,}000 \text{ meters}\right)$

Solution: In 1 minute the train travels $\left(25\right)\left(60\right) = 1{,}500$ meters, so in 5 minutes it travels 7,500 meters. Since 1 kilometer = 1,000 meters, it follows that 7,500 meters equals $\dfrac{7{,}500}{1{,}000}$, or 7.5 kilometers.

10. Data Interpretation

Occasionally a question or set of questions will be based on data provided in a table or graph. Some examples of tables and graphs are given below.

Example 1:

Population by Age Group (in thousands)	
Age	Population
17 years and under	63,376
18–44 years	86,738
45–64 years	43,845
65 years and over	24,054

How many people are 44 years old or younger?

Solution: The figures in the table are given in thousands. The answer in thousands can be obtained by adding 63,376 thousand and 86,738 thousand. The result is 150,114 thousand, which is 150,114,000.

Example 2:

AVERAGE TEMPERATURE AND PRECIPITATION IN CITY X

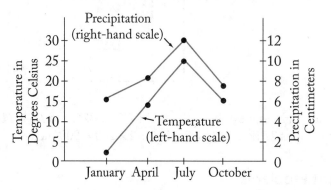

What are the average temperature and precipitation in City X during April?

Solution: Note that the scale on the left applies to the temperature line graph and the one on the right applies to the precipitation line graph. According to the graph, during April the average temperature is approximately 14° Celsius and the average precipitation is approximately 8 centimeters.

Example 3:

DISTRIBUTION OF AL'S WEEKLY NET SALARY

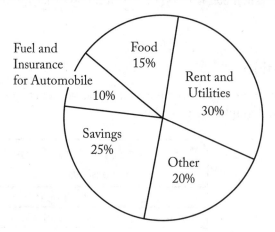

Al's weekly net salary is $350. To how many of the categories listed was at least $80 of Al's weekly net salary allocated?

Solution: In the circle graph, the relative sizes of the sectors are proportional to their corresponding values and the sum of the percents given is 100%. Note that $\frac{80}{350}$ is approximately 23%, so at least $80 was allocated to each of 2 categories—Rent and Utilities, and Savings—since their allocations are each greater than 23%.

4.0 Problem Solving

4.0 Problem Solving

The Quantitative section of the GMAT® test uses problem solving and data sufficiency questions to gauge your skill level. This chapter focuses on problem solving questions. Remember that quantitative questions require knowledge of the following:

- Arithmetic

- Elementary algebra

- Commonly known concepts of geometry

Problem solving questions are designed to test your basic mathematical skills and understanding of elementary mathematical concepts, as well as your ability to reason quantitatively, solve quantitative problems, and interpret graphic data. The mathematics knowledge required to answer the questions is no more advanced than what is generally taught in secondary school (or high school) mathematics classes.

In these questions, you are asked to solve each problem and select the best of the five answer choices given. Begin by reading the question thoroughly to determine exactly what information is given and to make sure you understand what is being asked. Scan the answer choices to understand your options. If the problem seems simple, take a few moments to see whether you can determine the answer. Then check your answer against the choices provided.

If you do not see your answer among the choices, or if the problem is complicated, take a closer look at the answer choices and think again about what the problem is asking. See whether you can eliminate some of the answer choices and narrow down your options. If you are still unable to narrow the answer down to a single choice, reread the question. Keep in mind that the answer will be based solely on the information provided in the question—don't allow your own experience and assumptions to interfere with your ability to find the correct answer to the question.

If you find yourself stuck on a question or unable to select the single correct answer, keep in mind that you have about two minutes to answer each quantitative question. You may run out of time if you take too long to answer any one question, so you may simply need to pick the answer that seems to make the most sense. Although guessing is generally not the best way to achieve a high GMAT score, making an educated guess is a good strategy for answering questions you are unsure of. Even if your answer to a particular question is incorrect, your answers to other questions will allow the test to accurately gauge your ability level.

The following pages include test-taking strategies, directions that will apply to questions of this type, sample questions, an answer key, and explanations for all the problems. These explanations present problem solving strategies that could be helpful in answering the questions.

4.1 Test-Taking Strategies

1. **Pace yourself.**
    Consult the on-screen timer periodically. Work as carefully as possible, but do not spend valuable time checking answers or pondering problems that you find difficult.

2. **Use the erasable notepad provided.**
    Working a problem out may help you avoid errors in solving the problem. If diagrams or figures are not presented, it may help if you draw your own.

3. **Read each question carefully to determine what is being asked.**
    For word problems, take one step at a time, reading each sentence carefully and translating the information into equations or other useful mathematical representations.

4. **Scan the answer choices before attempting to answer a question.**
    Scanning the answers can prevent you from putting answers in a form that is not given (e.g., finding the answer in decimal form, such as 0.25, when the choices are given in fractional form, such as $\frac{1}{4}$). Also, if the question requires approximations, a shortcut could serve well (e.g., you may be able to approximate 48 percent of a number by using half).

5. **Don't waste time trying to solve a problem that is too difficult for you.**
    Make your best guess and move on to the next question.

4.2 The Directions

These directions are very similar to those you will see for problem solving questions when you take the GMAT test. If you read them carefully and understand them clearly before sitting for the GMAT test, you will not need to spend too much time reviewing them once the test begins.

Solve the problem and indicate the best of the answer choices given.

Numbers: All numbers used are real numbers.

Figures: A figure accompanying a problem solving question is intended to provide information useful in solving the problem. Figures are drawn as accurately as possible. Exceptions will be clearly noted. Lines shown as straight are straight, and lines that appear jagged are also straight. The positions of points, angles, regions, etc., exist in the order shown, and angle measures are greater than zero. All figures lie in a plane unless otherwise indicated.

To register for the GMAT test go to www.mba.com

4.3 Sample Questions

Solve the problem and indicate the best of the answer choices given.

<u>Numbers:</u> All numbers used are real numbers.

<u>Figures:</u> A figure accompanying a problem solving question is intended to provide information useful in solving the problem. Figures are drawn as accurately as possible. Exceptions will be clearly noted. Lines shown as straight are straight, and lines that appear jagged are also straight. The positions of points, angles, regions, etc., exist in the order shown, and angle measures are greater than zero. All figures lie in a plane unless otherwise indicated.

1. The maximum recommended pulse rate R, when exercising, for a person who is x years of age is given by the equation $R = 176 - 0.8x$. What is the age, in years, of a person whose maximum recommended pulse rate when exercising is 140 ?

 (A) 40
 (B) 45
 (C) 50
 (D) 55
 (E) 60

2. If $\frac{x}{4}$ is 2 more than $\frac{x}{8}$, then $x =$

 (A) 4
 (B) 8
 (C) 16
 (D) 32
 (E) 64

3. If Mario was 32 years old 8 years ago, how old was he x years ago?

 (A) $x - 40$
 (B) $x - 24$
 (C) $40 - x$
 (D) $24 - x$
 (E) $24 + x$

4. If k is an integer and 0.0010101×10^k is greater than 1,000, what is the least possible value of k ?

 (A) 2
 (B) 3
 (C) 4
 (D) 5
 (E) 6

5. If $\left(b - 3\right)\left(4 + \dfrac{2}{b}\right) = 0$ and $b \neq 3$, then $b =$

 (A) -8
 (B) -2
 (C) $-\dfrac{1}{2}$
 (D) $\dfrac{1}{2}$
 (E) 2

6. The number $2 - 0.5$ is how many times the number $1 - 0.5$?

 (A) 2
 (B) 2.5
 (C) 3
 (D) 3.5
 (E) 4

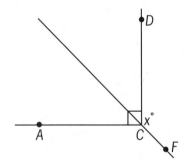

7. In the figure above, if F is a point on the line that bisects angle ACD and the measure of angle DCF is $x°$, which of the following is true of x ?

 (A) $90 \leq x < 100$
 (B) $100 \leq x < 110$
 (C) $110 \leq x < 120$
 (D) $120 \leq x < 130$
 (E) $130 \leq x < 140$

8. In which of the following pairs are the two numbers reciprocals of each other?

I. 3 and $\frac{1}{3}$

II. $\frac{1}{17}$ and $\frac{-1}{17}$

III. $\sqrt{3}$ and $\frac{\sqrt{3}}{3}$

(A) I only
(B) II only
(C) I and II
(D) I and III
(E) II and III

9. The price of a certain television set is discounted by 10 percent, and the reduced price is then discounted by 10 percent. This series of successive discounts is equivalent to a single discount of

(A) 20%
(B) 19%
(C) 18%
(D) 11%
(E) 10%

10. If there are 664,579 prime numbers among the first 10 million positive integers, approximately what percent of the first 10 million positive integers are prime numbers?

(A) 0.0066%
(B) 0.066%
(C) 0.66%
(D) 6.6%
(E) 66%

11. How many multiples of 4 are there between 12 and 96, inclusive?

(A) 21
(B) 22
(C) 23
(D) 24
(E) 25

12. In Country X a returning tourist may import goods with a total value of $500 or less tax free, but must pay an 8 percent tax on the portion of the total value in excess of $500. What tax must be paid by a returning tourist who imports goods with a total value of $730 ?

(A) $58.40
(B) $40.00
(C) $24.60
(D) $18.40
(E) $16.00

13. The number of rooms at Hotel G is 10 less than twice the number of rooms at Hotel H. If the total number of rooms at Hotel G and Hotel H is 425, what is the number of rooms at Hotel G ?

(A) 140
(B) 180
(C) 200
(D) 240
(E) 280

14. Which of the following is greater than $\frac{2}{3}$?

(A) $\frac{33}{50}$

(B) $\frac{8}{11}$

(C) $\frac{3}{5}$

(D) $\frac{13}{27}$

(E) $\frac{5}{8}$

15. If 60 percent of a rectangular floor is covered by a rectangular rug that is 9 feet by 12 feet, what is the area, in square feet, of the floor?

(A) 65
(B) 108
(C) 180
(D) 270
(E) 300

16. Three machines, individually, can do a certain job in 4, 5, and 6 hours, respectively. What is the greatest part of the job that can be done in one hour by two of the machines working together at their respective rates?

    (A) $\frac{11}{30}$

    (B) $\frac{9}{20}$

    (C) $\frac{3}{5}$

    (D) $\frac{11}{15}$

    (E) $\frac{5}{6}$

17. The value of $-3-(-10)$ is how much greater than the value of $-10-(-3)$?

    (A) 0
    (B) 6
    (C) 7
    (D) 14
    (E) 26

18. If X and Y are sets of integers, $X \triangle Y$ denotes the set of integers that belong to set X or set Y, but not both. If X consists of 10 integers, Y consists of 18 integers, and 6 of the integers are in both X and Y, then $X \triangle Y$ consists of how many integers?

    (A) 6
    (B) 16
    (C) 22
    (D) 30
    (E) 174

		x
37	38	15
		y

19. In the figure above, the sum of the three numbers in the horizontal row equals the product of the three numbers in the vertical column. What is the value of xy?

    (A) 6
    (B) 15
    (C) 35
    (D) 75
    (E) 90

20. $(1+\sqrt{5})(1-\sqrt{5})=$

    (A) -4
    (B) 2
    (C) 6
    (D) $-4-2\sqrt{5}$
    (E) $6-2\sqrt{5}$

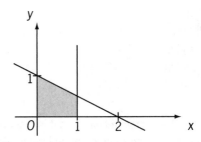

21. In the rectangular coordinate system above, the shaded region is bounded by straight lines. Which of the following is NOT an equation of one of the boundary lines?

    (A) $x=0$
    (B) $y=0$
    (C) $x=1$
    (D) $x-y=0$
    (E) $x+2y=2$

22. A certain population of bacteria doubles every 10 minutes. If the number of bacteria in the population initially was 10^4, what was the number in the population 1 hour later?

    (A) $2(10^4)$
    (B) $6(10^4)$
    (C) $(2^6)(10^4)$
    (D) $(10^6)(10^4)$
    (E) $(10^4)^6$

23. How many minutes does it take to travel 120 miles at 400 miles per hour?

    (A) 3

    (B) $3\frac{1}{3}$

    (C) $8\frac{2}{3}$

    (D) 12

    (E) 18

24. If the perimeter of a rectangular garden plot is 34 feet and its area is 60 square feet, what is the length of each of the longer sides?

   (A)   5 ft
   (B)   6 ft
   (C)   10 ft
   (D)   12 ft
   (E)   15 ft

25. A certain manufacturer produces items for which the production costs consist of annual fixed costs totaling $130,000 and variable costs averaging $8 per item. If the manufacturer's selling price per item is $15, how many items must the manufacturer produce and sell to earn an annual profit of $150,000 ?

   (A)   2,858
   (B)   18,667
   (C)   21,429
   (D)   35,000
   (E)   40,000

26. In a poll of 66,000 physicians, only 20 percent responded; of these, 10 percent disclosed their preference for pain reliever X. How many of the physicians who responded did <u>not</u> disclose a preference for pain reliever X ?

   (A)   1,320
   (B)   5,280
   (C)   6,600
   (D)   10,560
   (E)   11,880

27. $\dfrac{3}{100} + \dfrac{5}{1,000} + \dfrac{7}{100,000} =$

   (A)   0.357
   (B)   0.3507
   (C)   0.35007
   (D)   0.0357
   (E)   0.03507

28. If the number n of calculators sold per week varies with the price p in dollars according to the equation $n = 300 - 20p$, what would be the total weekly revenue from the sale of $10 calculators?

   (A) $ 100
   (B) $ 300
   (C) $1,000
   (D) $2,800
   (E) $3,000

29. Which of the following fractions is equal to the decimal 0.0625 ?

   (A) $\dfrac{5}{8}$

   (B) $\dfrac{3}{8}$

   (C) $\dfrac{1}{16}$

   (D) $\dfrac{1}{18}$

   (E) $\dfrac{3}{80}$

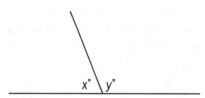

30. In the figure above, if $\dfrac{x}{x+y} = \dfrac{3}{8}$, then $x =$

   (A)   60
   (B)   67.5
   (C)   72
   (D)   108
   (E)   112.5

31. If positive integers x and y are not both odd, which of the following must be even?

   (A) xy
   (B) $x+y$
   (C) $x-y$
   (D) $x+y-1$
   (E) $2(x+y)-1$

32. On 3 sales John has received commissions of $240, $80, and $110, and he has 1 additional sale pending. If John is to receive an average (arithmetic mean) commission of exactly $150 on the 4 sales, then the 4th commission must be

    (A) $164
    (B) $170
    (C) $175
    (D) $182
    (E) $185

33. The annual budget of a certain college is to be shown on a circle graph. If the size of each sector of the graph is to be proportional to the amount of the budget it represents, how many degrees of the circle should be used to represent an item that is 15 percent of the budget?

    (A) 15°
    (B) 36°
    (C) 54°
    (D) 90°
    (E) 150°

34. During a two-week period, the price of an ounce of silver increased by 25 percent by the end of the first week and then decreased by 20 percent of this new price by the end of the second week. If the price of silver was x dollars per ounce at the beginning of the two-week period, what was the price, in dollars per ounce, by the end of the period?

    (A) 0.8x
    (B) 0.95x
    (C) x
    (D) 1.05x
    (E) 1.25x

35. In a certain pond, 50 fish were caught, tagged, and returned to the pond. A few days later, 50 fish were caught again, of which 2 were found to have been tagged. If the percent of tagged fish in the second catch approximates the percent of tagged fish in the pond, what is the approximate number of fish in the pond?

    (A) 400
    (B) 625
    (C) 1,250
    (D) 2,500
    (E) 10,000

36. $\sqrt{16 + 16} =$

    (A) $4\sqrt{2}$
    (B) $8\sqrt{2}$
    (C) $16\sqrt{2}$
    (D) 8
    (E) 16

37. An automobile's gasoline mileage varies, depending on the speed of the automobile, between 18.0 and 22.4 miles per gallon, inclusive. What is the maximum distance, in miles, that the automobile could be driven on 15 gallons of gasoline?

    (A) 336
    (B) 320
    (C) 303
    (D) 284
    (E) 270

38. The organizers of a fair projected a 25 percent increase in attendance this year over that of last year, but attendance this year actually decreased by 20 percent. What percent of the projected attendance was the actual attendance?

    (A) 45%
    (B) 56%
    (C) 64%
    (D) 75%
    (E) 80%

39. What is the ratio of $\frac{3}{4}$ to the product $4\left(\frac{3}{4}\right)$?

    (A) $\frac{1}{4}$

    (B) $\frac{1}{3}$

    (C) $\frac{4}{9}$

    (D) $\frac{9}{4}$

    (E) 4

40. If $3 - x = 2x - 3$, then $4x =$

    (A) −24
    (B) −8
    (C) 0
    (D) 8
    (E) 24

$$2x + 2y = -4$$
$$4x + y = 1$$

41. In the system of equations above, what is the value of x?

    (A) −3
    (B) −1
    (C) $\dfrac{2}{5}$
    (D) 1
    (E) $1\dfrac{3}{4}$

42. If $x > 3{,}000$, then the value of $\dfrac{x}{2x+1}$ is closest to

    (A) $\dfrac{1}{6}$
    (B) $\dfrac{1}{3}$
    (C) $\dfrac{10}{21}$
    (D) $\dfrac{1}{2}$
    (E) $\dfrac{3}{2}$

43. If 18 is 15 percent of 30 percent of a certain number, what is the number?

    (A) 9
    (B) 36
    (C) 40
    (D) 81
    (E) 400

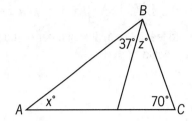

44. In $\triangle ABC$ above, what is x in terms of z?

    (A) $z + 73$
    (B) $z - 73$
    (C) $70 - z$
    (D) $z - 70$
    (E) $73 - z$

45. $\dfrac{(3)(0.072)}{0.54} =$

    (A) 0.04
    (B) 0.3
    (C) 0.4
    (D) 0.8
    (E) 4.0

46. What is the maximum number of $1\dfrac{1}{4}$ foot pieces of wire that can be cut from a wire that is 24 feet long?

    (A) 11
    (B) 18
    (C) 19
    (D) 20
    (E) 30

$$\frac{61.24 \times (0.998)^2}{\sqrt{403}}$$

47. The expression above is approximately equal to

    (A) 1
    (B) 3
    (C) 4
    (D) 5
    (E) 6

48. If the numbers $\frac{17}{24}$, $\frac{1}{2}$, $\frac{3}{8}$, $\frac{3}{4}$, and $\frac{9}{16}$ were ordered from greatest to least, the middle number of the resulting sequence would be

   (A) $\frac{17}{24}$

   (B) $\frac{1}{2}$

   (C) $\frac{3}{8}$

   (D) $\frac{3}{4}$

   (E) $\frac{9}{16}$

49. Last year if 97 percent of the revenues of a company came from domestic sources and the remaining revenues, totaling $450,000, came from foreign sources, what was the total of the company's revenues?

   (A) $ 1,350,000
   (B) $ 1,500,000
   (C) $ 4,500,000
   (D) $ 15,000,000
   (E) $150,000,000

50. $\frac{2+2\sqrt{6}}{2} =$

   (A) $\sqrt{6}$
   (B) $2\sqrt{6}$
   (C) $1+\sqrt{6}$
   (D) $1+2\sqrt{6}$
   (E) $2+\sqrt{6}$

51. A certain fishing boat is chartered by 6 people who are to contribute equally to the total charter cost of $480. If each person contributes equally to a $150 down payment, how much of the charter cost will each person still owe?

   (A) $80
   (B) $66
   (C) $55
   (D) $50
   (E) $45

52. Craig sells major appliances. For each appliance he sells, Craig receives a commission of $50 plus 10 percent of the selling price. During one particular week Craig sold 6 appliances for selling prices totaling $3,620. What was the total of Craig's commissions for that week?

   (A) $412
   (B) $526
   (C) $585
   (D) $605
   (E) $662

53. What number when multiplied by $\frac{4}{7}$ yields $\frac{6}{7}$ as the result?

   (A) $\frac{2}{7}$

   (B) $\frac{3}{3}$

   (C) $\frac{3}{2}$

   (D) $\frac{24}{7}$

   (E) $\frac{7}{2}$

54. If 3 pounds of dried apricots that cost x dollars per pound are mixed with 2 pounds of prunes that cost y dollars per pound, what is the cost, in dollars, per pound of the mixture?

   (A) $\frac{3x+2y}{5}$

   (B) $\frac{3x+2y}{x+y}$

   (C) $\frac{3x+2y}{xy}$

   (D) $5(3x+2y)$

   (E) $3x+2y$

55. Which of the following must be equal to zero for all real numbers x ?

   I. $-\dfrac{1}{x}$

   II. $x+(-x)$

   III. x^0

   (A)   I only
   (B)   II only
   (C)   I and III only
   (D)   II and III only
   (E)   I, II, and III

	City A	City B	City C	City D	City E	City F
City A						
City B						
City C						
City D						
City E						
City F						

56. In the table above, what is the least number of table entries that are needed to show the mileage between each city and each of the other five cities?

   (A)   15
   (B)   21
   (C)   25
   (D)   30
   (E)   36

57. If $(t-8)$ is a factor of $t^2 - kt - 48$, then $k =$

   (A)   –6
   (B)   –2
   (C)   2
   (D)   6
   (E)   14

58. $\dfrac{31}{125} =$

   (A)   0.248
   (B)   0.252
   (C)   0.284
   (D)   0.312
   (E)   0.320

59. Members of a social club met to address 280 newsletters. If they addressed $\dfrac{1}{4}$ of the newsletters during the first hour and $\dfrac{2}{5}$ of the remaining newsletters during the second hour, how many newsletters did they address during the second hour?

   (A)   28
   (B)   42
   (C)   63
   (D)   84
   (E)   112

60. $\dfrac{1}{3-\dfrac{1}{3-\dfrac{1}{3-1}}} =$

   (A) $\dfrac{7}{23}$

   (B) $\dfrac{5}{13}$

   (C) $\dfrac{2}{3}$

   (D) $\dfrac{23}{7}$

   (E) $\dfrac{13}{5}$

61. After 4,000 gallons of water were added to a large water tank that was already filled to $\dfrac{3}{4}$ of its capacity, the tank was then at $\dfrac{4}{5}$ of its capacity. How many gallons of water does the tank hold when filled to capacity?

   (A)   5,000
   (B)   6,200
   (C)   20,000
   (D)   40,000
   (E)   80,000

62. The sum of three integers is 40. The largest integer is 3 times the middle integer, and the smallest integer is 23 less than the largest integer. What is the product of the three integers?

   (A)   1,104
   (B)   972
   (C)   672
   (D)   294
   (E)   192

63. If $S = \{0, 4, 5, 2, 11, 8\}$, how much greater than the median of the numbers in S is the mean of the numbers in S?

    (A)   0.5
    (B)   1.0
    (C)   1.5
    (D)   2.0
    (E)   2.5

64. At a monthly meeting, $\frac{2}{5}$ of the attendees were males and $\frac{7}{8}$ of the male attendees arrived on time. If $\frac{9}{10}$ of the female attendees arrived on time, what fraction of the attendees at the monthly meeting did not arrive on time?

    (A) $\frac{11}{100}$

    (B) $\frac{3}{25}$

    (C) $\frac{7}{50}$

    (D) $\frac{3}{20}$

    (E) $\frac{4}{25}$

65. If $d = 2.0453$ and d^* is the decimal obtained by rounding d to the nearest hundredth, what is the value of $d^* - d$?

    (A)   −0.0053
    (B)   −0.0003
    (C)   0.0007
    (D)   0.0047
    (E)   0.0153

66. Company K's earnings were $12 million last year. If this year's earnings are projected to be 150 percent greater than last year's earnings, what are Company K's projected earnings this year?

    (A) $13.5 million
    (B) $15 million
    (C) $18 million
    (D) $27 million
    (E) $30 million

67. The sequence a_1, a_2, a_3, a_4, a_5 is such that $a_n = a_{n-1} + 5$ for $2 \leq n \leq 5$. If $a_5 = 31$, what is the value of a_1?

    (A)   1
    (B)   6
    (C)   11
    (D)   16
    (E)   21

68. When positive integer n is divided by 5, the remainder is 1. When n is divided by 7, the remainder is 3. What is the smallest positive integer k such that $k + n$ is a multiple of 35?

    (A)   3
    (B)   4
    (C)   12
    (D)   32
    (E)   35

69. Of the goose eggs laid at a certain pond, $\frac{2}{3}$ hatched, and $\frac{3}{4}$ of the geese that hatched from those eggs survived the first month. Of the geese that survived the first month, $\frac{3}{5}$ did not survive the first year. If 120 geese survived the first year and if no more than one goose hatched from each egg, how many goose eggs were laid at the pond?

    (A)   280
    (B)   400
    (C)   540
    (D)   600
    (E)   840

70. List S consists of 10 consecutive odd integers, and list T consists of 5 consecutive even integers. If the least integer in S is 7 more than the least integer in T, how much greater is the average (arithmetic mean) of the integers in S than the average of the integers in T?

    (A)   2
    (B)   7
    (C)   8
    (D)   12
    (E)   22

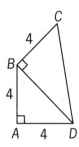

71. In the figure above, what is the area of triangular region *BCD*?

    (A) $4\sqrt{2}$
    (B)   8
    (C) $8\sqrt{2}$
    (D)   16
    (E) $16\sqrt{2}$

72. If $x^2 - 2x - 15 = 0$ and $x > 0$, which of the following must be equal to 0 ?

    I. $x^2 - 6x + 9$
    II. $x^2 - 7x + 10$
    III. $x^2 - 10x + 25$

    (A)   I only
    (B)   II only
    (C)   III only
    (D)   II and III only
    (E)   I, II, and III

73. If Mel saved more than $10 by purchasing a sweater at a 15 percent discount, what is the smallest amount the original price of the sweater could be, to the nearest dollar?

    (A)   45
    (B)   67
    (C)   75
    (D)   83
    (E)   150

74. If $x = -1$, then $-\left(x^4 + x^3 + x^2 + x\right) =$

    (A)   −10
    (B)   −4
    (C)   0
    (D)   4
    (E)   10

75. Today Rose is twice as old as Sam and Sam is 3 years younger than Tina. If Rose, Sam, and Tina are all alive 4 years from today, which of the following must be true on that day?

    I.   Rose is twice as old as Sam.
    II.   Sam is 3 years younger than Tina.
    III. Rose is older than Tina.

    (A)   I only
    (B)   II only
    (C)   III only
    (D)   I and II
    (E)   II and III

76. If a square region has area *n*, what is the length of the diagonal of the square in terms of *n*?

    (A) $\sqrt{2n}$
    (B) $\sqrt{n}$
    (C) $2\sqrt{n}$
    (D) $2n$
    (E) $2n^2$

77. Temperatures in degrees Celsius (*C*) can be converted to temperatures in degrees Fahrenheit (*F*) by the formula $F = \dfrac{9}{5}C + 32$. What is the temperature at which $F = C$?

    (A) $20°$
    (B) $\left(\dfrac{32}{5}\right)°$
    (C) $0°$
    (D) $-20°$
    (E) $-40°$

78. The "prime sum" of an integer *n* greater than 1 is the sum of all the prime factors of *n*, including repetitions. For example, the prime sum of 12 is 7, since $12 = 2 \times 2 \times 3$ and $2 + 2 + 3 = 7$. For which of the following integers is the prime sum greater than 35 ?

    (A)   440
    (B)   512
    (C)   620
    (D)   700
    (E)   750

79. If x is to be chosen at random from the set {1, 2, 3, 4} and y is to be chosen at random from the set {5, 6, 7}, what is the probability that xy will be even?

(A) $\frac{1}{6}$

(B) $\frac{1}{3}$

(C) $\frac{1}{2}$

(D) $\frac{2}{3}$

(E) $\frac{5}{6}$

80. At a garage sale, all of the prices of the items sold were different. If the price of a radio sold at the garage sale was both the 15th highest price and the 20th lowest price among the prices of the items sold, how many items were sold at the garage sale?

(A) 33
(B) 34
(C) 35
(D) 36
(E) 37

81. Ada and Paul received their scores on three tests. On the first test, Ada's score was 10 points higher than Paul's score. On the second test, Ada's score was 4 points higher than Paul's score. If Paul's average (arithmetic mean) score on the three tests was 3 points higher than Ada's average score on the three tests, then Paul's score on the third test was how many points higher than Ada's score?

(A) 9
(B) 14
(C) 17
(D) 23
(E) 25

82. Three business partners, Q, R, and S, agree to divide their total profit for a certain year in the ratios 2:5:8, respectively. If Q's share was $4,000, what was the total profit of the business partners for the year?

(A) $ 26,000
(B) $ 30,000
(C) $ 52,000
(D) $ 60,000
(E) $300,000

83. Which of the following lines in the xy-plane does not contain any point with integers as both coordinates?

(A) $y = x$

(B) $y = x + \frac{1}{2}$

(C) $y = x + 5$

(D) $y = \frac{1}{2}x$

(E) $y = \frac{1}{2}x + 5$

84. The average (arithmetic mean) of 6 numbers is 8.5. When one number is discarded, the average of the remaining numbers becomes 7.2. What is the discarded number?

(A) 7.8
(B) 9.8
(C) 10.0
(D) 12.4
(E) 15.0

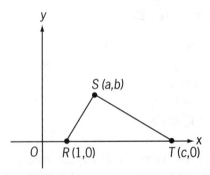

85. In the rectangular coordinate system above, the area of $\triangle RST$ is

(A) $\frac{bc}{2}$

(B) $\frac{b(c-1)}{2}$

(C) $\frac{c(b-1)}{2}$

(D) $\frac{a(c-1)}{2}$

(E) $\frac{c(a-1)}{2}$

86. What is the largest integer n such that $\frac{1}{2^n} > 0.01$?

    (A)   5
    (B)   6
    (C)   7
    (D)   10
    (E)   51

87. One inlet pipe fills an empty tank in 5 hours. A second inlet pipe fills the same tank in 3 hours. If both pipes are used together, how long will it take to fill $\frac{2}{3}$ of the tank?

    (A) $\frac{8}{15}$ hr

    (B) $\frac{3}{4}$ hr

    (C) $\frac{5}{4}$ hr

    (D) $\frac{15}{8}$ hr

    (E) $\frac{8}{3}$ hr

88. $\left(\frac{1}{5}\right)^2 - \left(\frac{1}{5}\right)\left(\frac{1}{4}\right) =$

    (A) $-\frac{1}{20}$

    (B) $-\frac{1}{100}$

    (C) $\frac{1}{100}$

    (D) $\frac{1}{20}$

    (E) $\frac{1}{5}$

89. If the length and width of a rectangular garden plot were each increased by 20 percent, what would be the percent increase in the area of the plot?

    (A)   20%
    (B)   24%
    (C)   36%
    (D)   40%
    (E)   44%

90. The population of a bacteria culture doubles every 2 minutes. Approximately how many minutes will it take for the population to grow from 1,000 to 500,000 bacteria?

    (A)   10
    (B)   12
    (C)   14
    (D)   16
    (E)   18

91. For a light that has an intensity of 60 candles at its source, the intensity in candles, S, of the light at a point d feet from the source is given by the formula $S = \frac{60k}{d^2}$, where k is a constant. If the intensity of the light is 30 candles at a distance of 2 feet from the source, what is the intensity of the light at a distance of 20 feet from the source?

    (A) $\frac{3}{10}$ candle

    (B) $\frac{1}{2}$ candle

    (C)   1 candle
    (D)   2 candles
    (E)   3 candles

92. If $b < 2$ and $2x - 3b = 0$, which of the following must be true?

    (A) $x > -3$
    (B) $x < 2$
    (C) $x = 3$
    (D) $x < 3$
    (E) $x > 3$

93. $\dfrac{(-1.5)(1.2) - (4.5)(0.4)}{30} =$

    (A) -1.2
    (B) -0.12
    (C)   0
    (D)   0.12
    (E)   1.2

94. René earns $8.50 per hour on days other than Sundays and twice that rate on Sundays. Last week she worked a total of 40 hours, including 8 hours on Sunday. What were her earnings for the week?

   (A) $272
   (B) $340
   (C) $398
   (D) $408
   (E) $476

95. In a shipment of 120 machine parts, 5 percent were defective. In a shipment of 80 machine parts, 10 percent were defective. For the two shipments combined, what percent of the machine parts were defective?

   (A) 6.5%
   (B) 7.0%
   (C) 7.5%
   (D) 8.0%
   (E) 8.5%

96. If $8^{2x + 3} = 2^{3x + 6}$, then $x =$

   (A) −3
   (B) −1
   (C) 0
   (D) 1
   (E) 3

97. Of the following, the closest approximation to $\sqrt{\dfrac{5.98(601.5)}{15.79}}$ is

   (A) 5
   (B) 15
   (C) 20
   (D) 25
   (E) 225

98. Which of the following CANNOT be the greatest common divisor of two positive integers x and y ?

   (A) 1
   (B) x
   (C) y
   (D) $x - y$
   (E) $x + y$

99. If a, b, and c are nonzero numbers and $a + b = c$, which of the following is equal to 1 ?

   (A) $\dfrac{a - b}{c}$
   (B) $\dfrac{a - c}{b}$
   (C) $\dfrac{b - c}{a}$
   (D) $\dfrac{b - a}{c}$
   (E) $\dfrac{c - b}{a}$

100. Last year Carlos saved 10 percent of his annual earnings. This year he earned 5 percent more than last year and he saved 12 percent of his annual earnings. The amount saved this year was what percent of the amount saved last year?

   (A) 122%
   (B) 124%
   (C) 126%
   (D) 128%
   (E) 130%

101. A corporation that had $115.19 billion in profits for the year paid out $230.10 million in employee benefits. Approximately what percent of the profits were the employee benefits? (Note: 1 billion $= 10^9$)

   (A) 50%
   (B) 20%
   (C) 5%
   (D) 2%
   (E) 0.2%

102. In the coordinate plane, line k passes through the origin and has slope 2. If points $(3,y)$ and $(x,4)$ are on line k, then $x + y =$

   (A) 3.5
   (B) 7
   (C) 8
   (D) 10
   (E) 14

103. If a, b, and c are constants, $a > b > c$, and $x^3 - x = (x - a)(x - b)(x - c)$ for all numbers x, what is the value of b ?

    (A)   −3
    (B)   −1
    (C)   0
    (D)   1
    (E)   3

104. If $x + y = 8z$, then which of the following represents the average (arithmetic mean) of x, y, and z, in terms of z ?

    (A) $2z + 1$
    (B) $3z$
    (C) $5z$
    (D) $\dfrac{z}{3}$
    (E) $\dfrac{3z}{2}$

105. On the number line, if $r < s$, if p is halfway between r and s, and if t is halfway between p and r, then $\dfrac{s - t}{t - r} =$

    (A) $\dfrac{1}{4}$
    (B) $\dfrac{1}{3}$
    (C) $\dfrac{4}{3}$
    (D)   3
    (E)   4

106. If x and y are different integers and $x^2 = xy$, which of the following must be true?

    I. $x = 0$
    II. $y = 0$
    III. $x = -y$

    (A)   I only
    (B)   II only
    (C)   III only
    (D)   I and III only
    (E)   I, II, and III

107. If $\dfrac{3}{x} = 2$ and $\dfrac{y}{4} = 3$, then $\dfrac{3 + y}{x + 4} =$

    (A) $\dfrac{10}{9}$
    (B) $\dfrac{3}{2}$
    (C) $\dfrac{20}{11}$
    (D) $\dfrac{30}{11}$
    (E)   5

108. $17^3 + 17^4 =$

    (A) 17^7
    (B) $17^3(18)$
    (C) $17^6(18)$
    (D) $2(17^3) + 17$
    (E) $2(17^3) - 17$

109. Which of the following CANNOT yield an integer when divided by 10 ?

    (A)   The sum of two odd integers
    (B)   An integer less than 10
    (C)   The product of two primes
    (D)   The sum of three consecutive integers
    (E)   An odd integer

110. A certain clock marks every hour by striking a number of times equal to the hour, and the time required for a stroke is exactly equal to the time interval between strokes. At 6:00 the time lapse between the beginning of the first stroke and the end of the last stroke is 22 seconds. At 12:00, how many seconds elapse between the beginning of the first stroke and the end of the last stroke?

    (A)   72
    (B)   50
    (C)   48
    (D)   46
    (E)   44

111. If $k \neq 0$ and $k - \dfrac{3 - 2k^2}{k} = \dfrac{x}{k}$, then $x =$

    (A) $-3 - k^2$
    (B) $k^2 - 3$
    (C) $3k^2 - 3$
    (D) $k - 3 - 2k^2$
    (E) $k - 3 + 2k^2$

112. What is the greatest number of identical bouquets that can be made out of 21 white and 91 red tulips if no flowers are to be left out? (Two bouquets are identical whenever the number of red tulips in the two bouquets is equal and the number of white tulips in the two bouquets is equal.)

    (A) 3
    (B) 4
    (C) 5
    (D) 6
    (E) 7

113. For all numbers s and t, the operation $*$ is defined by $s * t = (s - 1)(t + 1)$. If $(-2) * x = -12$, then $x =$

    (A) 2
    (B) 3
    (C) 5
    (D) 6
    (E) 11

114. Salesperson A's compensation for any week is $360 plus 6 percent of the portion of A's total sales above $1,000 for that week. Salesperson B's compensation for any week is 8 percent of B's total sales for that week. For what amount of total weekly sales would both salespeople earn the same compensation?

    (A) $21,000
    (B) $18,000
    (C) $15,000
    (D) $ 4,500
    (E) $ 4,000

115. The sum of the ages of Doris and Fred is y years. If Doris is 12 years older than Fred, how many years old will Fred be y years from now, in terms of y?

    (A) $y - 6$
    (B) $2y - 6$
    (C) $\dfrac{y}{2} - 6$
    (D) $\dfrac{3y}{2} - 6$
    (E) $\dfrac{5y}{2} - 6$

116. If a basketball team scores an average (arithmetic mean) of x points per game for n games and then scores y points in its next game, what is the team's average score for the $n + 1$ games?

    (A) $\dfrac{nx + y}{n + 1}$
    (B) $x + \dfrac{y}{n + 1}$
    (C) $x + \dfrac{y}{n}$
    (D) $\dfrac{n(x + y)}{n + 1}$
    (E) $\dfrac{x + ny}{n + 1}$

117. If $xy > 0$ and $yz < 0$, which of the following must be negative?

    (A) xyz
    (B) xyz^2
    (C) xy^2z
    (D) xy^2z^2
    (E) $x^2y^2z^2$

118. At a certain pizzeria, $\frac{1}{8}$ of the pizzas sold in one week were mushroom and $\frac{1}{3}$ of the <u>remaining</u> pizzas sold were pepperoni. If n of the pizzas sold were pepperoni, how many were mushroom?

    (A) $\frac{3}{8}n$

    (B) $\frac{3}{7}n$

    (C) $\frac{7}{16}n$

    (D) $\frac{7}{8}n$

    (E) $3n$

119. Two trains, X and Y, started simultaneously from opposite ends of a 100-mile route and traveled toward each other on parallel tracks. Train X, traveling at a constant rate, completed the 100-mile trip in 5 hours; Train Y, traveling at a constant rate, completed the 100-mile trip in 3 hours. How many miles had Train X traveled when it met Train Y ?

    (A) 37.5
    (B) 40.0
    (C) 60.0
    (D) 62.5
    (E) 77.5

120. One week a certain truck rental lot had a total of 20 trucks, all of which were on the lot Monday morning. If 50 percent of the trucks that were rented out during the week were returned to the lot on or before Saturday morning of that week, and if there were at least 12 trucks on the lot that Saturday morning, what is the greatest number of different trucks that could have been rented out during the week?

    (A) 18
    (B) 16
    (C) 12
    (D) 8
    (E) 4

121. What is the value of $2x^2 - 2.4x - 1.7$ for $x = 0.7$?

    (A) −0.72
    (B) −1.42
    (C) −1.98
    (D) −2.40
    (E) −2.89

122. If s, u, and v are positive integers and $2s = 2u + 2v$, which of the following must be true?

    I. $s = u$
    II. $u \neq v$
    III. $s > v$

    (A) None
    (B) I only
    (C) II only
    (D) III only
    (E) II and III

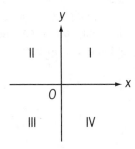

123. In the rectangular coordinate system shown above, which quadrant, if any, contains no point (x,y) that satisfies the inequality $2x - 3y \leq -6$?

    (A) None
    (B) I
    (C) II
    (D) III
    (E) IV

124. The cost to rent a small bus for a trip is x dollars, which is to be shared equally among the people taking the trip. If 10 people take the trip rather than 16, how many more dollars, in terms of x, will it cost per person?

    (A) $\frac{x}{6}$

    (B) $\frac{x}{10}$

    (C) $\frac{x}{16}$

    (D) $\frac{3x}{40}$

    (E) $\frac{3x}{80}$

125. If x is an integer and $y = 3x + 2$, which of the following CANNOT be a divisor of y?

    (A) 4
    (B) 5
    (C) 6
    (D) 7
    (E) 8

126. A certain electronic component is sold in boxes of 54 for $16.20 and in boxes of 27 for $13.20. A customer who needed only 54 components for a project had to buy 2 boxes of 27 because boxes of 54 were unavailable. Approximately how much more did the customer pay for each component due to the unavailability of the larger boxes?

    (A) $0.33
    (B) $0.19
    (C) $0.11
    (D) $0.06
    (E) $0.03

127. As a salesperson, Phyllis can choose one of two methods of annual payment: either an annual salary of $35,000 with no commission or an annual salary of $10,000 plus a 20 percent commission on her total annual sales. What must her total annual sales be to give her the same annual pay with either method?

    (A) $100,000
    (B) $120,000
    (C) $125,000
    (D) $130,000
    (E) $132,000

128. If $\dfrac{x+y}{xy} = 1$, then $y =$

    (A) $\dfrac{x}{x-1}$

    (B) $\dfrac{x}{x+1}$

    (C) $\dfrac{x-1}{x}$

    (D) $\dfrac{x+1}{x}$

    (E) x

129. Last year Department Store X had a sales total for December that was 4 times the average (arithmetic mean) of the monthly sales totals for January through November. The sales total for December was what fraction of the sales total for the year?

    (A) $\dfrac{1}{4}$

    (B) $\dfrac{4}{15}$

    (C) $\dfrac{1}{3}$

    (D) $\dfrac{4}{11}$

    (E) $\dfrac{4}{5}$

130. Working alone, Printers X, Y, and Z can do a certain printing job, consisting of a large number of pages, in 12, 15, and 18 hours, respectively. What is the ratio of the time it takes Printer X to do the job, working alone at its rate, to the time it takes Printers Y and Z to do the job, working together at their individual rates?

    (A) $\dfrac{4}{11}$

    (B) $\dfrac{1}{2}$

    (C) $\dfrac{15}{22}$

    (D) $\dfrac{22}{15}$

    (E) $\dfrac{11}{4}$

131. In the sequence x_0, x_1, x_2, ..., x_n, each term from x_1 to x_k is 3 greater than the previous term, and each term from x_{k+1} to x_n is 3 less than the previous term, where n and k are positive integers and $k < n$. If $x_0 = x_n = 0$ and if $x_k = 15$, what is the value of n?

    (A) 5
    (B) 6
    (C) 9
    (D) 10
    (E) 15

132. A company that ships boxes to a total of 12 distribution centers uses color coding to identify each center. If either a single color or a pair of two different colors is chosen to represent each center and if each center is uniquely represented by that choice of one or two colors, what is the minimum number of colors needed for the coding? (Assume that the order of the colors in a pair does not matter.)

    (A)   4
    (B)   5
    (C)   6
    (D)   12
    (E)   24

133. If $x \neq 2$, then $\dfrac{3x^2(x-2)-x+2}{x-2} =$

    (A) $3x^2 - x + 2$
    (B) $3x^2 + 1$
    (C) $3x^2$
    (D) $3x^2 - 1$
    (E) $3x^2 - 2$

134. If $d > 0$ and $0 < 1 - \dfrac{c}{d} < 1$, which of the following must be true?

    I. $c > 0$
    II. $\dfrac{c}{d} < 1$
    III. $c^2 + d^2 > 1$

    (A)   I only
    (B)   II only
    (C)   I and II only
    (D)   II and III only
    (E)   I, II, and III

Note: Not drawn to scale.

135. In the figure shown above, line segment QR has length 12, and rectangle $MPQT$ is a square. If the area of rectangular region $MPRS$ is 540, what is the area of rectangular region $TQRS$?

    (A)   144
    (B)   216
    (C)   324
    (D)   360
    (E)   396

136. A train travels from New York City to Chicago, a distance of approximately 840 miles, at an average rate of 60 miles per hour and arrives in Chicago at 6:00 in the evening, Chicago time. At what hour in the morning, New York City time, did the train depart for Chicago? (<u>Note:</u> Chicago time is one hour earlier than New York City time.)

    (A)   4:00
    (B)   5:00
    (C)   6:00
    (D)   7:00
    (E)   8:00

137. Last year Manfred received 26 paychecks. Each of his first 6 paychecks was $750; each of his remaining paychecks was $30 more than each of his first 6 paychecks. To the nearest dollar, what was the average (arithmetic mean) amount of his paychecks for the year?

    (A) $752
    (B) $755
    (C) $765
    (D) $773
    (E) $775

138. If 25 percent of p is equal to 10 percent of q, and $pq \neq 0$, then p is what percent of q ?

 (A)   2.5%
 (B)   15%
 (C)   20%
 (D)   35%
 (E)   40%

139. If the length of an edge of cube X is twice the length of an edge of cube Y, what is the ratio of the volume of cube Y to the volume of cube X ?

 (A) $\dfrac{1}{2}$

 (B) $\dfrac{1}{4}$

 (C) $\dfrac{1}{6}$

 (D) $\dfrac{1}{8}$

 (E) $\dfrac{1}{27}$

140. Machines A and B always operate independently and at their respective constant rates. When working alone, Machine A can fill a production lot in 5 hours, and Machine B can fill the same lot in x hours. When the two machines operate simultaneously to fill the production lot, it takes them 2 hours to complete the job. What is the value of x ?

 (A) $3\dfrac{1}{3}$

 (B) 3

 (C) $2\dfrac{1}{2}$

 (D) $2\dfrac{1}{3}$

 (E) $1\dfrac{1}{2}$

141. An artist wishes to paint a circular region on a square poster that is 2 feet on a side. If the area of the circular region is to be $\dfrac{1}{2}$ the area of the poster, what must be the radius of the circular region in feet?

 (A) $\dfrac{1}{\pi}$

 (B) $\sqrt{\dfrac{2}{\pi}}$

 (C) 1

 (D) $\dfrac{2}{\sqrt{\pi}}$

 (E) $\dfrac{\pi}{2}$

142. A driver completed the first 20 miles of a 40-mile trip at an average speed of 50 miles per hour. At what average speed must the driver complete the remaining 20 miles to achieve an average speed of 60 miles per hour for the entire 40-mile trip? (Assume that the driver did not make any stops during the 40-mile trip.)

 (A)   65 mph
 (B)   68 mph
 (C)   70 mph
 (D)   75 mph
 (E)   80 mph

143. A $500 investment and a $1,500 investment have a combined yearly return of 8.5 percent of the total of the two investments. If the $500 investment has a yearly return of 7 percent, what percent yearly return does the $1,500 investment have?

 (A)   9%
 (B)   10%

 (C) $10\dfrac{5}{8}\%$

 (D)   11%

 (E)   12%

144. For any integer n greater than 1, $\lfloor n$ denotes the product of all the integers from 1 to n, inclusive. How many prime numbers are there between $\lfloor 6 + 2$ and $\lfloor 6 + 6$, inclusive?

    (A) None
    (B) One
    (C) Two
    (D) Three
    (E) Four

145. The figure shown above consists of three identical circles that are tangent to each other. If the area of the shaded region is $64\sqrt{3} - 32\pi$, what is the radius of each circle?

    (A) 4
    (B) 8
    (C) 16
    (D) 24
    (E) 32

146. On a certain transatlantic crossing, 20 percent of a ship's passengers held round-trip tickets and also took their cars aboard the ship. If 60 percent of the passengers with round-trip tickets did <u>not</u> take their cars aboard the ship, what percent of the ship's passengers held round-trip tickets?

    (A) $33\frac{1}{3}\%$
    (B) 40%
    (C) 50%
    (D) 60%
    (E) $66\frac{2}{3}\%$

147. If x and k are integers and $(12^x)(4^{2x+1}) = (2^k)(3^2)$, what is the value of k ?

    (A) 5
    (B) 7
    (C) 10
    (D) 12
    (E) 14

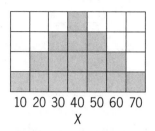

10 20 30 40 50 60 70
X

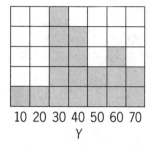

10 20 30 40 50 60 70
Y

10 20 30 40 50 60 70
Z

148. If the variables, X, Y, and Z take on only the values 10, 20, 30, 40, 50, 60, or 70 with frequencies indicated by the shaded regions above, for which of the frequency distributions is the mean equal to the median?

    (A) X only
    (B) Y only
    (C) Z only
    (D) X and Y
    (E) X and Z

149. For every even positive integer m, f(m) represents the product of all even integers from 2 to m, inclusive. For example, $f(12) = 2 \times 4 \times 6 \times 8 \times 10 \times 12$. What is the greatest prime factor of f(24) ?

    (A) 23
    (B) 19
    (C) 17
    (D) 13
    (E) 11

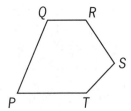

Note: Not drawn to scale.

150. In pentagon PQRST, PQ = 3, QR = 2, RS = 4, and ST = 5. Which of the lengths 5, 10, and 15 could be the value of PT ?

   (A)   5 only
   (B)   15 only
   (C)   5 and 10 only
   (D)   10 and 15 only
   (E)   5, 10, and 15

151. A certain university will select 1 of 7 candidates eligible to fill a position in the mathematics department and 2 of 10 candidates eligible to fill 2 identical positions in the computer science department. If none of the candidates is eligible for a position in both departments, how many different sets of 3 candidates are there to fill the 3 positions?

   (A)   42
   (B)   70
   (C)   140
   (D)   165
   (E)   315

$$2x + y = 12$$
$$|y| \leq 12$$

152. For how many ordered pairs (x,y) that are solutions of the system above are x and y both integers?

   (A)   7
   (B)   10
   (C)   12
   (D)   13
   (E)   14

153. The points R, T, and U lie on a circle that has radius 4. If the length of arc RTU is $\frac{4\pi}{3}$, what is the length of line segment RU ?

   (A) $\frac{4}{3}$

   (B) $\frac{8}{3}$

   (C)   3
   (D)   4
   (E)   6

154. A survey of employers found that during 1993 employment costs rose 3.5 percent, where employment costs consist of salary costs and fringe-benefit costs. If salary costs rose 3 percent and fringe-benefit costs rose 5.5 percent during 1993, then fringe-benefit costs represented what percent of employment costs at the beginning of 1993 ?

   (A)   16.5%
   (B)   20%
   (C)   35%
   (D)   55%
   (E)   65%

155. A certain company that sells only cars and trucks reported that revenues from car sales in 1997 were down 11 percent from 1996 and revenues from truck sales in 1997 were up 7 percent from 1996. If total revenues from car sales and truck sales in 1997 were up 1 percent from 1996, what is the ratio of revenue from car sales in 1996 to revenue from truck sales in 1996 ?

   (A)   1:2
   (B)   4:5
   (C)   1:1
   (D)   3:2
   (E)   5:3

156. If $4 < \frac{7-x}{3}$, which of the following must be true?

   I. $5 < x$
   II. $|x + 3| > 2$
   III. $-(x + 5)$ is positive.

   (A)   II only
   (B)   III only
   (C)   I and II only
   (D)   II and III only
   (E)   I, II, and III

157. A certain right triangle has sides of length x, y, and z, where $x < y < z$. If the area of this triangular region is 1, which of the following indicates all of the possible values of y?

    (A) $y > \sqrt{2}$

    (B) $\dfrac{\sqrt{3}}{2} < y < \sqrt{2}$

    (C) $\dfrac{\sqrt{2}}{3} < y < \dfrac{\sqrt{3}}{2}$

    (D) $\dfrac{\sqrt{3}}{4} < y < \dfrac{\sqrt{2}}{3}$

    (E) $y < \dfrac{\sqrt{3}}{4}$

158. A set of numbers has the property that for any number t in the set, $t + 2$ is in the set. If -1 is in the set, which of the following must also be in the set?

    I. -3
    II. 1
    III. 5

    (A) I only
    (B) II only
    (C) I and II only
    (D) II and III only
    (E) I, II, and III

159. A group of store managers must assemble 280 displays for an upcoming sale. If they assemble 25 percent of the displays during the first hour and 40 percent of the remaining displays during the second hour, how many of the displays will <u>not</u> have been assembled by the end of the second hour?

    (A) 70
    (B) 98
    (C) 126
    (D) 168
    (E) 182

160. A couple decides to have 4 children. If they succeed in having 4 children and each child is equally likely to be a boy or a girl, what is the probability that they will have exactly 2 girls and 2 boys?

    (A) $\dfrac{3}{8}$

    (B) $\dfrac{1}{4}$

    (C) $\dfrac{3}{16}$

    (D) $\dfrac{1}{8}$

    (E) $\dfrac{1}{16}$

$$3, k, 2, 8, m, 3$$

161. The arithmetic mean of the list of numbers above is 4. If k and m are integers and $k \neq m$, what is the median of the list?

    (A) 2
    (B) 2.5
    (C) 3
    (D) 3.5
    (E) 4

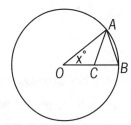

162. In the figure above, point O is the center of the circle and $OC = AC = AB$. What is the value of x?

    (A) 40
    (B) 36
    (C) 34
    (D) 32
    (E) 30

163. $\dfrac{\left(8^2\right)\left(3^3\right)\left(2^4\right)}{96^2} =$

    (A) 3
    (B) 6
    (C) 9
    (D) 12
    (E) 18

164. When 10 is divided by the positive integer n, the remainder is $n - 4$. Which of the following could be the value of n?

    (A) 3
    (B) 4
    (C) 7
    (D) 8
    (E) 12

165. If $\frac{1}{2}$ of the money in a certain trust fund was invested in stocks, $\frac{1}{4}$ in bonds, $\frac{1}{5}$ in a mutual fund, and the remaining \$10,000 in a government certificate, what was the total amount of the trust fund?

    (A) \$ 100,000
    (B) \$ 150,000
    (C) \$ 200,000
    (D) \$ 500,000
    (E) \$2,000,000

166. If m is an integer such that $(-2)^{2m} = 2^{9-m}$, then $m =$

    (A) 1
    (B) 2
    (C) 3
    (D) 4
    (E) 6

167. In a mayoral election, Candidate X received $\frac{1}{3}$ more votes than Candidate Y, and Candidate Y received $\frac{1}{4}$ fewer votes than Candidate Z . If Candidate Z received 24,000 votes, how many votes did Candidate X receive?

    (A) 18,000
    (B) 22,000
    (C) 24,000
    (D) 26,000
    (E) 32,000

168. An airline passenger is planning a trip that involves three connecting flights that leave from Airports A, B, and C, respectively. The first flight leaves Airport A every hour, beginning at 8:00 a.m., and arrives at Airport B $2\frac{1}{2}$ hours later. The second flight leaves Airport B every 20 minutes, beginning at 8:00 a.m., and arrives at Airport C $1\frac{1}{6}$ hours later. The third flight leaves Airport C every hour, beginning at 8:45 a.m. What is the least total amount of time the passenger must spend between flights if all flights keep to their schedules?

    (A) 25 min
    (B) 1 hr 5 min
    (C) 1 hr 15 min
    (D) 2 hr 20 min
    (E) 3 hr 40 min

169. If n is a positive integer and n^2 is divisible by 72, then the largest positive integer that must divide n is

    (A) 6
    (B) 12
    (C) 24
    (D) 36
    (E) 48

170. If n is a positive integer and $k + 2 = 3^n$, which of the following could NOT be a value of k?

    (A) 1
    (B) 4
    (C) 7
    (D) 25
    (E) 79

171. A certain grocery purchased x pounds of produce for p dollars per pound. If y pounds of the produce had to be discarded due to spoilage and the grocery sold the rest for s dollars per pound, which of the following represents the gross profit on the sale of the produce?

    (A) $(x - y)s - xp$
    (B) $(x - y)p - ys$
    (C) $(s - p)y - xp$
    (D) $xp - ys$
    (E) $(x - y)(s - p)$

172. If x, y, and z are positive integers such that x is a factor of y, and x is a multiple of z, which of the following is NOT necessarily an integer?

(A) $\dfrac{x+z}{z}$

(B) $\dfrac{y+z}{x}$

(C) $\dfrac{x+y}{z}$

(D) $\dfrac{xy}{z}$

(E) $\dfrac{yz}{x}$

173. Running at their respective constant rates, Machine X takes 2 days longer to produce w widgets than Machine Y. At these rates, if the two machines together produce $\dfrac{5}{4}w$ widgets in 3 days, how many days would it take Machine X alone to produce 2w widgets?

(A) 4
(B) 6
(C) 8
(D) 10
(E) 12

$$\begin{array}{r} \square\triangle \\ \times\ \triangle\square \\ \hline \end{array}$$

174. The product of the two-digit numbers above is the three-digit number $\square\Diamond\square$, where $\square$, $\triangle$, and $\Diamond$, are three different nonzero digits. If $\square \times \triangle < 10$, what is the two-digit number $\square\triangle$?

(A) 11
(B) 12
(C) 13
(D) 21
(E) 31

175. A square wooden plaque has a square brass inlay in the center, leaving a wooden strip of uniform width around the brass square. If the ratio of the brass area to the wooden area is 25 to 39, which of the following could be the width, in inches, of the wooden strip?

I. 1
II. 3
III. 4

(A) I only
(B) II only
(C) I and II only
(D) I and III only
(E) I, II, and III

176. $\dfrac{2\frac{3}{5} - 1\frac{2}{3}}{\frac{2}{3} - \frac{3}{5}} =$

(A) 16
(B) 14
(C) 3
(D) 1
(E) −1

4.4 Answer Key

1.	B	36.	A	71.	C	106.	A	141.	B
2.	C	37.	A	72.	D	107.	D	142.	D
3.	C	38.	C	73.	B	108.	B	143.	A
4.	E	39.	A	74.	C	109.	E	144.	A
5.	C	40.	D	75.	B	110.	D	145.	B
6.	C	41.	D	76.	A	111.	C	146.	C
7.	E	42.	D	77.	E	112.	E	147.	E
8.	D	43.	E	78.	C	113.	B	148.	E
9.	B	44.	E	79.	D	114.	C	149.	E
10.	D	45.	C	80.	B	115.	D	150.	C
11.	B	46.	C	81.	D	116.	A	151.	E
12.	D	47.	B	82.	B	117.	C	152.	D
13.	E	48.	E	83.	B	118.	B	153.	D
14.	B	49.	D	84.	E	119.	A	154.	B
15.	C	50.	C	85.	B	120.	B	155.	A
16.	B	51.	C	86.	B	121.	D	156.	D
17.	D	52.	E	87.	C	122.	D	157.	A
18.	B	53.	C	88.	B	123.	E	158.	D
19.	A	54.	A	89.	E	124.	E	159.	C
20.	A	55.	B	90.	E	125.	C	160.	A
21.	D	56.	A	91.	A	126.	B	161.	C
22.	C	57.	C	92.	D	127.	C	162.	B
23.	E	58.	A	93.	B	128.	A	163.	A
24.	D	59.	D	94.	D	129.	B	164.	C
25.	E	60.	B	95.	B	130.	D	165.	C
26.	E	61.	E	96.	B	131.	D	166.	C
27.	E	62.	B	97.	B	132.	B	167.	C
28.	C	63.	A	98.	E	133.	D	168.	B
29.	C	64.	A	99.	E	134.	C	169.	B
30.	B	65.	D	100.	C	135.	B	170.	B
31.	A	66.	E	101.	E	136.	B	171.	A
32.	B	67.	C	102.	C	137.	D	172.	B
33.	C	68.	B	103.	C	138.	E	173.	E
34.	C	69.	D	104.	B	139.	D	174.	D
35.	C	70.	D	105.	D	140.	A	175.	E
								176.	B

4.5 Answer Explanations

The following discussion is intended to familiarize you with the most efficient and effective approaches to the kinds of problems common to problem solving questions. The particular questions in this chapter are generally representative of the kinds of problem solving questions you will encounter on the GMAT. Remember that it is the problem solving strategy that is important, not the specific details of a particular question.

1. The maximum recommended pulse rate R, when exercising, for a person who is x years of age is given by the equation $R = 176 - 0.8x$. What is the age, in years, of a person whose maximum recommended pulse rate when exercising is 140 ?

   (A) 40
   (B) 45
   (C) 50
   (D) 55
   (E) 60

   Algebra Substitution; Operations with rational numbers

   Substitute 140 for R in the given equation and solve for x.

   $$140 = 176 - 0.8x$$
   $$-36 = -0.8x$$
   $$\frac{-36}{-0.8} = x$$
   $$45 = x$$

   The correct answer is B.

2. If $\frac{x}{4}$ is 2 more than $\frac{x}{8}$, then $x =$

   (A)   4
   (B)   8
   (C) 16
   (D) 32
   (E) 64

   Algebra First-degree equations

   Write an equation for the given information and solve for x.

$$\frac{x}{4} = 2 + \frac{x}{8}$$
$$(8)\left(\frac{x}{4}\right) = (8)\left(2 + \frac{x}{8}\right)$$
$$2x = 16 + x$$
$$x = 16$$

The correct answer is C.

3. If Mario was 32 years old 8 years ago, how old was he x years ago?

   (A) $x - 40$
   (B) $x - 24$
   (C) $40 - x$
   (D) $24 - x$
   (E) $24 + x$

   Arithmetic Operations on rational numbers

   Since Mario was 32 years old 8 years ago, his age now is $32 + 8 = 40$ years old. Therefore, x years ago Mario was $40 - x$ years old.

   The correct answer is C.

4. If k is an integer and 0.0010101×10^k is greater than 1,000, what is the least possible value of k ?

   (A) 2
   (B) 3
   (C) 4
   (D) 5
   (E) 6

Arithmetic Operations on rational numbers

Multiplying any number by 10^k, where k is a positive integer, will move the decimal point of the number k places to the right. For example, if $k = 5$, $0.0010101 \times 10^5 = 101.01$. But $101.01 < 1{,}000$ so k needs to be greater than 5 if 0.0010101×10^k is to be greater than 1,000. If $k = 6$, then $0.0010101 \times 10^6 = 1{,}010.1$ and $1{,}010.1 > 1{,}000$. Therefore, 6 is the least possible value for k.

The correct answer is E.

5.   If $\left(b - 3\right)\left(4 + \dfrac{2}{b}\right) = 0$ and $b \neq 3$, then $b =$

   (A) -8

   (B) -2

   (C) $-\dfrac{1}{2}$

   (D) $\dfrac{1}{2}$

   (E) 2

Algebra Second-degree equations

If $\left(b - 3\right)\left(4 + \dfrac{2}{b}\right) = 0$, then $b - 3 = 0$ or $4 + \dfrac{2}{b} = 0$. Since $b \neq 3$, then $b - 3 \neq 0$ and so $4 + \dfrac{2}{b} = 0$. Solve for b.

$$4 + \frac{2}{b} = 0$$

$$\frac{2}{b} = -4$$

$$2 = -4b$$

$$-\frac{1}{2} = b$$

The correct answer is C.

6.   The number $2 - 0.5$ is how many times the number $1 - 0.5$?

   (A)   2

   (B)   2.5

   (C)   3

   (D)   3.5

   (E)   4

Arithmetic Operations on rational numbers

Set up an equation in the order given in the problem, and solve for x.

$$\left(2 - 0.5\right) = \left(1 - 0.5\right)x$$

$$1.5 = 0.5x$$

$$3 = x$$

The correct answer is C.

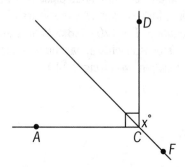

7.   In the figure above, if F is a point on the line that bisects angle ACD and the measure of angle DCF is $x°$, which of the following is true of x?

   (A) $90 \leq x < 100$

   (B) $100 \leq x < 110$

   (C) $110 \leq x < 120$

   (D) $120 \leq x < 130$

   (E) $130 \leq x < 140$

Geometry Angles

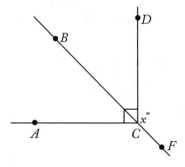

As shown in the figure above, if B is on the line that bisects $\angle ACD$, then the degree measure of $\angle DCB$ is $\dfrac{90}{2} = 45$. Then because B, C, and F are collinear, the sum of the degree measures of $\angle BCD$ and $\angle DCF$ is 180. Therefore, $x = 180 - 45 = 135$ and $130 \leq 135 < 140$.

The correct answer is E.

8. In which of the following pairs are the two numbers reciprocals of each other?

    I. 3 and $\frac{1}{3}$

    II. $\frac{1}{17}$ and $\frac{-1}{17}$

    III. $\sqrt{3}$ and $\frac{\sqrt{3}}{3}$

    (A) I only
    (B) II only
    (C) I and II
    (D) I and III
    (E) II and III

Arithmetic Properties of numbers (reciprocals)

Two numbers are reciprocals of each other if and only if their product is 1.

I. $3\left(\frac{1}{3}\right) = 1$ reciprocals

II. $\left(\frac{1}{17}\right)\left(-\frac{1}{17}\right) = -\frac{1}{(17)(17)}$ not reciprocals

III. $\left(\sqrt{3}\right)\left(\frac{\sqrt{3}}{3}\right) = \frac{3}{3} = 1$ reciprocals

The correct answer is D.

9. The price of a certain television set is discounted by 10 percent, and the reduced price is then discounted by 10 percent. This series of successive discounts is equivalent to a single discount of

    (A) 20%
    (B) 19%
    (C) 18%
    (D) 11%
    (E) 10%

Arithmetic Percents

If P represents the original price of the television, then after a discount of 10 percent, the reduced price is $(1 - 0.10)P = 0.90P$. When the reduced price is discounted by 10 percent, the resulting price is $(1 - 0.10)(0.90P) = (0.90)(0.90P) = 0.81P = (1 - 0.19)P$. This price is the original price of the television discounted by 19 percent.

The correct answer is B.

10. If there are 664,579 prime numbers among the first 10 million positive integers, approximately what percent of the first 10 million positive integers are prime numbers?

    (A) 0.0066%
    (B) 0.066%
    (C) 0.66%
    (D) 6.6%
    (E) 66%

Arithmetic Percents

To convert the ratio of 664,579 to 10 million to a percent, solve the proportion $\frac{664,579}{10,000,000} = \frac{x}{100}$.

$$\frac{664,579}{10,000,000} = \frac{x}{100}$$

$$x = 100\left(\frac{664,579}{10,000,000}\right)$$

$$= \left(\frac{66,457,900}{10,000,000}\right)$$

$$\approx \left(\frac{66,000,000}{10,000,000}\right)$$

$$= \frac{66}{10}$$

$$= 6.6$$

The correct answer is D.

11. How many multiples of 4 are there between 12 and 96, inclusive?

    (A) 21
    (B) 22
    (C) 23
    (D) 24
    (E) 25

Arithmetic Properties of numbers

Since 12 is the 3rd multiple of 4 $(12 = 3 \times 4)$ and 96 is the 24th multiple of 4 $(96 = 24 \times 4)$, the number of multiples of 4 between 12 and 96, inclusive, is the same as the number of integers between 3 and 24, inclusive, namely, $24 - 3 + 1 = 22$.

The correct answer is B.

12. In Country X a returning tourist may import goods with a total value of $500 or less tax free, but must pay an 8 percent tax on the portion of the total value in excess of $500. What tax must be paid by a returning tourist who imports goods with a total value of $730 ?

    (A) $58.40
    (B) $40.00
    (C) $24.60
    (D) $18.40
    (E) $16.00

    Arithmetic Percents

    The tourist must pay tax on $730 − $500 = $230. The amount of the tax is $0.08($230$) = $18.40.

    The correct answer is D.

13. The number of rooms at Hotel G is 10 less than twice the number of rooms at Hotel H. If the total number of rooms at Hotel G and Hotel H is 425, what is the number of rooms at Hotel G ?

    (A) 140
    (B) 180
    (C) 200
    (D) 240
    (E) 280

    Algebra Simultaneous equations

    Let G be the number of rooms in Hotel G and let H be the number of rooms in Hotel H. Expressed in symbols, the given information is the following system of equations

    $$\begin{cases} G = 2H - 10 \\ 425 = G + H \end{cases}$$

    Solving the second equation for H gives $H = 425 - G$. Then, substituting $425 - G$ for H in the first equation gives

    $$G = 2(425 - G) - 10$$
    $$G = 850 - 2G - 10$$
    $$G = 840 - 2G$$
    $$3G = 840$$
    $$G = 280$$

    The correct answer is E.

14. Which of the following is greater than $\frac{2}{3}$?

    (A) $\frac{33}{50}$

    (B) $\frac{8}{11}$

    (C) $\frac{3}{5}$

    (D) $\frac{13}{27}$

    (E) $\frac{5}{8}$

    Arithmetic Properties of numbers

    Let $\frac{a}{b}$ be a fraction in which a and b are both positive. Then, $\frac{a}{b} > \frac{2}{3}$ if and only if $3a > 2b$, and $\frac{a}{b} < \frac{2}{3}$ if and only if $3a < 2b$. Test each of the given fractions.

    For $\frac{33}{50}$, since $3(33) = 99$, $2(50) = 100$, and $99 < 100$, then $\frac{33}{50} < \frac{2}{3}$.

    For $\frac{8}{11}$, since $3(8) = 24$, $2(11) = 22$, and $24 > 22$, then $\frac{8}{11} > \frac{2}{3}$.

    Because only one of the five fractions is greater than $\frac{2}{3}$, the fractions given in C, D, and E need not be tested. However, for completeness, $\frac{3}{5} < \frac{2}{3}$ because $3(3) < 2(5)$; $\frac{13}{27} < \frac{2}{3}$ because $3(13) < 2(27)$; and $\frac{5}{8} < \frac{2}{3}$ because $3(5) < 2(8)$.

    The correct answer is B.

15. If 60 percent of a rectangular floor is covered by a rectangular rug that is 9 feet by 12 feet, what is the area, in square feet, of the floor?

    (A) 65
    (B) 108
    (C) 180
    (D) 270
    (E) 300

Geometry; Arithmetic Area; Percents

First, calculate the area of the rug. Using the formula area $=$ (width)(length), the area of the rug is thus $9(12) = 108$ square feet.

Then, letting $x =$ the area of the floor in square feet, build an equation to express the given information that the rug's area is equal to 60 percent of the floor area, and work the problem.

$108 = 0.6x$ 　　　　solve for x

$180 = x$

The correct answer is C.

16. Three machines, individually, can do a certain job in 4, 5, and 6 hours, respectively. What is the greatest part of the job that can be done in one hour by two of the machines working together at their respective rates?

(A) $\dfrac{11}{30}$

(B) $\dfrac{9}{20}$

(C) $\dfrac{3}{5}$

(D) $\dfrac{11}{15}$

(E) $\dfrac{5}{6}$

Arithmetic Applied problems; Operations on rational numbers

The two fastest machines will be able to do the greatest part of the job in one hour. The fastest machine, which can do the whole job in 4 hours, can do $\dfrac{1}{4}$ of the job in one hour. The next fastest machine, which can do the whole job in 5 hours, can do $\dfrac{1}{5}$ of the job in one hour. Together, these machines can do $\dfrac{1}{4} + \dfrac{1}{5} = \dfrac{5}{20} + \dfrac{4}{20} = \dfrac{9}{20}$ of the job in one hour.

The correct answer is B.

17. The value of $-3-(-10)$ is how much greater than the value of $-10-(-3)$?

(A)   0
(B)   6
(C)   7
(D)   14
(E)   26

Arithmetic Operations on rational numbers

Work the problem.

$-3-(-10) = 7$

$-10-(-3) = -7$

$7-(-7) = 14$

The correct answer is D.

18. If X and Y are sets of integers, $X \triangle Y$ denotes the set of integers that belong to set X or set Y, but not both. If X consists of 10 integers, Y consists of 18 integers, and 6 of the integers are in both X and Y, then $X \triangle Y$ consists of how many integers?

(A)   6
(B)   16
(C)   22
(D)   30
(E)   174

Arithmetic Properties of numbers

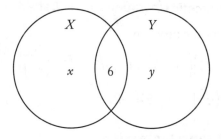

Consider the Venn diagram above, where x represents the number of integers in set X only, y represents the number of integers in set Y only, and there are 6 integers in both X and Y. The number of integers in $X \triangle Y$ is $x + y$. Since there are 10 integers in X, $x + 6 = 10$, from which $x = 4$. Since there are 18 integers in Y, $y + 6 = 18$, from which $y = 12$. Then $x + y = 4 + 12 = 16$.

The correct answer is B.

		x
37	38	15
		y

19. In the figure above, the sum of the three numbers in the horizontal row equals the product of the three numbers in the vertical column. What is the value of xy?

(A)   6
(B)   15
(C)   35
(D)   75
(E)   90

Arithmetic Operations on rational numbers

The sum of the three numbers in the horizontal row is $37 + 38 + 15$, or 90. The product of the three numbers in the vertical column is $15xy$. Thus, $15xy = 90$, or the value of $xy = 6$.

The correct answer is A.

20. $\left(1+\sqrt{5}\right)\left(1-\sqrt{5}\right) =$

(A) -4
(B)   2
(C)   6
(D) $-4-2\sqrt{5}$
(E) $6-2\sqrt{5}$

Arithmetic Operations on radical expressions

Work the problem.

$$\left(1+\sqrt{5}\right)\left(1-\sqrt{5}\right) = 1^2 + \sqrt{5} - \sqrt{5} - \left(\sqrt{5}\right)^2 =$$
$$1 - \left(\sqrt{5}\right)^2 = 1 - 5 = -4$$

The correct answer is A.

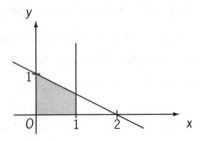

21. In the rectangular coordinate system above, the shaded region is bounded by straight lines. Which of the following is NOT an equation of one of the boundary lines?

(A) $x = 0$
(B) $y = 0$
(C) $x = 1$
(D) $x - y = 0$
(E) $x + 2y = 2$

Geometry Simple coordinate geometry

The left boundary of the shaded region is the y-axis, which has equation $x = 0$. The bottom boundary of the shaded region is the x-axis, which has equation $y = 0$. The right boundary of the shaded region is the vertical line that has equation $x = 1$ since it goes through $(1,0)$. The top boundary of the shaded region is the line that goes through $(0,1)$ and $(2,0)$. The equation of this line CANNOT be $x - y = 0$ because $0 - 1 \neq 0$ and also $2 - 0 \neq 0$. The equation of this line is $x + 2y = 2$ since both $(0,1)$ and $(2,0)$ are on this line (i.e., $0 + 2\left(1\right) = 2$ and $2 + 2\left(0\right) = 2$).

The correct answer is D.

22. A certain population of bacteria doubles every 10 minutes. If the number of bacteria in the population initially was 10^4, what was the number in the population 1 hour later?

(A) $2(10^4)$
(B) $6(10^4)$
(C) $(2^6)(10^4)$
(D) $(10^6)(10^4)$
(E) $(10^4)^6$

Arithmetic Operations on rational numbers

If the population of bacteria doubles every 10 minutes, it doubles 6 times in one hour. This doubling action can be expressed as $(2)(2)(2)(2)(2)(2)$ or 2^6. Thus, if the initial population is 10^4, the population will be $(2^6)(10^4)$ after one hour.

The correct answer is C.

23. How many minutes does it take to travel 120 miles at 400 miles per hour?

    (A) 3
    (B) $3\frac{1}{3}$
    (C) $8\frac{2}{3}$
    (D) 12
    (E) 18

Arithmetic Operations on rational numbers

Using distance = rate × time, or $D = rt$, transformed into the equivalent equation $t = \dfrac{D}{r}$,

$t = (120 \text{ miles}) \div \left(\dfrac{400 \text{ miles}}{1 \text{ hour}}\right)$

$= (120 \text{ miles}) \times \left(\dfrac{1 \text{ hour}}{400 \text{ miles}}\right) =$

$\dfrac{120}{400}$ hour $= \dfrac{3}{10}$ hour.

Then $\left(\dfrac{3}{10} \text{ hour}\right)\left(\dfrac{60 \text{ minutes}}{1 \text{ hour}}\right) =$

$\dfrac{3(60)}{10}$ minutes = 18 minutes.

The correct answer is E.

24. If the perimeter of a rectangular garden plot is 34 feet and its area is 60 square feet, what is the length of each of the longer sides?

    (A) 5 ft
    (B) 6 ft
    (C) 10 ft
    (D) 12 ft
    (E) 15 ft

Geometry; Algebra Perimeter; Area; Simultaneous equations

Letting x represent the length of the rectangular garden and y represent the width of the garden in the formulas for calculating perimeter and area, the given information can be expressed as:

Perimeter $= 2(\text{length}) + 2(\text{width})$ $\quad 34 = 2x + 2y$

or

$17 = x + y$

Area $= (\text{length})(\text{width})$ $\quad 60 = xy$

This reduces the problem to finding two numbers whose sum is 17 and whose product is 60. It can be seen by inspection that the two numbers are 5 and 12, so the length of each of the longer sides of the garden is 12 ft.

It is also possible to solve $x + y = 17$ for y and substitute the value of $y = 17 - x$ in the equation for the area and solve for x:

$xy = 60$

$x(17 - x) = 60$

$17x - x^2 = 60$

$0 = x^2 - 17x + 60$

$0 = (x - 12)(x - 5)$

$x = 12 \text{ or } 5$

$y = 5 \text{ or } 12$

Thus, the length of each of the longer sides of the garden must be 12 ft.

The correct answer is D.

25. A certain manufacturer produces items for which the production costs consist of annual fixed costs totaling $130,000 and variable costs averaging $8 per item. If the manufacturer's selling price per item is $15, how many items must the manufacturer produce and sell to earn an annual profit of $150,000 ?

    (A) 2,858
    (B) 18,667
    (C) 21,429
    (D) 35,000
    (E) 40,000

Algebra Applied problems

If x is the number of items the manufacturer must produce and sell, then the profit, $P(x)$, is defined as revenue, $R(x)$, minus cost, $C(x)$, or $P(x) = R(x) - C(x)$. From the given information,

$P(x) = 150,000$ profit

$R(x) = 15x$ revenue

$C(x) = 8x + 130,000$ cost = variable costs + fixed costs

Then

$$150,000 = 15x - (8x + 130,000)$$

$$150,000 = 7x - 130,000$$

$$280,000 = 7x$$

$$40,000 = x$$

The correct answer is E.

26. In a poll of 66,000 physicians, only 20 percent responded; of these, 10 percent disclosed their preference for pain reliever X. How many of the physicians who responded did <u>not</u> disclose a preference for pain reliever X ?

(A)   1,320
(B)   5,280
(C)   6,600
(D)   10,560
(E)   11,880

Arithmetic Percents

The number of physicians who responded to the poll was $0.2(66,000) = 13,200$. If 10 percent of the respondents disclosed a preference for X, then 90 percent did not disclose a preference for X. Thus, the number of respondents who did not disclose a preference is $0.9(13,200) = 11,880$.

The correct answer is E.

27. $\dfrac{3}{100} + \dfrac{5}{1,000} + \dfrac{7}{100,000} =$

(A)   0.357
(B)   0.3507
(C)   0.35007
(D)   0.0357
(E)   0.03507

Arithmetic Operations on rational numbers

If each fraction is written in decimal form, the sum to be found is

$$0.03$$
$$0.005$$
$$\underline{+\ 0.00007}$$
$$0.03507$$

The correct answer is E.

28. If the number n of calculators sold per week varies with the price p in dollars according to the equation $n = 300 - 20p$, what would be the total weekly revenue from the sale of $10 calculators?

(A) $ 100
(B) $ 300
(C) $1,000
(D) $2,800
(E) $3,000

Algebra First-degree equations

Using the given equation, substitute 10 for p and solve for n to determine the number of calculators sold.

$n = 300 - 20p$

$n = 300 - 20(10)$

$n = 300 - 200$

$n = 100$

Then, the revenue from the sale of n calculators $= (10)(100) = 1,000$.

The correct answer is C.

29. Which of the following fractions is equal to the decimal 0.0625 ?

    (A) $\dfrac{5}{8}$

    (B) $\dfrac{3}{8}$

    (C) $\dfrac{1}{16}$

    (D) $\dfrac{1}{18}$

    (E) $\dfrac{3}{80}$

    Arithmetic Operations on rational numbers

    Work the problem.

    $$0.0625 = \frac{625}{10,000} = \frac{1}{16}$$

    The correct answer is C.

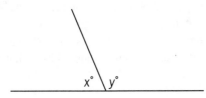

30. In the figure above, if $\dfrac{x}{x+y} = \dfrac{3}{8}$, then $x =$

    (A) 60
    (B) 67.5
    (C) 72
    (D) 108
    (E) 112.5

    Geometry; Algebra Angle measures;
        Simultaneous equations

    Since the angles x and y form a straight line, $x + y = 180$. Work the problem by substituting 180 for $x + y$ and then solving for x.

$$\frac{x}{x+y} = \frac{3}{8}$$

$\dfrac{x}{180} = \dfrac{3}{8}$	substitution
$8x = 540$	cross multiply
$x = 67.5$	divide both sides by 8

The correct answer is B.

31. If positive integers x and y are not both odd, which of the following must be even?

    (A) xy
    (B) $x + y$
    (C) $x - y$
    (D) $x + y - 1$
    (E) $2(x + y) - 1$

    Arithmetic Properties of numbers

    Since it is given that x and y are NOT both odd, either both x and y are even or one is even and the other one is odd. The following table clearly shows that only the product of x and y must be even.

	Both x and y even	One of x or y even, the other odd
xy	Even	Even
$x + y$	Even	Odd
$x - y$	Even	Odd
$x + y - 1$	Odd	Even
$2(x + y) - 1$	Odd	Odd

The correct answer is A.

32. On 3 sales John has received commissions of $240, $80, and $110, and he has 1 additional sale pending. If John is to receive an average (arithmetic mean) commission of exactly $150 on the 4 sales, then the 4th commission must be

    (A) $164
    (B) $170
    (C) $175
    (D) $182
    (E) $185

Arithmetic Statistics

Letting x equal the value of John's 4th commission, and using the formula

$$\text{average} = \frac{\text{sum of values}}{\text{number of values}}, \text{ the given}$$

information can be expressed in the following equation, which can then be solved for x:

$$\frac{240 + 80 + 110 + x}{4} = 150$$

$430 + x = 600$ simplify numerator; multiply both sides by 4

$x = 170$ subtract 430 from both sides

The correct answer is B.

33. The annual budget of a certain college is to be shown on a circle graph. If the size of each sector of the graph is to be proportional to the amount of the budget it represents, how many degrees of the circle should be used to represent an item that is 15 percent of the budget?

    (A) 15°
    (B) 36°
    (C) 54°
    (D) 90°
    (E) 150°

Arithmetic Percents; Interpretation of graphs

Since there are 360 degrees in a circle, the measure of the central angle in the circle should be $0.15(360°) = 54°$.

The correct answer is C.

34. During a two-week period, the price of an ounce of silver increased by 25 percent by the end of the first week and then decreased by 20 percent of this new price by the end of the second week. If the price of silver was x dollars per ounce at the beginning of the two-week period, what was the price, in dollars per ounce, by the end of the period?

    (A) 0.8x
    (B) 0.95x
    (C) x
    (D) 1.05x
    (E) 1.25x

Arithmetic Percents

At the end of the first week the price of an ounce of silver was $1.25x$. At the end of the second week, the price was 20 percent less than this, or 80 percent of $1.25x$, which is $(0.80)(1.25)x$, which is in turn equal to x.

The correct answer is C.

35. In a certain pond, 50 fish were caught, tagged, and returned to the pond. A few days later, 50 fish were caught again, of which 2 were found to have been tagged. If the percent of tagged fish in the second catch approximates the percent of tagged fish in the pond, what is the approximate number of fish in the pond?

    (A) 400
    (B) 625
    (C) 1,250
    (D) 2,500
    (E) 10,000

Algebra Applied problems

To solve this problem, it is necessary to determine two fractions: the fraction of fish tagged and the fraction of fish then caught that were already tagged. These two fractions can then be set equal in a proportion, and the problem can be solved.

Letting N be the approximate total number of fish in the pond, then $\frac{50}{N}$ is the fraction of fish in the pond that were tagged in the first catch. Then, the fraction of tagged fish in the sample of 50 that were caught in the second catch can be expressed as $\frac{2}{50}$, or $\frac{1}{25}$. Therefore, $\frac{50}{N} = \frac{1}{25}$, or $N = (50)(25) = 1,250.$

The correct answer is C.

36. $\sqrt{16+16} =$

(A) $4\sqrt{2}$
(B) $8\sqrt{2}$
(C) $16\sqrt{2}$
(D)   8
(E)   16

Arithmetic Operations on radical expressions

Working this problem gives

$$\sqrt{16+16} = \sqrt{(16)(2)} = \left(\sqrt{16}\right)\left(\sqrt{2}\right) = 4\sqrt{2}$$

The correct answer is A.

37. An automobile's gasoline mileage varies, depending on the speed of the automobile, between 18.0 and 22.4 miles per gallon, inclusive. What is the maximum distance, in miles, that the automobile could be driven on 15 gallons of gasoline?

(A)   336
(B)   320
(C)   303
(D)   284
(E)   270

Arithmetic Operations on rational numbers

The maximum distance would occur at the maximum mileage per gallon. Thus, the maximum distance would be

$(22.4 \text{ miles per gallon}) \times (15 \text{ gallons})$
$= 336$ miles.

The correct answer is A.

38. The organizers of a fair projected a 25 percent increase in attendance this year over that of last year, but attendance this year actually decreased by 20 percent. What percent of the projected attendance was the actual attendance?

(A)   45%
(B)   56%
(C)   64%
(D)   75%
(E)   80%

Arithmetic Percents

Letting A be last year's attendance, set up the given information, and work the problem.

$$\frac{\text{Actual Attendance}}{\text{Projected Attendance}} = \frac{0.80A}{1.25A} = 0.64 = 64\%$$

The correct answer is C.

39. What is the ratio of $\frac{3}{4}$ to the product $4\left(\frac{3}{4}\right)$?

(A) $\frac{1}{4}$

(B) $\frac{1}{3}$

(C) $\frac{4}{9}$

(D) $\frac{9}{4}$

(E)   4

Arithmetic Operations on rational numbers

Work the problem.

$$\frac{\frac{3}{4}}{4\left(\frac{3}{4}\right)} = \frac{\frac{3}{4}}{\frac{12}{4}} = \frac{\frac{3}{4}}{3} = \frac{3}{4} \times \frac{1}{3} = \frac{1}{4}$$

The correct answer is A.

40. If $3 - x = 2x - 3$, then $4x =$

    (A) −24
    (B) −8
    (C) 0
    (D) 8
    (E) 24

    Algebra First-degree equations

    Work the problem.

    $3 - x = 2x - 3$

    $\quad 6 = 3x \qquad$ add 3 to both sides;
    $\qquad\qquad\qquad$ add x to both sides

    $\quad 2 = x \qquad$ divide both sides by 3

    Therefore, $4x = 4(2) = 8$.

    The correct answer is D.

    $$2x + 2y = -4$$
    $$4x + y = 1$$

41. In the system of equations above, what is the value of x?

    (A) −3
    (B) −1
    (C) $\dfrac{2}{5}$
    (D) 1
    (E) $1\dfrac{3}{4}$

    Algebra Simultaneous equations

    Solving the second equation for y gives $y = 1 - 4x$. Then, substituting $1 - 4x$ for y in the first equation gives

    $$2x + 2(1 - 4x) = -4$$
    $$2x + 2 - 8x = -4$$
    $$-6x + 2 = -4$$
    $$-6x = -6$$
    $$x = 1$$

    The correct answer is D.

42. If $x > 3{,}000$, then the value of $\dfrac{x}{2x+1}$ is closest to

    (A) $\dfrac{1}{6}$

    (B) $\dfrac{1}{3}$

    (C) $\dfrac{10}{21}$

    (D) $\dfrac{1}{2}$

    (E) $\dfrac{3}{2}$

    Algebra Simplifying algebraic expressions

    For all large values of x, the value of $\dfrac{x}{2x+1}$ is going to be very close to the value of $\dfrac{x}{2x}$, which is equal to $\dfrac{1}{2}$.

    The correct answer is D.

43. If 18 is 15 percent of 30 percent of a certain number, what is the number?

    (A) 9
    (B) 36
    (C) 40
    (D) 81
    (E) 400

    Arithmetic Percents

    Letting n be the number, the given information can be expressed as $18 = 0.15(0.30n)$. Solve this equation for n.

    $18 = 0.15(0.30n)$

    $18 = 0.045n$

    $400 = n$

    The correct answer is E.

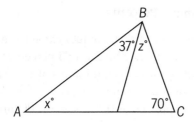

44. In $\triangle ABC$ above, what is x in terms of z ?

(A) $z + 73$
(B) $z - 73$
(C) $70 - z$
(D) $z - 70$
(E) $73 - z$

Geometry Angle measure in degrees

Since the sum of the degree measures of the angles in a triangle equals $180°$,
$x + 37 + z + 70 = 180$. Solve this equation for x.

$$x + 37 + z + 70 = 180$$
$$x + z + 107 = 180$$
$$x + z = 73$$
$$x = 73 - z$$

The correct answer is E.

45. $\dfrac{(3)(0.072)}{0.54} =$

(A) 0.04
(B) 0.3
(C) 0.4
(D) 0.8
(E) 4.0

Arithmetic Operations on rational numbers

To clear the decimals, multiply the given

expression by $1 = \dfrac{1,000}{1,000}$. Then,

$$\frac{(3)(0.072)}{0.54} \times \frac{1,000}{1,000} = \frac{3(72)}{540} = \frac{3(4)(18)}{3(10)(18)} = \frac{4}{10} = 0.4$$

The correct answer is C.

46. What is the maximum number of $1\frac{1}{4}$ foot pieces of wire that can be cut from a wire that is 24 feet long?

(A) 11
(B) 18
(C) 19
(D) 20
(E) 30

Arithmetic Operations on rational numbers

In working the problem,

$24 \div 1\frac{1}{4} = 24 \div \frac{5}{4} = 24 \times \frac{4}{5} = \frac{96}{5} = 19.2$. Since full

$1\frac{1}{4}$ foot pieces of wire are needed, 19 pieces can

be cut.

The correct answer is C.

$$\frac{61.24 \times (0.998)^2}{\sqrt{403}}$$

47. The expression above is approximately equal to

(A) 1
(B) 3
(C) 4
(D) 5
(E) 6

Arithmetic Operations on radical expressions

Simplify the expression using approximations.

$$\frac{61.24 \times (0.998)^2}{\sqrt{403}} \approx \frac{60 \times 1^2}{\sqrt{400}} = \frac{60}{20} = 3$$

The correct answer is B.

48. If the numbers $\frac{17}{24}$, $\frac{1}{2}$, $\frac{3}{8}$, $\frac{3}{4}$, and $\frac{9}{16}$ were ordered from greatest to least, the middle number of the resulting sequence would be

(A) $\frac{17}{24}$

(B) $\frac{1}{2}$

(C) $\frac{3}{8}$

(D) $\frac{3}{4}$

(E) $\frac{9}{16}$

Arithmetic Operations on rational numbers

The least common denominator for all the fractions in the problem is 48. Work out their equivalencies to see clearly their relative values:

$\frac{17}{24} = \frac{34}{48}$, $\frac{1}{2} = \frac{24}{48}$, $\frac{3}{8} = \frac{18}{48}$, $\frac{3}{4} = \frac{36}{48}$, $\frac{9}{16} = \frac{27}{48}$

In descending order, they are

$\frac{36}{48}$, $\frac{34}{48}$, $\frac{27}{48}$, $\frac{24}{48}$, $\frac{18}{48}$, and the middle

number is $\frac{27}{48} = \frac{9}{16}$.

The correct answer is E.

49. Last year if 97 percent of the revenues of a company came from domestic sources and the remaining revenues, totaling $450,000, came from foreign sources, what was the total of the company's revenues?

(A) $ 1,350,000
(B) $ 1,500,000
(C) $ 4,500,000
(D) $ 15,000,000
(E) $150,000,000

Arithmetic Percents

If 97 percent of the revenues came from domestic sources, then the remaining 3 percent, totaling $450,000, came from foreign sources. Letting x represent the total revenue, this information can be expressed as $0.03x = 450,000$, and thus

$$x = \frac{450,000}{.03} = \frac{45,000,000}{3} = 15,000,000.$$

The correct answer is D.

50. $\frac{2+2\sqrt{6}}{2} =$

(A) $\sqrt{6}$
(B) $2\sqrt{6}$
(C) $1+\sqrt{6}$
(D) $1+2\sqrt{6}$
(E) $2+\sqrt{6}$

Arithmetic Operations on radical expressions

Rewrite the expression to eliminate the denominator.

$$\frac{2+2\sqrt{6}}{2} = \frac{2\left(1+\sqrt{6}\right)}{2} = 1+\sqrt{6}$$

or

$$\frac{2+2\sqrt{6}}{2} = \frac{2}{2} + \frac{2\sqrt{6}}{2} = 1+\sqrt{6}$$

The correct answer is C.

51. A certain fishing boat is chartered by 6 people who are to contribute equally to the total charter cost of $480. If each person contributes equally to a $150 down payment, how much of the charter cost will each person still owe?

(A) $80
(B) $66
(C) $55
(D) $50
(E) $45

Arithmetic Operations on rational numbers

Since each of the 6 individuals contributes equally to the $150 down payment, and since it is given that the total cost of the chartered boat is $480, each person still owes $\frac{\$480 - \$150}{6} = \$55$.

The correct answer is C.

52. Craig sells major appliances. For each appliance he sells, Craig receives a commission of $50 plus 10 percent of the selling price. During one particular week Craig sold 6 appliances for selling prices totaling $3,620. What was the total of Craig's commissions for that week?

    (A) $412
    (B) $526
    (C) $585
    (D) $605
    (E) $662

Arithmetic Percents

Since Craig receives a commission of $50 on each appliance plus a 10 percent commission on total sales, his commission for that week was $6(\$50) + (0.1)(\$3,620) = \$662$.

The correct answer is E.

53. What number when multiplied by $\frac{4}{7}$ yields $\frac{6}{7}$ as the result?

    (A) $\frac{2}{7}$

    (B) $\frac{3}{3}$

    (C) $\frac{3}{2}$

    (D) $\frac{24}{7}$

    (E) $\frac{7}{2}$

Algebra Applied problems

Letting n represent the number, this problem can be expressed as $\frac{4}{7}n = \frac{6}{7}$, which can be solved for n by multiplying both sides by $\frac{7}{4}$:

$$\frac{4}{7}n = \frac{6}{7}$$

$$n = \frac{42}{28} \qquad \text{multiply both sides by } \frac{7}{4}$$

$$n = \frac{3}{2} \qquad \text{reduce the fraction}$$

The correct answer is C.

54. If 3 pounds of dried apricots that cost x dollars per pound are mixed with 2 pounds of prunes that cost y dollars per pound, what is the cost, in dollars, per pound of the mixture?

    (A) $\dfrac{3x + 2y}{5}$

    (B) $\dfrac{3x + 2y}{x + y}$

    (C) $\dfrac{3x + 2y}{xy}$

    (D) $5(3x + 2y)$

    (E) $3x + 2y$

Algebra Applied problems; Simplifying algebraic expressions

The total number of pounds in the mixture is $3 + 2 = 5$ pounds, and the total cost of the mixture is $3x + 2y$ dollars. Therefore, the cost per pound of the mixture is $\dfrac{3x + 2y}{5}$ dollars.

The correct answer is A.

55. Which of the following must be equal to zero for all real numbers x ?

I. $-\dfrac{1}{x}$

II. $x+(-x)$

III. x^0

(A) I only
(B) II only
(C) I and III only
(D) II and III only
(E) I, II, and III

Arithmetic Properties of numbers

Consider the numeric properties of each answer choice.

I. $-\dfrac{1}{x} \neq 0$ for all real numbers x.

II. $x+(-x) = 0$ for all real numbers x

III. $x^0 = 1 \neq 0$ for all nonzero real numbers x

Thus, only the expression in II must be equal to zero for all real numbers x.

The correct answer is B.

	City A	City B	City C	City D	City E	City F
City A						
City B						
City C						
City D						
City E						
City F						

56. In the table above, what is the least number of table entries that are needed to show the mileage between each city and each of the other five cities?

(A) 15
(B) 21
(C) 25
(D) 30
(E) 36

Arithmetic Interpretation of tables

Since there is no mileage between a city and itself and since the mileage for each pair of cities needs to be entered only once, only those boxes below (or above) the diagonal from the upper left to the lower right need entries. This gives $1 + 2 + 3 + 4 + 5 = 15$ entries.

The correct answer is A.

57. If $(t-8)$ is a factor of $t^2 - kt - 48$, then $k =$

(A) −6
(B) −2
(C) 2
(D) 6
(E) 14

Algebra Second-degree equations

If $(t-8)$ is a factor of the expression $t^2 - kt - 48$, then $t = 8$ is a solution of the equation $t^2 - kt - 48 = 0$. So,

$$8^2 - 8k - 48 = 0$$
$$64 - 8k - 48 = 0$$
$$16 - 8k = 0$$
$$16 = 8k$$
$$2 = k$$

The correct answer is C.

58. $\dfrac{31}{125} =$

(A) 0.248
(B) 0.252
(C) 0.284
(D) 0.312
(E) 0.320

Arithmetic Operations on rational numbers

To avoid long division, multiply the given fraction by 1 using a form for 1 that will result in a power of 10 in the denominator.

$$\frac{31}{125} = \frac{31}{5^3} = \frac{31}{5^3} \times \frac{2^3}{2^3} = \frac{(31)(8)}{10^3} = \frac{248}{1{,}000} = 0.248$$

The correct answer is A.

59. Members of a social club met to address 280 newsletters. If they addressed $\frac{1}{4}$ of the newsletters during the first hour and $\frac{2}{5}$ of the remaining newsletters during the second hour, how many newsletters did they address during the second hour?

    (A) 28
    (B) 42
    (C) 63
    (D) 84
    (E) 112

Arithmetic Operations on rational numbers

Since $\frac{1}{4}$ of the newsletters were addressed during the first hour, $\frac{3}{4}(280) = 210$ newsletters were NOT addressed during the first hour and remained to be done in the second hour. Therefore, $\frac{2}{5}(210) = 84$ newsletters were addressed during the second hour.

The correct answer is D.

60. $\dfrac{1}{3 - \dfrac{1}{3 - \dfrac{1}{3 - 1}}} =$

    (A) $\dfrac{7}{23}$

    (B) $\dfrac{5}{13}$

    (C) $\dfrac{2}{3}$

    (D) $\dfrac{23}{7}$

    (E) $\dfrac{13}{5}$

Arithmetic Operations with rational numbers

Perform each subtraction beginning at the lowest level in the fraction and proceeding upward.

$$\dfrac{1}{3 - \dfrac{1}{3 - \dfrac{1}{3 - 1}}} = \dfrac{1}{3 - \dfrac{1}{3 - \dfrac{1}{2}}}$$

$$= \dfrac{1}{3 - \dfrac{1}{\dfrac{6}{2} - \dfrac{1}{2}}}$$

$$= \dfrac{1}{3 - \dfrac{1}{\dfrac{5}{2}}}$$

$$= \dfrac{1}{3 - \dfrac{2}{5}}$$

$$= \dfrac{1}{\dfrac{15}{5} - \dfrac{2}{5}}$$

$$= \dfrac{1}{\dfrac{13}{5}}$$

$$= \dfrac{5}{13}$$

The correct answer is B.

61. After 4,000 gallons of water were added to a large water tank that was already filled to $\frac{3}{4}$ of its capacity, the tank was then at $\frac{4}{5}$ of its capacity. How many gallons of water does the tank hold when filled to capacity?

    (A) 5,000
    (B) 6,200
    (C) 20,000
    (D) 40,000
    (E) 80,000

Algebra First-degree equations

Let C be the capacity of the tank. In symbols, the given information is $4{,}000 + \frac{3}{4}C = \frac{4}{5}C$. Solve for C.

$$4{,}000 + \frac{3}{4}C = \frac{4}{5}C$$

$$4{,}000 = \left(\frac{4}{5} - \frac{3}{4}\right)C$$

$$4{,}000 = \frac{16-15}{20}C$$

$$4{,}000 = \frac{1}{20}C$$

$$20(4{,}000) = C$$

$$80{,}000 = C$$

The correct answer is E.

62. The sum of three integers is 40. The largest integer is 3 times the middle integer, and the smallest integer is 23 less than the largest integer. What is the product of the three integers?

(A) 1,104
(B) 972
(C) 672
(D) 294
(E) 192

Algebra Simultaneous equations

Let the three integers be x, y, and z, where $x < y < z$. Then, in symbols the given information is

$$\begin{cases} x + y + z = 40 \\ z = 3y \\ x = z - 23 \end{cases}$$

Substituting $3y$ for z in the third equation gives $x = 3y - 23$. Then, substituting $(3y - 23)$ for x and $3y$ for z into the first equation gives

$$(3y - 23) + y + 3y = 40$$

$$7y - 23 = 40$$

$$7y = 63$$

$$y = 9$$

From $y = 9$, it follows that $z = 3(9) = 27$ and $x = 27 - 23 = 4$. Thus, the product of x, y, and z is $(4)(9)(27) = 972$.

The correct answer is B.

63. If $S = \{0, 4, 5, 2, 11, 8\}$, how much greater than the median of the numbers in S is the mean of the numbers in S?

(A) 0.5
(B) 1.0
(C) 1.5
(D) 2.0
(E) 2.5

Arithmetic; Algebra Statistics; Concepts of sets

The median of S is found by ordering the values according to size $(0, 2, 4, 5, 8, 11)$ and taking the average of the two middle numbers: $\frac{4+5}{2} = 4.5$.

The mean is $\frac{\text{sum of } n \text{ values}}{n} =$

$$\frac{0 + 4 + 5 + 2 + 11 + 8}{6} = 5.$$

The difference between the mean and the median is $5 - 4.5 = 0.5$.

The correct answer is A.

64. At a monthly meeting, $\frac{2}{5}$ of the attendees were males and $\frac{7}{8}$ of the male attendees arrived on time. If $\frac{9}{10}$ of the female attendees arrived on time, what fraction of the attendees at the monthly meeting did <u>not</u> arrive on time?

(A) $\frac{11}{100}$

(B) $\frac{3}{25}$

(C) $\frac{7}{50}$

(D) $\frac{3}{20}$

(E) $\frac{4}{25}$

Arithmetic Operations with rational numbers

Let T be the total number of attendees at the meeting. Then, $\frac{2}{5}T$ is the number of male attendees. Of these, $\frac{7}{8}$ arrived on time, so $\frac{7}{8}\left(\frac{2}{5}T\right) = \frac{7}{20}T$ is the number of male attendees who arrived on time. Since $\frac{2}{5}T$ of the attendees were male, the number of female attendees is $T - \frac{2}{5}T = \frac{3}{5}T$. Of these $\frac{9}{10}$ arrived on time, so $\frac{9}{10}\left(\frac{3}{5}T\right) = \frac{27}{50}T$ is the number of female attendees who arrived on time. The total number of attendees who arrived on time is therefore $\frac{7}{20}T + \frac{27}{50}T = \left(\frac{35+54}{100}\right)T = \frac{89}{100}T$. Thus, the number of attendees who did NOT arrive on time is $T - \frac{89}{100}T = \frac{11}{100}T$, so the fraction of attendees who did not arrive on time is $\frac{11}{100}$.

The correct answer is A.

65. If $d = 2.0453$ and d^* is the decimal obtained by rounding d to the nearest hundredth, what is the value of $d^* - d$?

(A) -0.0053
(B) -0.0003
(C) 0.0007
(D) 0.0047
(E) 0.0153

Arithmetic Operations on rational numbers

Since $d = 2.0453$ rounded to the nearest hundredth is 2.05, $d^* = 2.05$; therefore, $d^* - d = 2.05 - 2.0453 = 0.0047$.

The correct answer is D.

66. Company K's earnings were $12 million last year. If this year's earnings are projected to be 150 percent greater than last year's earnings, what are Company K's projected earnings this year?

(A) $13.5 million
(B) $15 million
(C) $18 million
(D) $27 million
(E) $30 million

Arithmetic Percents

If one quantity x is p percent **greater** than another quantity y, then $x = y + \left(\frac{p}{100}\right)y$. Let y represent last year's earnings and x represent this year's earnings, which are projected to be 150 percent greater than last year's earnings. Then, $x = y + \left(\frac{150}{100}\right)y = y + 1.5y = 2.5y$. Since last year's earnings were $12 million, this year's earnings are projected to be $2.5(\$12 \text{ million}) = \$30 \text{ million}$.

The correct answer is E.

67. The sequence a_1, a_2, a_3, a_4, a_5 is such that $a_n = a_{n-1} + 5$ for $2 \leq n \leq 5$. If $a_5 = 31$, what is the value of a_1?

(A) 1
(B) 6
(C) 11
(D) 16
(E) 21

Algebra Sequences

Since $a_n = a_{n-1} + 5$, then $a_n - a_{n-1} = 5$. So,

$a_5 - a_4 = 5$

$a_4 - a_3 = 5$

$a_3 - a_2 = 5$

$a_2 - a_1 = 5$

Adding the equations gives

$a_5 - a_4 + a_4 - a_3 + a_3 - a_2 + a_2 - a_1 = 5 + 5 + 5 + 5$

$$a_5 - a_1 = 20$$

and substituting 31 for a_5 gives

$31 - a_1 = 20$

$a_1 = 11$.

The correct answer is C.

68. When positive integer n is divided by 5, the remainder is 1. When n is divided by 7, the remainder is 3. What is the smallest positive integer k such that $k + n$ is a multiple of 35 ?

    (A)   3
    (B)   4
    (C)   12
    (D)   32
    (E)   35

Arithmetic Properties of numbers

Given that the remainder is 1 when the positive integer n is divided by 5, it follows that $n = 5p + 1$ for some positive integer p. Likewise, the remainder is 3 when n is divided by 7, so $n = 7q + 3$ for some positive integer q. Equating the two expressions for n gives $5p + 1 = 7q + 3$ or $5p = 7q + 2$. Since the units digit of each multiple of 5 is either 5 or 0, the units digit of $7q + 2$ must be 5 or 0 and the units digit of $7q$ must be 3 or 8. Therefore, $7q = 28, 63, 98, 133, \ldots$, and so $q = 4, 9, 14, 19, \ldots$. Thus, $q = 5m + 4$ for some positive integer m. Then, $n = 7q + 3 = 7(5m + 4) + 3 = 35m + 28 + 3 = 35m + 31$. Therefore, if k is a positive integer, $n + k$ is a multiple of 35 when $k = 4, 39, 74, \ldots$ and the smallest of these values of k is 4.

The correct answer is B.

69. Of the goose eggs laid at a certain pond, $\frac{2}{3}$ hatched, and $\frac{3}{4}$ of the geese that hatched from those eggs survived the first month. Of the geese that survived the first month, $\frac{3}{5}$ did <u>not</u> survive the first year. If 120 geese survived the first year and if no more than one goose hatched from each egg, how many goose eggs were laid at the pond?

    (A)   280
    (B)   400
    (C)   540
    (D)   600
    (E)   840

Arithmetic Operations with rational numbers

Let N represent the number of eggs laid at the pond. Then $\frac{2}{3}N$ eggs hatched and $\frac{3}{4}\left(\frac{2}{3}N\right)$ goslings (baby geese) survived the first month. Since $\frac{3}{5}$ of these goslings did not survive the first year, then $\frac{2}{5}$ did survive the first year. This means that $\frac{2}{5}\left(\frac{3}{4}\left(\frac{2}{3}N\right)\right)$ goslings survived the first year. But this number is 120 and so, $\frac{2}{5}\left(\frac{3}{4}\left(\frac{2}{3}N\right)\right) = 120$, $\frac{1}{5}N = 120$, and $N = 5(120) = 600$.

The correct answer is D.

70. List S consists of 10 consecutive odd integers, and list T consists of 5 consecutive even integers. If the least integer in S is 7 more than the least integer in T, how much greater is the average (arithmetic mean) of the integers in S than the average of the integers in T?

    (A)   2
    (B)   7
    (C)   8
    (D)   12
    (E)   22

Arithmetic Statistics

Let the integers in S be $s, s + 2, s + 4, \ldots, s + 18$, where s is odd. Let the integers in T be $t, t + 2, t + 4, t + 6, t + 8$, where t is even. Given that $s = t + 7$, it follows that $s - t = 7$. The average of the integers in S is $\frac{10s + 90}{10} = s + 9$, and, similarly, the average of the integers in T is $\frac{5t + 20}{5} = t + 4$. The difference in these averages is $(s + 9) - (t + 4) = (s - t) + (9 - 4) = 7 + 5 = 12$. Thus, the average of the integers in S is 12 greater than the average of the integers in T.

The correct answer is D.

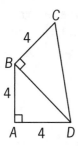

71. In the figure above, what is the area of triangular region *BCD* ?

    (A) $4\sqrt{2}$
    (B)   8
    (C) $8\sqrt{2}$
    (D)   16
    (E) $16\sqrt{2}$

    Geometry Triangles; Area

    By the Pythagorean theorem, $BD = \sqrt{4^2 + 4^2} = 4\sqrt{2}$.

    Then the area of $\triangle BCD$ is $\frac{1}{2}\left(4\sqrt{2}\right)\left(4\right) = 8\sqrt{2}$.

    The correct answer is C.

72. If $x^2 - 2x - 15 = 0$ and $x > 0$, which of the following must be equal to 0 ?

    I. $x^2 - 6x + 9$
    II. $x^2 - 7x + 10$
    III. $x^2 - 10x + 25$

    (A)   I only
    (B)   II only
    (C)   III only
    (D)   II and III only
    (E)   I, II, and III

    Algebra Second-degree equations

    Since $x^2 - 2x - 15 = 0$, then $\left(x - 5\right)\left(x + 3\right) = 0$, so $x = 5$ or $x = -3$. Since $x > 0$, then $x = 5$.

    I. $5^2 - 6\left(5\right) + 9 = 25 - 30 + 9 = 4 \neq 0$

    II. $5^2 - 7\left(5\right) + 10 = 25 - 35 + 10 = 0$

    III. $5^2 - 10\left(5\right) + 25 = 25 - 50 + 25 = 0$

    The correct answer is D.

73. If Mel saved more than $10 by purchasing a sweater at a 15 percent discount, what is the smallest amount the original price of the sweater could be, to the nearest dollar?

    (A)   45
    (B)   67
    (C)   75
    (D)   83
    (E)   150

    Arithmetic; Algebra Percents; Inequalities; Applied problems

    Letting P be the original price of the sweater in dollars, the given information can be expressed as $\left(0.15\right)P > 10$. Solving for P gives

    $$\left(0.15\right)P > 10$$
    $$P > \frac{10}{0.15} = \frac{1,000}{15} = \frac{200}{3}$$
    $$P > 66\frac{2}{3}$$

    Thus, to the nearest dollar, the smallest amount P could have been is $67.

    The correct answer is B.

74. If $x = -1$, then $-\left(x^4 + x^3 + x^2 + x\right) =$

    (A) -10
    (B) -4
    (C) 0
    (D) 4
    (E) 10

    Arithmetic Operations on rational numbers

    Substituting -1 for x throughout the expression gives

    $$-\left(x^4 + x^3 + x^2 + x\right) = -\left(\left(-1\right)^4 + \left(-1\right)^3 + \left(-1\right)^2 + \left(-1\right)\right)$$
    $$= -\left(1 - 1 + 1 - 1\right)$$
    $$= -0$$
    $$= 0$$

    The correct answer is C.

75. Today Rose is twice as old as Sam and Sam is 3 years younger than Tina. If Rose, Sam, and Tina are all alive 4 years from today, which of the following must be true on that day?

    I.   Rose is twice as old as Sam.
    II.   Sam is 3 years younger than Tina.
    III. Rose is older than Tina.

    (A) I only
    (B) II only
    (C) III only
    (D) I and II
    (E) II and III

Algebra Applied problems

Letting R, S, and T represent Rose's, Sam's, and Tina's ages today, the given information is summarized by the following table:

	Today	4 years from today
Rose	$2S$	$2S + 4$
Sam	S	$S + 4$
Tina	$S + 3$	$(S + 3) + 4 = S + 7$

I.   Four years from today, Rose will be twice as old as Sam, only if
$2S + 4 = 2(S + 4)$ or $2S + 4 = 2S + 8$.
But, this is NEVER true.

II. Four years from today, Sam will be 3 years younger than Tina since $S + 4 = (S + 7) - 3$ for all values of S. Therefore, II MUST be true.

(Note: Two people who are 3 years apart in age will remain so their entire lives.)

III. Four years from today, Rose will be older than Tina only if $2S + 4 > S + 7$ or only if $S > 3$. Therefore, depending on how old Sam is today, III need not be true.

Thus, II must be true, but I and III need not be true.

The correct answer is B.

76. If a square region has area n, what is the length of the diagonal of the square in terms of n?

    (A) $\sqrt{2n}$
    (B) $\sqrt{n}$
    (C) $2\sqrt{n}$
    (D) $2n$
    (E) $2n^2$

Geometry Area; Pythagorean theorem

If s represents the side length of the square, then $n = s^2$. By the Pythagorean theorem, the length of the diagonal of the square is $\sqrt{s^2 + s^2} = \sqrt{n + n} = \sqrt{2n}$.

The correct answer is A.

77. Temperatures in degrees Celsius (C) can be converted to temperatures in degrees Fahrenheit (F) by the formula $F = \dfrac{9}{5}C + 32$. What is the temperature at which $F = C$?

    (A) $20°$
    (B) $\left(\dfrac{32}{5}\right)°$
    (C) $0°$
    (D) $-20°$
    (E) $-40°$

Algebra First-degree equations

For $F = C$, substitute F for C in the formula, and solve for F.

$$F = \frac{9}{5}C + 32$$

$$F = \frac{9}{5}F + 32 \qquad \text{substitution}$$

$$-\frac{4}{5}F = 32 \qquad \text{subtract } \frac{9}{5}F \text{ from both sides}$$

$$F = -40 \qquad \text{divide both sides by } -\frac{4}{5}$$

The correct answer is E.

78. The "prime sum" of an integer n greater than 1 is the sum of all the prime factors of n, including repetitions. For example, the prime sum of 12 is 7, since $12 = 2 \times 2 \times 3$ and $2 + 2 + 3 = 7$. For which of the following integers is the prime sum greater than 35 ?

    (A) 440
    (B) 512
    (C) 620
    (D) 700
    (E) 750

Arithmetic Properties of numbers

A Since $440 = 2 \times 2 \times 2 \times 5 \times 11$, the prime sum of 440 is $2 + 2 + 2 + 5 + 11 = 22$, which is not greater than 35.

B Since $512 = 2^9$, the prime sum of 512 is $9(2) = 18$, which is not greater than 35.

C Since $620 = 2 \times 2 \times 5 \times 31$, the prime sum of 620 is $2 + 2 + 5 + 31 = 40$, which is greater than 35.

Because there can be only one correct answer, D and E need not be checked. However, for completeness,

D Since $700 = 2 \times 2 \times 5 \times 5 \times 7$, the prime sum of 700 is $2 + 2 + 5 + 5 + 7 = 21$, which is not greater than 35.

E Since $750 = 2 \times 3 \times 5 \times 5 \times 5$, the prime sum of 750 is $2 + 3 + 5 + 5 + 5 = 20$, which is not greater than 35.

The correct answer is C.

79. If x is to be chosen at random from the set {1, 2, 3, 4} and y is to be chosen at random from the set {5, 6, 7}, what is the probability that xy will be even?

    (A) $\frac{1}{6}$

    (B) $\frac{1}{3}$

    (C) $\frac{1}{2}$

    (D) $\frac{2}{3}$

    (E) $\frac{5}{6}$

Arithmetic; Algebra Probability; Concepts of sets

By the principle of multiplication, since there are 4 elements in the first set and 3 elements in the second set, there are $(4)(3) = 12$ possible products of xy, where x is chosen from the first set and y is chosen from the second set. These products will be even EXCEPT when both x and y are odd. Since there are 2 odd numbers in the first set and 2 odd numbers in the second set, there are $(2)(2) = 4$ products of x and y that are odd. This means that the remaining $12 - 4 = 8$ products are even. Thus, the probability that xy is even is $\frac{8}{12} = \frac{2}{3}$.

The correct answer is D.

80. At a garage sale, all of the prices of the items sold were different. If the price of a radio sold at the garage sale was both the 15th highest price and the 20th lowest price among the prices of the items sold, how many items were sold at the garage sale?

    (A) 33
    (B) 34
    (C) 35
    (D) 36
    (E) 37

Arithmetic Operations with integers

If the price of the radio was the 15th highest price, there were 14 items that sold for prices higher than the price of the radio. If the price of the radio was the 20th lowest price, there were 19 items that sold for prices lower than the price of the radio. Therefore, the total number of items sold is $14 + 1 + 19 = 34$.

The correct answer is B.

81. Ada and Paul received their scores on three tests. On the first test, Ada's score was 10 points higher than Paul's score. On the second test, Ada's score was 4 points higher than Paul's score. If Paul's average (arithmetic mean) score on the three tests was 3 points higher than Ada's average score on the three tests, then Paul's score on the third test was how many points higher than Ada's score?

   (A)   9
   (B)   14
   (C)   17
   (D)   23
   (E)   25

Algebra Statistics

Let a_1, a_2, and a_3 be Ada's scores on the first, second, and third tests, respectively, and let p_1, p_2, and p_3 be Paul's scores on the first, second, and third tests, respectively. Then, Ada's average score is $\dfrac{a_1 + a_2 + a_3}{3}$ and Paul's average score is $\dfrac{p_1 + p_2 + p_3}{3}$. But, Paul's average score is 3 points higher than Ada's average score, so $\dfrac{p_1 + p_2 + p_3}{3} = \dfrac{a_1 + a_2 + a_3}{3} + 3$. Also, it is given that $a_1 = p_1 + 10$ and $a_2 = p_2 + 4$, so by substitution,

$$\frac{p_1 + p_2 + p_3}{3} = \frac{(p_1 + 10) + (p_2 + 4) + a_3}{3} + 3.$$ Then,

$p_1 + p_2 + p_3 = (p_1 + 10) + (p_2 + 4) + a_3 + 9$ and so $p_3 = a_3 + 23$. On the third test, Paul's score was 23 points higher than Ada's score.

The correct answer is D.

82. Three business partners, Q, R, and S, agree to divide their total profit for a certain year in the ratios 2:5:8, respectively. If Q's share was $4,000, what was the total profit of the business partners for the year?

   (A) $ 26,000
   (B) $ 30,000
   (C) $ 52,000
   (D) $ 60,000
   (E) $300,000

Algebra Applied problems

Letting T represent the total profit and using the given ratios, Q's share is $\dfrac{2}{2 + 5 + 8}T = \dfrac{2}{15}T$. Since Q's share is $4,000, then $\dfrac{2}{15}T = 4,000$ and $T = \dfrac{15}{2}(4,000) = 30,000$.

The correct answer is B.

83. Which of the following lines in the xy-plane does not contain any point with integers as both coordinates?

   (A) $y = x$
   (B) $y = x + \dfrac{1}{2}$
   (C) $y = x + 5$
   (D) $y = \dfrac{1}{2}x$
   (E) $y = \dfrac{1}{2}x + 5$

Algebra; Arithmetic Substitution; Operations with rational numbers

A   If x is an integer, y is an integer since $y = x$. Thus, the line given by $y = x$ contains points with integers as both coordinates.

B   If x is an integer, then if y were an integer, then $y - x$ would be an integer. But,

$y - x = \dfrac{1}{2}$ and $\dfrac{1}{2}$ is NOT an integer. Since assuming that y is an integer leads to a contradiction, then y cannot be an integer and the line given by $y = x + \dfrac{1}{2}$ does NOT contain any points with integers as both coordinates.

Since there can be only one correct answer, the lines in C, D, and E need not be checked, but for completeness,

C   If x is an integer, $x + 5$ is an integer and so y is an integer since $y = x + 5$. Thus, the line given by $y = x + 5$ contains points with integers as both coordinates.

D   If x is an even integer, $\frac{1}{2}x$ is an integer and so y is an integer since $y = \frac{1}{2}x$. Thus, the line given by $y = \frac{1}{2}x$ contains points with integers as both coordinates.

E   If x is an even integer, $\frac{1}{2}x$ is an integer and $\frac{1}{2}x + 5$ is also an integer so y is an integer since $y = \frac{1}{2}x + 5$. Thus, the line given by $y = \frac{1}{2}x + 5$ contains points with integers as both coordinates.

The correct answer is B.

84.   The average (arithmetic mean) of 6 numbers is 8.5. When one number is discarded, the average of the remaining numbers becomes 7.2. What is the discarded number?

(A)   7.8
(B)   9.8
(C)   10.0
(D)   12.4
(E)   15.0

Arithmetic Statistics

The average, or arithmetic mean, of a data set is the sum of the values in the data set divided by the number of values in the data set:

$$\text{Average} = \frac{\text{sum of } v \text{ values}}{v}.$$

In the original data set, $\frac{\text{sum of 6 values}}{6} = 8.5$, and thus the sum of the 6 values is $6(8.5) = 51.0$.

Letting x represent the discarded number, the average for the altered data set is

$$\frac{\text{sum of 5 values}}{5} = \frac{\text{sum of 6 values} - x}{5} =$$

$\frac{51 - x}{5} = 7.2$. Then $51 - x = 5(7.2) = 36$ and $x = 51 - 36 = 15$.

The correct answer is E.

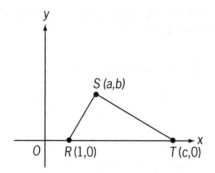

85.   In the rectangular coordinate system above, the area of $\triangle RST$ is

(A) $\dfrac{bc}{2}$

(B) $\dfrac{b(c-1)}{2}$

(C) $\dfrac{c(b-1)}{2}$

(D) $\dfrac{a(c-1)}{2}$

(E) $\dfrac{c(a-1)}{2}$

Geometry Simple-coordinate geometry

Letting $\overline{RT}$ be the base of the triangle, since $RT = c - 1$, the length of the base of $\triangle RST$ is $c - 1$. The altitude to the base $\overline{RT}$ is a perpendicular dropped from S to the x-axis. The length of this perpendicular is $b - 0 = b$. Using the formula for the area, A, of a triangle, $A = \frac{1}{2}bh$, where b is the length of the base and h is the length of the altitude to that base, the area of $\triangle RST$ is

$$\frac{1}{2}(c-1)(b) \text{ or } \frac{b(c-1)}{2}.$$

The correct answer is B.

86.   What is the largest integer n such that $\frac{1}{2^n} > 0.01$?

(A)   5
(B)   6
(C)   7
(D)   10
(E)   51

Arithmetic Exponents; Operations with rational numbers

Since $\frac{1}{2^n} > 0.01$ is equivalent to $2^n < 100$, find the largest integer n such that $2^n < 100$. Using trial and error, $2^6 = 64$ and $64 < 100$, but $2^7 = 128$ and $128 > 100$. Therefore, 6 is the largest integer such that $\frac{1}{2^n} > 0.01$.

The correct answer is B.

87. One inlet pipe fills an empty tank in 5 hours. A second inlet pipe fills the same tank in 3 hours. If both pipes are used together, how long will it take to fill $\frac{2}{3}$ of the tank?

(A) $\frac{8}{15}$ hr

(B) $\frac{3}{4}$ hr

(C) $\frac{5}{4}$ hr

(D) $\frac{15}{8}$ hr

(E) $\frac{8}{3}$ hr

Algebra Applied problems

If the first pipe fills the tank in 5 hours, then it fills $\frac{1}{5}$ of the tank in one hour. If the second pipe fills the tank in 3 hours, then it fills $\frac{1}{3}$ of the tank in one hour. Together, the two pipes fill $\frac{1}{5} + \frac{1}{3} = \frac{8}{15}$ of the tank in one hour, which means they fill the whole tank in $\frac{15}{8}$ hours. To fill $\frac{2}{3}$ of the tank at this constant rate would then take $\left(\frac{2}{3}\right)\left(\frac{15}{8}\right) = \frac{5}{4}$ hours.

The correct answer is C.

88. $\left(\frac{1}{5}\right)^2 - \left(\frac{1}{5}\right)\left(\frac{1}{4}\right) =$

(A) $-\frac{1}{20}$

(B) $-\frac{1}{100}$

(C) $\frac{1}{100}$

(D) $\frac{1}{20}$

(E) $\frac{1}{5}$

Arithmetic Operations on rational numbers

$$\left(\frac{1}{5}\right)^2 - \left(\frac{1}{5}\right)\left(\frac{1}{4}\right) = \frac{1}{25} - \frac{1}{20}$$

$$= \frac{4}{100} - \frac{5}{100}$$

$$= -\frac{1}{100}$$

The correct answer is B.

89. If the length and width of a rectangular garden plot were each increased by 20 percent, what would be the percent increase in the area of the plot?

(A) 20%
(B) 24%
(C) 36%
(D) 40%
(E) 44%

Geometry Area

If L represents the length of the original plot and W represents the width of the original plot, the area of the original plot is LW. To get the dimensions of the plot after the increase, multiply each dimension of the original plot by $(1 + 0.2) = 1.2$ to reflect the 20 percent increase.

Then, the area of the plot after the increase is $(1.2L)(1.2W) = 1.44LW$ or 144 percent of the area of the original plot, which is an increase of 44 percent over the area of the original plot.

The correct answer is E.

90. The population of a bacteria culture doubles every 2 minutes. Approximately how many minutes will it take for the population to grow from 1,000 to 500,000 bacteria?

(A) 10
(B) 12
(C) 14
(D) 16
(E) 18

Arithmetic Estimation

Set up a table of values to see how the culture grows.

Number of Minutes	Bacteria Population
0	1,000
2	2,000
4	4,000
6	8,000
8	16,000
10	32,000
12	64,000
14	128,000
16	256,000
18	512,000

At 18 minutes, the population of bacteria is just over 500,000.

The correct answer is E.

91. For a light that has an intensity of 60 candles at its source, the intensity in candles, S, of the light at a point d feet from the source is given by the formula $S = \dfrac{60k}{d^2}$, where k is a constant. If the intensity of the light is 30 candles at a distance of 2 feet from the source, what is the intensity of the light at a distance of 20 feet from the source?

(A) $\dfrac{3}{10}$ candle

(B) $\dfrac{1}{2}$ candle

(C) 1 candle
(D) 2 candles
(E) 3 candles

Algebra Applied problems

First, solve the equation for the constant k using the values where both the intensity (S) and distance (d) are known.

$$S = \frac{60k}{d^2}$$

$$30 = \frac{60k}{2^2} \qquad \text{substitute } S = 30 \text{ candles and } d = 2 \text{ feet}$$

$$120 = 60k \qquad \text{solve for } k$$

$$2 = k$$

Then, with this known value of k, solve the equation for S where only the distance (d) is known.

$$S = \frac{60k}{d^2}$$

$$S = \frac{60(2)}{20^2} \qquad \text{substitute } k = 2 \text{ and } d = 20 \text{ feet}$$

$$S = \frac{120}{400} = \frac{3}{10}$$

The correct answer is A.

92. If $b < 2$ and $2x - 3b = 0$, which of the following must be true?

    (A) $x > -3$
    (B) $x < 2$
    (C) $x = 3$
    (D) $x < 3$
    (E) $x > 3$

Algebra Inequalities

First, solve the equation for b.

$$2x - 3b = 0$$

$$2x = 3b$$

$$\frac{2}{3}x = b$$

Then, by substitution, the inequality $b < 2$ becomes

$$\frac{2}{3}x < 2$$

$$x < \left(\frac{3}{2}\right)(2)$$

$$x < 3$$

The correct answer is D.

93. $\dfrac{(-1.5)(1.2) - (4.5)(0.4)}{30} =$

    (A) -1.2
    (B) -0.12
    (C) 0
    (D) 0.12
    (E) 1.2

Arithmetic Operations on rational numbers

Simplify the expression.

$$\frac{(-1.5)(1.2) - (4.5)(0.4)}{30} =$$

$$\frac{-1.80 - 1.80}{30} = \frac{-3.60}{30} = -0.12$$

The correct answer is B.

94. René earns $8.50 per hour on days other than Sundays and twice that rate on Sundays. Last week she worked a total of 40 hours, including 8 hours on Sunday. What were her earnings for the week?

    (A) $272
    (B) $340
    (C) $398
    (D) $408
    (E) $476

Arithmetic Operations on rational numbers

René worked a total of $40 - 8 = 32$ hours at a rate of $8.50 per hour during the week. On Sunday she worked 8 hours at a rate of $8.50(2) = $17.00 per hour. Her total earnings for the week were thus $32($8.50) + 8($17) = 408.

The correct answer is D.

95. In a shipment of 120 machine parts, 5 percent were defective. In a shipment of 80 machine parts, 10 percent were defective. For the two shipments combined, what percent of the machine parts were defective?

    (A) 6.5%
    (B) 7.0%
    (C) 7.5%
    (D) 8.0%
    (E) 8.5%

Arithmetic Percents

The number of defective parts in the first shipment was $120(0.05) = 6$. The number of defective parts in the second shipment was $80(0.10) = 8$. The percent of machine parts that were defective in the two shipments combined was therefore $\frac{6+8}{120+80} = \frac{14}{200} = \frac{7}{100} = 7\%$.

The correct answer is B.

96. If $8^{2x+3} = 2^{3x+6}$, then $x =$

   (A) -3
   (B) -1
   (C) 0
   (D) 1
   (E) 3

Algebra First-degree equations

To work the problem, create a common base so that the exponents can be set equal to each other.

$$8^{2x+3} = 2^{3x+6}$$
$$\left(2^3\right)^{2x+3} = 2^{3x+6} \quad \text{since } 8 = 2 \times 2 \times 2, \text{ can be expressed as } 2^3$$
$$2^{6x+9} = 2^{3x+6} \quad \text{multiply exponents}$$
$$6x+9 = 3x+6 \quad \text{set exponents equal since they are on a common base (2)}$$
$$3x = -3 \quad \text{solve for } x$$
$$x = -1$$

The correct answer is B.

97. Of the following, the closest approximation to $\sqrt{\dfrac{5.98(601.5)}{15.79}}$ is

   (A) 5
   (B) 15
   (C) 20
   (D) 25
   (E) 225

Arithmetic Estimation

$$\sqrt{\frac{5.98(601.5)}{15.79}} \approx \sqrt{\frac{6(600)}{16}} =$$
$$\sqrt{\frac{3,600}{16}} = \frac{\sqrt{3,600}}{\sqrt{16}} = \frac{60}{4} = 15$$

The correct answer is B.

98. Which of the following CANNOT be the greatest common divisor of two positive integers x and y ?

   (A) 1
   (B) x
   (C) y
   (D) $x - y$
   (E) $x + y$

Arithmetic Properties of numbers

One example is sufficient to show that a statement CAN be true.

A   The greatest common divisor (gcd) of $x = 3$ and $y = 2$ is 1 and, therefore, 1 can be the gcd of the two positive integers x and y.

B   The greatest common divisor (gcd) of $x = 3$ and $y = 6$ is 3 and therefore x can be the gcd of the two positive integers x and y.

C   The greatest common divisor (gcd) of $x = 6$ and $y = 3$ is 3 and therefore y can be the gcd of the two positive integers x and y.

D   The greatest common divisor (gcd) of $x = 3$ and $y = 2$ is 1. Since $3 - 2 = 1$, $x - y$ can be the gcd of the two positive integers x and y.

By the process of elimination, $x + y$ CANNOT be the gcd of the two positive integers x and y.

Algebraically, since $x > 0$, $x + y > y$. Also, since $y > 0$, $x + y > x$. The greatest divisor of x is x, so $x + y$ cannot be a divisor of x. Likewise, the greatest divisor of y is y, so $x + y$ cannot be a divisor of y. Therefore, $x + y$ cannot be a divisor of either x or y and thus cannot be a common divisor of x and y.

The correct answer is E.

99. If a, b, and c are nonzero numbers and $a + b = c$, which of the following is equal to 1 ?

   (A) $\dfrac{a-b}{c}$

   (B) $\dfrac{a-c}{b}$

   (C) $\dfrac{b-c}{a}$

   (D) $\dfrac{b-a}{c}$

   (E) $\dfrac{c-b}{a}$

Arithmetic Operations on rational numbers

The equation $a + b = c$ can be manipulated in several ways to get an expression with value 1. For example, divide both sides by c to get $\dfrac{a+b}{c} = 1$. The expression $\dfrac{a+b}{c}$ is not among the answer choices, but it serves to eliminate answer choices A and D because neither $a - b$ nor $b - a$ is necessarily equal to $a + b$. Next, try subtracting a from both sides and dividing the result by b to get $\dfrac{c-a}{b} = 1$. The expression $\dfrac{c-a}{b}$ is not among the answer choices, but it serves to eliminate answer choice B because $a - c$ is not necessarily equal to $c - a$. Next, try subtracting b from both sides and dividing the result by a to get $\dfrac{c-b}{a} = 1$. The expression $\dfrac{c-b}{a}$ is answer choice E and it also serves to eliminate answer choice C because $b - c$ is not necessarily equal to $c - b$.

The correct answer is E.

100. Last year Carlos saved 10 percent of his annual earnings. This year he earned 5 percent more than last year and he saved 12 percent of his annual earnings. The amount saved this year was what percent of the amount saved last year?

   (A) 122%
   (B) 124%
   (C) 126%
   (D) 128%
   (E) 130%

Arithmetic Percents

Let x represent the amount of Carlos's annual earnings last year.

Carlos's savings last year = $0.1x$

Carlos's earnings this year = $1.05x$

Carlos's savings this year = $(1.05x)(0.12) = 0.126x$

The amount saved this year as a percent of the amount saved last year is $\dfrac{0.126x}{0.1x} = 1.26 = 126\%$.

The correct answer is C.

101. A corporation that had $115.19 billion in profits for the year paid out $230.10 million in employee benefits. Approximately what percent of the profits were the employee benefits? (Note: 1 billion $= 10^9$)

   (A) 50%
   (B) 20%
   (C) 5%
   (D) 2%
   (E) 0.2%

Arithmetic Percents; Estimation

The employee benefits as a fraction of profits can be expressed as

$$\frac{230.10 \times 10^6}{115.19 \times 10^9} \approx \frac{230 \times 10^6}{115 \times 10^9}$$

$$= \frac{230}{115} \times \frac{10^6}{10^9}$$

$$= 2 \times 10^{-3}$$

$$= 0.002$$

$$= 0.2\%$$

The correct answer is E.

102. In the coordinate plane, line k passes through the origin and has slope 2. If points $(3, y)$ and $(x, 4)$ are on line k, then $x + y =$

   (A) 3.5
   (B) 7
   (C) 8
   (D) 10
   (E) 14

Algebra Simple coordinate geometry

Since line k has slope 2 and passes through the origin, the equation of line k is $y = 2x$. If the point $(3, y)$ is on line k, then $y = 2(3) = 6$. If the point $(x, 4)$ is on line k, then $4 = 2x$ and so $x = 2$. Therefore, $x + y = 2 + 6 = 8$.

The correct answer is C.

103. If a, b, and c are constants, $a > b > c$, and $x^3 - x = (x - a)(x - b)(x - c)$ for all numbers x, what is the value of b ?

(A) −3
(B) −1
(C) 0
(D) 1
(E) 3

Algebra Simplifying algebraic expressions

Since $(x - a)(x - b)(x - c) = x^3 - x = x(x^2 - 1)$ $= x(x + 1)(x - 1) = (x - 0)(x - 1)(x + 1)$ then a, b, and c are 0, 1, and −1 in some order. Since $a > b > c$, it follows that $a = 1$, $b = 0$, and $c = -1$.

The correct answer is C.

104. If $x + y = 8z$, then which of the following represents the average (arithmetic mean) of x, y, and z, in terms of z ?

(A) $2z + 1$
(B) $3z$
(C) $5z$
(D) $\dfrac{z}{3}$
(E) $\dfrac{3z}{2}$

Arithmetic; Algebra Statistics; Simplifying algebraic expressions

Since the average of three values is equal to $\dfrac{\text{sum of the values}}{3}$, the average of x, y, and z is $\dfrac{x + y + z}{3}$. Substituting $8z$ for $x + y$ in this equation gives $\dfrac{8z + z}{3} = \dfrac{9z}{3} = 3z$.

The correct answer is B.

105. On the number line, if $r < s$, if p is halfway between r and s, and if t is halfway between p and r, then $\dfrac{s - t}{t - r} =$

(A) $\dfrac{1}{4}$

(B) $\dfrac{1}{3}$

(C) $\dfrac{4}{3}$

(D) 3

(E) 4

Algebra Factoring; Simplifying algebraic expressions

Using a number line makes it possible to see these relationships more readily:

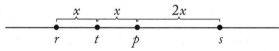

The given relative distances between r, s, t, and p are shown in the number line above. The distance between s and t can be expressed as $s - t$, or as $x + 2x$. The distance between t and r can be expressed as $t - r$, or as x. Thus, by substitution into the given equation:

$$\frac{s - t}{t - r} = \frac{x + 2x}{x} = \frac{3x}{x} = 3.$$

The correct answer is D.

106. If x and y are different integers and $x^2 = xy$, which of the following must be true?

   I. $x = 0$
   II. $y = 0$
   III. $x = -y$

   (A) I only
   (B) II only
   (C) III only
   (D) I and III only
   (E) I, II, and III

Arithmetic; Algebra Operations on rational numbers; Second-degree equations

If $x^2 = xy$, then $x^2 - xy = 0$ and so $x(x - y) = 0$. Then $x = 0$ or $x - y = 0$. Since x and y are different integers, $x - y \neq 0$. Therefore, the statement $x = 0$ MUST be true. Furthermore, the statement $y = 0$ cannot be true because, if it were true, then x and y would be the same integer. Likewise, the statement $x = -y$ cannot be true because, if it were true, then $-y$ would be 0, which means that y would be 0 and, again, x and y would be the same integer. Thus, only Statement I must be true.

The correct answer is A.

107. If $\frac{3}{x} = 2$ and $\frac{y}{4} = 3$, then $\frac{3+y}{x+4} =$

   (A) $\frac{10}{9}$
   (B) $\frac{3}{2}$
   (C) $\frac{20}{11}$
   (D) $\frac{30}{11}$
   (E) 5

Algebra First-degree equations; Simplifying algebraic expressions

Solving $\frac{3}{x} = 2$ and $\frac{y}{4} = 3$ for x and y, respectively, gives $x = \frac{3}{2}$ and $y = 12$. Then substituting these into the given expression gives

$$\frac{3+y}{x+4} = \frac{3+12}{\frac{3}{2}+4} = \frac{3+12}{\frac{3}{2}+\frac{8}{2}} = \frac{15}{\frac{11}{2}} = \frac{15 \times 2}{11} = \frac{30}{11}$$

The correct answer is D.

108. $17^3 + 17^4 =$

   (A) 17^7
   (B) $17^3(18)$
   (C) $17^6(18)$
   (D) $2(17^3) + 17$
   (E) $2(17^3) - 17$

Arithmetic Exponents

Since $17^3 = 17^3 \times 1$ and $17^4 = 17^3 \times 17$, then 17^3 may be factored out of each term. It follows that $17^3 + 17^4 = 17^3(1 + 17) = 17^3(18)$.

The correct answer is B.

109. Which of the following CANNOT yield an integer when divided by 10?

   (A) The sum of two odd integers
   (B) An integer less than 10
   (C) The product of two primes
   (D) The sum of three consecutive integers
   (E) An odd integer

Arithmetic Operations on rational numbers

Test each answer choice with values that satisfy the condition in order to determine which one does NOT yield an integer when divided by 10.

A 3 and 7 are both odd integers, and
   $\dfrac{3+7}{10} = 1$ IS an integer

B −10 is an integer that is less than 10,
   and $\dfrac{-10}{10} = 1$ IS an integer

C 2 and 5 are primes, and
   $\dfrac{(5)(2)}{10} = 1$ IS an integer

D 9, 10, and 11 are three consecutive integers,
   and $\dfrac{9+10+11}{10} = 3$ IS an integer

E All multiples of 10 are
   even integers; therefore,
   an odd integer divided
   by 10 CANNOT yield
   an integer.

The correct answer is E.

110. A certain clock marks every hour by striking a number
of times equal to the hour, and the time required for
a stroke is exactly equal to the time interval between
strokes. At 6:00 the time lapse between the beginning
of the first stroke and the end of the last stroke is
22 seconds. At 12:00, how many seconds elapse
between the beginning of the first stroke and the end
of the last stroke?

(A) 72
(B) 50
(C) 48
(D) 46
(E) 44

Arithmetic Operations on rational numbers

At 6:00 there are 6 strokes and 5 intervals
between strokes. Thus, there are 11 equal time
intervals in the 22 seconds between the beginning
of the first stroke and the end of the last stroke.
Therefore, each time interval is $\dfrac{22}{11} = 2$ seconds
long. At 12:00 there are 12 strokes and 11
intervals between strokes. Thus, there are 23
equal 2-second time intervals, or $23 \times 2 = 46$
seconds, between the beginning of the first stroke
and the end of the last stroke.

The correct answer is D.

111. If $k \neq 0$ and $k - \dfrac{3-2k^2}{k} = \dfrac{x}{k}$, then $x =$

(A) $-3 - k^2$
(B) $k^2 - 3$
(C) $3k^2 - 3$
(D) $k - 3 - 2k^2$
(E) $k - 3 + 2k^2$

Algebra Second-degree equations

Solve the equation for x.

$$k - \dfrac{3-2k^2}{k} = \dfrac{x}{k}$$
$$k^2 - (3 - 2k^2) = x \qquad \text{multiply through by } k$$
$$k^2 - 3 + 2k^2 = x \qquad \text{simplify}$$
$$3k^2 - 3 = x$$

The correct answer is C.

112. What is the greatest number of identical bouquets that
can be made out of 21 white and 91 red tulips if no
flowers are to be left out? (Two bouquets are identical
whenever the number of red tulips in the two bouquets
is equal and the number of white tulips in the two
bouquets is equal.)

(A) 3
(B) 4
(C) 5
(D) 6
(E) 7

Arithmetic Properties of numbers

Since the question asks for the greatest number of
bouquets that can be made using all of the
flowers, the number of bouquets will need to be
the greatest common factor of 21 and 91. Since
$21 = (3)(7)$ and $91 = (7)(13)$, the greatest common
factor of 21 and 91 is 7. Therefore, 7 bouquets can
be made, each with 3 white tulips and 13 red
tulips.

The correct answer is E.

113. For all numbers s and t, the operation $*$ is defined by $s*t = (s-1)(t+1)$. If $(-2)*x = -12$, then $x =$

    (A) 2
    (B) 3
    (C) 5
    (D) 6
    (E) 11

Algebra First-degree equations

The equivalent values established for this problem are $s = -2$ and $t = x$. So, substitute -2 for s and x for t in the given equation:

$$-2*x = -12$$
$$(-2-1)(x+1) = -12$$
$$(-3)(x+1) = -12$$
$$x+1 = 4$$
$$x = 3$$

The correct answer is B.

114. Salesperson A's compensation for any week is $360 plus 6 percent of the portion of A's total sales above $1,000 for that week. Salesperson B's compensation for any week is 8 percent of B's total sales for that week. For what amount of total weekly sales would both salespeople earn the same compensation?

    (A) $21,000
    (B) $18,000
    (C) $15,000
    (D) $ 4,500
    (E) $ 4,000

Algebra Applied problems; Simultaneous equations

Let x represent the total weekly sales amount at which both salespersons earn the same compensation. Then, the given information regarding when Salesperson A's weekly pay equals Salesperson B's weekly pay can be expressed as:

$$360 + 0.06(x - 1,000) = 0.08x$$
$$360 + 0.06x - 60 = 0.08x \qquad \text{solve for } x$$
$$300 = 0.02x$$
$$15,000 = x$$

The correct answer is C.

115. The sum of the ages of Doris and Fred is y years. If Doris is 12 years older than Fred, how many years old will Fred be y years from now, in terms of y?

    (A) $y - 6$

    (B) $2y - 6$

    (C) $\dfrac{y}{2} - 6$

    (D) $\dfrac{3y}{2} - 6$

    (E) $\dfrac{5y}{2} - 6$

Algebra Applied problems; Simultaneous equations

Letting d represent the current age of Doris and f represent the current age of Fred, the given information can be expressed as follows:

$d + f = y$ Doris's age + Fred's age = y

$d = f + 12$ Doris's age = Fred's age + 12

To find Fred's current age, substitute the value of d and solve for f:

$$(f + 12) + f = y$$
$$2f + 12 = y \qquad \text{combine like terms}$$
$$2f = y - 12 \qquad \text{subtract 12 from both sides}$$
$$f = \frac{y - 12}{2} \qquad \text{divide both sides by 2}$$
$$f = \frac{y}{2} - 6 \qquad \text{simplify}$$

Fred's age after y years can be expressed as $f + y$. First, substitute the value of $f = \dfrac{y}{2} - 6$ and then simplify. Thus, Fred's age y years from now will be:

$$\frac{y}{2} - 6 + y$$
$$= \frac{3y}{2} - 6$$

The correct answer is D.

116. If a basketball team scores an average (arithmetic mean) of x points per game for n games and then scores y points in its next game, what is the team's average score for the $n+1$ games?

    (A) $\dfrac{nx+y}{n+1}$

    (B) $x+\dfrac{y}{n+1}$

    (C) $x+\dfrac{y}{n}$

    (D) $\dfrac{n(x+y)}{n+1}$

    (E) $\dfrac{x+ny}{n+1}$

Arithmetic Statistics

Using the formula $\text{average} = \dfrac{\text{total points}}{\text{number of games}}$, the average number of points per game for the first n games can be expressed as $x = \dfrac{\text{total points for } n \text{ games}}{n}$. Solving this equation shows that the total points for n games $= nx$. Then, the total points for $n+1$ games can be expressed as $nx + y$, and the average number of points for $n+1$ games $= \dfrac{nx+y}{n+1}$.

The correct answer is A.

117. If $xy > 0$ and $yz < 0$, which of the following must be negative?

    (A) xyz
    (B) xyz^2
    (C) xy^2z
    (D) xy^2z^2
    (E) $x^2y^2z^2$

Arithmetic Properties of numbers

Since $xy > 0$ and $yz < 0$, $(xy)(yz) = xy^2z < 0$, and xy^2z is the expression given in answer choice C.

Alternatively, the chart below shows all possibilities for the algebraic signs of x, y, and z. Those satisfying $xy > 0$ are checked in the fourth column of the chart, and those satisfying $yz < 0$ are checked in the fifth column of the chart.

x	y	z	$xy > 0$	$yz < 0$
+	+	+	✓	
+	+	−	✓	✓
+	−	+		✓
+	−	−		
−	+	+		
−	+	−		✓
−	−	+	✓	✓
−	−	−	✓	

The chart below shows only the possibilities that satisfy both $xy > 0$ and $yz < 0$. Noting that the expression in answer choice E is the product of the squares of three nonzero numbers, which is always positive, extend the chart to include the algebraic sign of each of the other answer choices.

x	y	z	xyz	xyz^2	xy^2z	xy^2z^2
+	+	−	−	+	−	+
−	−	+	+	+	−	−

Only xy^2z is negative in both cases.

The correct answer is C.

118. At a certain pizzeria, $\dfrac{1}{8}$ of the pizzas sold in one week were mushroom and $\dfrac{1}{3}$ of the <u>remaining</u> pizzas sold were pepperoni. If n of the pizzas sold were pepperoni, how many were mushroom?

    (A) $\dfrac{3}{8}n$

    (B) $\dfrac{3}{7}n$

    (C) $\dfrac{7}{16}n$

    (D) $\dfrac{7}{8}n$

    (E) $3n$

Algebra Simplifying algebraic expressions

Let t represent the total number of pizzas sold.

Then $\frac{1}{8}t$ represents the number of mushroom

pizzas sold, $\frac{7}{8}t$ represents the number of

remaining pizzas sold, and $\frac{1}{3}\left(\frac{7}{8}t\right) = \frac{7}{24}t$

represents the number of pepperoni pizzas sold.

Then $n = \frac{7}{24}t$, $t = \frac{24}{7}n$, and $\frac{1}{8}t = \frac{1}{8}\left(\frac{24}{7}n\right) = \frac{3}{7}n$.

Thus, $\frac{3}{7}n$ mushroom pizzas were sold.

The correct answer is B.

119. Two trains, X and Y, started simultaneously from opposite ends of a 100-mile route and traveled toward each other on parallel tracks. Train X, traveling at a constant rate, completed the 100-mile trip in 5 hours; Train Y, traveling at a constant rate, completed the 100-mile trip in 3 hours. How many miles had Train X traveled when it met Train Y ?

   (A)   37.5
   (B)   40.0
   (C)   60.0
   (D)   62.5
   (E)   77.5

Algebra Applied problems

To solve this problem, use the formula distance = rate × time and its two equivalent forms

$\text{rate} = \dfrac{\text{distance}}{\text{time}}$ and $\text{time} = \dfrac{\text{distance}}{\text{rate}}$. Train X

traveled 100 miles in 5 hours so its rate was

$\dfrac{100}{5} = 20$ miles per hour. Train Y traveled

100 miles in 3 hours so its rate was $\dfrac{100}{3}$ miles per

hour. If t represents the number of hours the trains took to meet, then when the trains met, Train X had traveled a distance of $20t$ miles and

Train Y had traveled a distance of $\dfrac{100}{3}t$ miles.

Since the trains started at opposite ends of the 100-mile route, the sum of the distances they had traveled when they met was 100 miles. Therefore,

$$20t + \frac{100}{3}t = 100$$

$$\frac{160}{3}t = 100$$

$$t = 100\left(\frac{3}{160}\right)$$

$$= \frac{300}{160}$$

$$= \frac{15}{8}$$

Thus, Train X had traveled

$20t = 20\left(\dfrac{15}{8}\right) = \dfrac{75}{2} = 37.5$ miles when it met

Train Y.

The correct answer is A.

120. One week a certain truck rental lot had a total of 20 trucks, all of which were on the lot Monday morning. If 50 percent of the trucks that were rented out during the week were returned to the lot on or before Saturday morning of that week, and if there were at least 12 trucks on the lot that Saturday morning, what is the greatest number of different trucks that could have been rented out during the week?

   (A)   18
   (B)   16
   (C)   12
   (D)   8
   (E)   4

Arithmetic; Algebra Percents; Applied problems

Let x represent the number of trucks that were rented during the week. Then $20 - x$ represents the number of trucks that were not rented during the week and were still on the lot Saturday morning. In addition to these $20 - x$ trucks, $0.5x$ trucks (that is, 50 percent of the x trucks that were rented and were returned by Saturday morning) were also on the lot Saturday morning. Thus the total number of trucks on the lot on Saturday morning was $(20 - x) + 0.5x$ and this number was at least 12.

$$(20 - x) + 0.5x \geq 12$$

$$20 - 0.5x \geq 12$$

$$-0.5x \geq -8$$

$$x \leq 16$$

The correct answer is B.

121. What is the value of $2x^2 - 2.4x - 1.7$ for $x = 0.7$?

(A) −0.72
(B) −1.42
(C) −1.98
(D) −2.40
(E) −2.89

Algebra Simplifying algebraic expressions

Work the problem by substituting $x = 0.7$.

$2x^2 - 2.4x - 1.7$

$= 2(0.7)^2 - 2.4(0.7) - 1.7$

$= 2(0.49) - 1.68 - 1.7$

$= 0.98 - 1.68 - 1.7$

$= -2.40$

The correct answer is D.

122. If s, u, and v are positive integers and $2s = 2u + 2v$, which of the following must be true?

I. $s = u$
II. $u \neq v$
III. $s > v$

(A) None
(B) I only
(C) II only
(D) III only
(E) II and III

Arithmetic Operations on rational numbers

Since $2s = 2u + 2v$, then $2s = 2(u + v)$ and $s = u + v$. Test each statement to determine which must be true.

I.   If $s = u$, then $v = 0$, which is NOT true because v is a positive integer. Thus, it need NOT be true that $s = u$, and, in fact, it is never true when $s = u + v$.

II. If $u = v = 2$, for example, then $s = 2 + 2 = 4$ and 4 is a positive integer. Thus, it need NOT be true that $u \neq v$.

III. Since $s = u + v$, then $s - v = u$ and, since u is a positive integer, $s - v > 0$ and $s > v$. Thus, it MUST be true that $s > v$.

The correct answer is D.

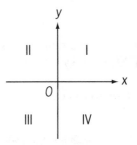

123. In the rectangular coordinate system shown above, which quadrant, if any, contains no point (x,y) that satisfies the inequality $2x - 3y \leq -6$?

(A) None
(B) I
(C) II
(D) III
(E) IV

Geometry Simple coordinate geometry

The region of the standard (x,y) coordinate plane containing points that satisfy the inequality $2x - 3y \leq -6$ is bounded by the line $2x - 3y = -6$. The intercepts of this line are $(0,2)$ (that is, if $x = 0$, then $y = 2$) and $(-3,0)$ (that is, if $y = 0$, then $x = -3$). Plot the intercepts and draw the line that goes through them. Next, test a point to see if it lies in the region satisfying the inequality $2x - 3y \leq -6$. For example, $(0,0)$ does not satisfy the inequality because $2(0) - 3(0) = 0$ and $0 \nleq -6$. Therefore, the region of the standard (x,y) coordinate plane containing points that satisfy $2x - 3y \leq -6$, shown shaded in the figure below, is on the other side of the line from $(0,0)$.

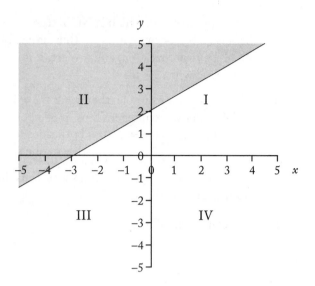

The shaded region contains points in every quadrant EXCEPT IV.

The correct answer is E.

124. The cost to rent a small bus for a trip is x dollars, which is to be shared equally among the people taking the trip. If 10 people take the trip rather than 16, how many more dollars, in terms of x, will it cost per person?

(A) $\dfrac{x}{6}$

(B) $\dfrac{x}{10}$

(C) $\dfrac{x}{16}$

(D) $\dfrac{3x}{40}$

(E) $\dfrac{3x}{80}$

Algebra Applied problems

If 16 take the trip, the cost per person would be $\dfrac{x}{16}$ dollars. If 10 take the trip, the cost per person would be $\dfrac{x}{10}$ dollars. (Note that the lowest common multiple of 10 and 16 is 80.)

Thus, if 10 take the trip, the increase in dollars per person would be $\dfrac{x}{10} - \dfrac{x}{16} = \dfrac{8x}{80} - \dfrac{5x}{80} = \dfrac{3x}{80}$.

The correct answer is E.

125. If x is an integer and $y = 3x + 2$, which of the following CANNOT be a divisor of y ?

(A) 4
(B) 5
(C) 6
(D) 7
(E) 8

Arithmetic Properties of numbers

Although $3x$ is always divisible by 3, $3x + 2$ cannot be divisible by 3 since 2 is not divisible by 3. Thus, $3x + 2$ cannot be divisible by any multiple of 3, including 6.

The correct answer is C.

126. A certain electronic component is sold in boxes of 54 for $16.20 and in boxes of 27 for $13.20. A customer who needed only 54 components for a project had to buy 2 boxes of 27 because boxes of 54 were unavailable. Approximately how much more did the customer pay for each component due to the unavailability of the larger boxes?

(A) $0.33
(B) $0.19
(C) $0.11
(D) $0.06
(E) $0.03

Arithmetic Operations of rational numbers

The customer paid $2(\$13.20) = \$26.40$ for the 2 boxes of 27 components. This is $\$26.40 - \$16.20 = \$10.20$ more than the cost of a single box of 54 components. So, the extra cost per component is $\dfrac{\$10.20}{54} = \$0.19$.

The correct answer is B.

127. As a salesperson, Phyllis can choose one of two methods of annual payment: either an annual salary of $35,000 with no commission or an annual salary of $10,000 plus a 20 percent commission on her total annual sales. What must her total annual sales be to give her the same annual pay with either method?

    (A) $100,000
    (B) $120,000
    (C) $125,000
    (D) $130,000
    (E) $132,000

Algebra Applied problems

Letting s be Phyllis's total annual sales needed to generate the same annual pay with either method, the given information can be expressed as $\$35,000 = \$10,000 + 0.2s$. Solve this equation for s.

$$\$35,000 = \$10,000 + 0.2s$$

$$\$25,000 = 0.2s$$

$$\$125,000 = s$$

The correct answer is C.

128. If $\dfrac{x+y}{xy} = 1$, then $y =$

    (A) $\dfrac{x}{x-1}$

    (B) $\dfrac{x}{x+1}$

    (C) $\dfrac{x-1}{x}$

    (D) $\dfrac{x+1}{x}$

    (E) x

Algebra First-degree equations

Solve the given equation for y.

$$\frac{x+y}{xy} = 1$$

$x + y = xy$	multiply both sides by xy
$x = xy - y$	subtract y from both sides to get all terms with y to one side
$x = y(x-1)$	factor out the y
$\dfrac{x}{x-1} = y$	divide both sides by $x-1$

The correct answer is A.

129. Last year Department Store X had a sales total for December that was 4 times the average (arithmetic mean) of the monthly sales totals for January through November. The sales total for December was what fraction of the sales total for the year?

    (A) $\dfrac{1}{4}$

    (B) $\dfrac{4}{15}$

    (C) $\dfrac{1}{3}$

    (D) $\dfrac{4}{11}$

    (E) $\dfrac{4}{5}$

Algebra; Arithmetic Applied problems; Statistics

Let A equal the average sales per month for the first 11 months. The given information about the total sales for the year can then be expressed as $11A + 4A = 15A$. Thus, $4A = (F)(15A)$, where F is the fraction of the sales total for the year that the sales total for December represents. Then $F = \dfrac{4A}{15A} = \dfrac{4}{15}$.

The correct answer is B.

130. Working alone, Printers X, Y, and Z can do a certain printing job, consisting of a large number of pages, in 12, 15, and 18 hours, respectively. What is the ratio of the time it takes Printer X to do the job, working alone at its rate, to the time it takes Printers Y and Z to do the job, working together at their individual rates?

(A) $\dfrac{4}{11}$

(B) $\dfrac{1}{2}$

(C) $\dfrac{15}{22}$

(D) $\dfrac{22}{15}$

(E) $\dfrac{11}{4}$

Arithmetic Operations on rational numbers

Since Printer Y can do the job in 15 hours, it can do $\dfrac{1}{15}$ of the job in 1 hour. Since Printer Z can do the job in 18 hours, it can do $\dfrac{1}{18}$ of the job in 1 hour. Together, Printers Y and Z can do

$$\left(\frac{1}{15}+\frac{1}{18}\right)=\left(\frac{6}{90}+\frac{5}{90}\right)=\frac{11}{90}$$ of the job in 1 hour,

which means that it takes them $\dfrac{90}{11}$ hours to complete the job. Since Printer X completes the job in 12 hours, the ratio of the time required for X to do the job to the time required for Y and Z working together to do the job is

$$\frac{\dfrac{12}{90}}{11}=\frac{12(11)}{90}=\frac{2(11)}{15}=\frac{22}{15}.$$

The correct answer is D.

131. In the sequence $x_0, x_1, x_2, \ldots, x_n$, each term from x_1 to x_k is 3 greater than the previous term, and each term from x_{k+1} to x_n is 3 less than the previous term, where n and k are positive integers and $k < n$. If $x_0 = x_n = 0$ and if $x_k = 15$, what is the value of n?

(A) 5
(B) 6
(C) 9
(D) 10
(E) 15

Algebra Sequences

Since $x_0 = 0$ and each term from x_1 to x_k is 3 greater than the previous term, then $x_k = 0 + (k)(3)$. Since $x_k = 15$, then $15 = 3k$ and $k = 5$. Since each term from x_{k+1} to x_n is 3 less than the previous term, then $x_n = x_k - (n-k)(3)$. Substituting the known values for x_k, x_n, and k gives $0 = 15 - (n-5)(3)$, from which it follows that $3n = 30$ and $n = 10$.

The correct answer is D.

132. A company that ships boxes to a total of 12 distribution centers uses color coding to identify each center. If either a single color or a pair of two different colors is chosen to represent each center and if each center is uniquely represented by that choice of one or two colors, what is the minimum number of colors needed for the coding? (Assume that the order of the colors in a pair does not matter.)

(A) 4
(B) 5
(C) 6
(D) 12
(E) 24

Arithmetic Elementary combinatorics

Since the problem asks for the minimum number of colors needed, start with the lowest answer choice available. Calculate each successive option until finding the minimum number of colors that can represent at least 12 distribution centers.

Note that $_nC_r = \dfrac{n!}{r!(n-r)!}$ for the combination of n things taken r at a time.

# of Colors	Number represented by one color	Number represented by two colors	Total represented
4	4	$_4C_2 = \dfrac{4!}{2!2!} = 6$	$4 + 6 = 10$
5	5	$_5C_2 = \dfrac{5!}{2!3!} =$ $\dfrac{(5)(4)}{2} = 10$	$5 + 10 = 15$

The correct answer is B.

133. If $x \neq 2$, then $\dfrac{3x^2(x-2)-x+2}{x-2} =$

    (A) $3x^2 - x + 2$
    (B) $3x^2 + 1$
    (C) $3x^2$
    (D) $3x^2 - 1$
    (E) $3x^2 - 2$

Algebra Simplifying algebraic expressions

When simplifying this expression, it is important to note that, as a first step, the numerator must be factored so that the numerator is the product of two or more expressions, one of which is $(x-2)$. This can be accomplished by rewriting the last two terms of the numerator as $(-1)(x-2)$. Then

$$\frac{3x^2(x-2)-x+2}{x-2} = \frac{3x^2(x-2)+(-1)(x-2)}{x-2}$$

$$= \frac{(x-2)(3x^2+(-1))}{x-2}$$

$$= 3x^2 + (-1)$$

$$= 3x^2 - 1$$

The correct answer is D.

134. If $d > 0$ and $0 < 1 - \dfrac{c}{d} < 1$, which of the following must be true?

    I. $c > 0$
    II. $\dfrac{c}{d} < 1$
    III. $c^2 + d^2 > 1$

    (A) I only
    (B) II only
    (C) I and II only
    (D) II and III only
    (E) I, II, and III

Algebra Inequalities

Consider each answer choice.

I. Since $1 - \dfrac{c}{d} < 1$, it follows that $-\dfrac{c}{d} < 0$ or $\dfrac{c}{d} > 0$.

    Since $d > 0$ and $\dfrac{c}{d} > 0$, then $c > 0$, and Statement I must be true.

II. Since $0 < 1 - \dfrac{c}{d} < 1$, it follows that

    $-1 < -\dfrac{c}{d} < 0$, or $0 < \dfrac{c}{d} < 1$, which means Statement II must be true.

III. By counterexample, if $c = \dfrac{1}{4}$ and $d = \dfrac{1}{3}$, then

    since $0 < 1 - \dfrac{\frac{1}{4}}{\frac{1}{3}} < 1$ or $0 < 1 - \dfrac{3}{4} < 1$, $c = \dfrac{1}{4}$ and

    $d = \dfrac{1}{3}$ satisfy Statement III. However,

    $c^2 + d^2 = \left(\dfrac{1}{4}\right)^2 + \left(\dfrac{1}{3}\right)^2 = \dfrac{1}{16} + \dfrac{1}{9}$, which is less

    than 1 because $\dfrac{1}{16} < \dfrac{1}{2}$ and $\dfrac{1}{9} < \dfrac{1}{2}$, and thus Statement III need not be true.

The correct answer is C.

Note: Not drawn to scale.

135. In the figure shown above, line segment QR has length 12, and rectangle $MPQT$ is a square. If the area of rectangular region $MPRS$ is 540, what is the area of rectangular region $TQRS$?

    (A) 144
    (B) 216
    (C) 324
    (D) 360
    (E) 396

Geometry; Algebra Area; Second-degree equations

Since $MPQT$ is a square, let $MP = PQ = x$. Then $PR = PQ + QR = x + 12$. The area of $MPRS$ can be expressed as $x(x + 12)$. Since the area of $MPRS$ is given to be 540,

$$x(x + 12) = 540$$

$$x^2 + 12x = 540$$

$$x^2 + 12x - 540 = 0$$

$$(x - 18)(x + 30) = 0$$

$$x = 18 \text{ or } x = -30$$

Since x represents a length and must be positive, $x = 18$. The area of $TQRS$ is then $(12)(18) = 216$.

As an alternative to solving the quadratic equation, look for a pair of positive numbers such that their product is 540 and one is 12 greater than the other. The pair is 18 and 30, so $x = 18$ and the area of $TQRS$ is then $(12)(18) = 216$.

The correct answer is B.

136. A train travels from New York City to Chicago, a distance of approximately 840 miles, at an average rate of 60 miles per hour and arrives in Chicago at 6:00 in the evening, Chicago time. At what hour in the morning, New York City time, did the train depart for Chicago? (<u>Note</u>: Chicago time is one hour earlier than New York City time.)

(A) 4:00
(B) 5:00
(C) 6:00
(D) 7:00
(E) 8:00

Arithmetic Operations on rational numbers

Using the formula $\dfrac{\text{distance}}{\text{rate}} = \text{time}$,

it can be calculated that it took the train

$\dfrac{840 \text{ miles}}{60 \text{ miles per hour}} = 14$ hours to travel from

New York City to Chicago. The train arrived in Chicago at 6:00 in the evening. Since it had departed 14 hours before that, it had therefore departed at 4:00 a.m. Chicago time. Then, since it is given that Chicago time is one hour earlier than New York City time, it had departed at 5:00 a.m. New York City time.

The correct answer is B.

137. Last year Manfred received 26 paychecks. Each of his first 6 paychecks was $750; each of his remaining paychecks was $30 more than each of his first 6 paychecks. To the nearest dollar, what was the average (arithmetic mean) amount of his paychecks for the year?

(A) $752
(B) $755
(C) $765
(D) $773
(E) $775

Arithmetic Statistics

In addition to the first 6 paychecks for $750 each, Manfred received $26 - 6 = 20$ paychecks for $750 + 30 or $780 each. Applying the formula

$\dfrac{\text{sum of values}}{\text{number of values}} = \text{average}$, this information

can be expressed in the following equation:

$$\frac{6(750) + 20(780)}{26} = \frac{20,100}{26} = 773.08$$

The correct answer is D.

138. If 25 percent of p is equal to 10 percent of q, and $pq \neq 0$, then p is what percent of q?

(A)   2.5%
(B)   15%
(C)   20%
(D)   35%
(E)   40%

Arithmetic; Algebra Percents; Applied problems

The given information can be expressed as follows and solved for p.

$$0.25p = 0.10q$$

$$p = \frac{0.10}{0.25}q$$

$$p = 0.40q$$

The correct answer is E.

139. If the length of an edge of cube X is twice the length of an edge of cube Y, what is the ratio of the volume of cube Y to the volume of cube X?

(A) $\frac{1}{2}$

(B) $\frac{1}{4}$

(C) $\frac{1}{6}$

(D) $\frac{1}{8}$

(E) $\frac{1}{27}$

Geometry Volume

When two similar three-dimensional objects are compared, the volume ratio will be the cube of the length ratio. Since it is given that the length of an edge of cube X is twice the length of an edge of cube Y, the length ratio for cube Y to cube X is $\frac{1}{2}$. This therefore makes the volume ratio $\left(\frac{1}{2}\right)^3 = \frac{1}{2} \times \frac{1}{2} \times \frac{1}{2} = \frac{1}{8}$.

The correct answer is D.

140. Machines A and B always operate independently and at their respective constant rates. When working alone, Machine A can fill a production lot in 5 hours, and Machine B can fill the same lot in x hours. When the two machines operate simultaneously to fill the production lot, it takes them 2 hours to complete the job. What is the value of x?

(A) $3\frac{1}{3}$

(B) 3

(C) $2\frac{1}{2}$

(D) $2\frac{1}{3}$

(E) $1\frac{1}{2}$

Algebra Applied problems

Since Machine A can fill a production lot in 5 hours, it can fill $\frac{1}{5}$ of the lot in 1 hour. Since Machine B can fill the same production lot in x hours, it can fill $\frac{1}{x}$ of the lot in 1 hour. The two machines operating simultaneously can fill $\frac{1}{5} + \frac{1}{x}$ of the lot in 1 hour. Since it takes them 2 hours to complete the lot together, they can fill $\frac{1}{2}$ of the lot in 1 hour and so $\frac{1}{5} + \frac{1}{x} = \frac{1}{2}$, which can be solved for x as follows:

$$\frac{1}{5} + \frac{1}{x} = \frac{1}{2}$$

$$10x\left(\frac{1}{5} + \frac{1}{x}\right) = 10x\left(\frac{1}{2}\right)$$

$$2x + 10 = 5x$$

$$10 = 3x$$

$$\frac{10}{3} = x$$

$$x = 3\frac{1}{3}$$

The correct answer is A.

141. An artist wishes to paint a circular region on a square poster that is 2 feet on a side. If the area of the circular region is to be $\frac{1}{2}$ the area of the poster, what must be the radius of the circular region in feet?

   (A) $\dfrac{1}{\pi}$

   (B) $\sqrt{\dfrac{2}{\pi}}$

   (C) 1

   (D) $\dfrac{2}{\sqrt{\pi}}$

   (E) $\dfrac{\pi}{2}$

Geometry Circles; Area

The area of the square poster is $2^2 = 4$ square feet. The area of a circle = πr^2, where r is the radius of the circle. The area of the circular region on the square poster can be expressed as $\pi r^2 = \frac{1}{2}(4)$, and this equation can be solved for r, the radius of the circular region:

$$\pi r^2 = 2$$
$$r^2 = \frac{2}{\pi}$$
$$r = \sqrt{\frac{2}{\pi}}$$

The correct answer is B.

142. A driver completed the first 20 miles of a 40-mile trip at an average speed of 50 miles per hour. At what average speed must the driver complete the remaining 20 miles to achieve an average speed of 60 miles per hour for the entire 40-mile trip? (Assume that the driver did not make any stops during the 40-mile trip.)

   (A) 65 mph
   (B) 68 mph
   (C) 70 mph
   (D) 75 mph
   (E) 80 mph

Algebra Applied problems

Using $D = rt$, where D represents distance, r represents average speed, and t represents time, and its equivalent formula $t = \dfrac{D}{r}$ to make a chart like the one below is often helpful in solving this type of problem.

	D	r	t
1st 20 miles	20	50	$\dfrac{20}{50} = \dfrac{2}{5}$
2nd 20 miles	20	r	$\dfrac{20}{r}$
Total trip	40	60	$\dfrac{40}{60} = \dfrac{2}{3}$

The total time for the trip is the sum of the times for the first 20 miles and the second 20 miles, so

$$\frac{2}{5} + \frac{20}{r} = \frac{2}{3}$$
$$(15r)\left(\frac{2}{5} + \frac{20}{r}\right) = (15r)\left(\frac{2}{3}\right)$$
$$6r + 300 = 10r$$
$$300 = 4r$$
$$75 = r$$

The correct answer is D.

143. A $500 investment and a $1,500 investment have a combined yearly return of 8.5 percent of the total of the two investments. If the $500 investment has a yearly return of 7 percent, what percent yearly return does the $1,500 investment have?

   (A) 9%
   (B) 10%
   (C) $10\frac{5}{8}$%
   (D) 11%
   (E) 12%

Algebra Percents

The total of the two investments is
$500 + $1,500 = $2,000, and the total yearly
return for the two investments is thus
$2,000(0.085) = 170. The return on the
$500 investment is $500(0.07) = 35, so the
return on the $1,500 investment is
$170 - $35 = $135. Then, $\frac{135}{1,500} = 0.09 = 9\%$
is the percent return on the $1,500 investment.

The correct answer is A.

144. For any integer n greater than 1, $\lfloor n$ denotes the
product of all the integers from 1 to n, inclusive. How
many prime numbers are there between $\lfloor 6 + 2$ and
$\lfloor 6 + 6$, inclusive?

(A) None
(B) One
(C) Two
(D) Three
(E) Four

Arithmetic Properties of numbers

Calculate the product of all the integers from
1 through 6, determine the values of $\lfloor 6 + 2$ and
$\lfloor 6 + 6$, and consider whether each number between
$\lfloor 6 + 2$ and $\lfloor 6 + 6$, inclusive, is a prime number.

$$\lfloor 6 = (6)(5)(4)(3)(2)(1) = 720$$

$$\lfloor 6 + 2 = 720 + 2 = 722$$

$$\lfloor 6 + 6 = 720 + 6 = 726$$

The range is thus 722 to 726, inclusive. The
numbers 722, 724, and 726 are divisible by 2, and
725 is divisible by 5. The only remaining number
is 723, which is divisible by 3.

Alternatively, $\lfloor 6$ has factors of 1, 2, 3, 4, 5, and 6,
among many other factors. Therefore, both $\lfloor 6$ and
$\lfloor 6 + 2$ have a factor of 2 so $\lfloor 6 + 2$ is divisible by 2
and not prime. Likewise, both $\lfloor 6$ and $\lfloor 6 + 3$ have a
factor of 3 so $\lfloor 6 + 3$ is divisible by 3 and not prime;
both $\lfloor 6$ and $\lfloor 6 + 4$ have a factor of 4 so $\lfloor 6 + 4$ is
divisible by 4 and not prime; both $\lfloor 6$ and $\lfloor 6 + 5$
have a factor of 5 so $\lfloor 6 + 5$ is divisible by 5 and not
prime; and both $\lfloor 6$ and $\lfloor 6 + 6$ have a factor of 6 so
$\lfloor 6 + 6$ is divisible by 6 and not prime.

The correct answer is A.

145. The figure shown above consists of three identical
circles that are tangent to each other. If the area of the
shaded region is $64\sqrt{3} - 32\pi$, what is the radius of
each circle?

(A) 4
(B) 8
(C) 16
(D) 24
(E) 32

Geometry Circles; Triangles; Area

Let r represent the radius of each circle. Then the
triangle shown dashed in the figure is equilateral
with sides $2r$ units long. The interior of the
triangle is comprised of the shaded region and
three circular sectors. The area of the shaded
region can be found as the area of the triangle
minus the sum of the areas of the three sectors.
Since the triangle is equilateral, its side lengths
are in the proportions as shown in the diagram
below. The area of the interior of the triangle is
$\frac{1}{2}(2r)(r\sqrt{3}) = r^2\sqrt{3}$.

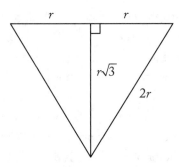

Each of the three sectors has a central angle of $60°$ because the central angle is an angle of the equilateral triangle. Therefore, the area of each sector is $\frac{60}{360} = \frac{1}{6}$ of the area of the circle. The sum of the areas of the three sectors is then

$3\left(\frac{1}{6}\pi r^2\right) = \frac{1}{2}\pi r^2$. Thus, the area of the shaded region is $r^2\sqrt{3} - \frac{1}{2}\pi r^2 = r^2\left(\sqrt{3} - \frac{1}{2}\pi\right)$. But, this area is given as $64\sqrt{3} - 32\pi = 64\left(\sqrt{3} - \frac{1}{2}\pi\right)$. Thus $r^2 = 64$, and $r = 8$.

The correct answer is B.

146. On a certain transatlantic crossing, 20 percent of a ship's passengers held round-trip tickets and also took their cars aboard the ship. If 60 percent of the passengers with round-trip tickets did <u>not</u> take their cars aboard the ship, what percent of the ship's passengers held round-trip tickets?

(A) $33\frac{1}{3}\%$
(B) 40%
(C) 50%
(D) 60%
(E) $66\frac{2}{3}\%$

Arithmetic Percents

Since the number of passengers on the ship is immaterial, let the number of passengers on the ship be 100 for convenience. Let x be the number of passengers that held round-trip tickets. Then, since 20 percent of the passengers held a round-trip ticket and took their cars aboard the ship, $0.20(100) = 20$ passengers held round-trip tickets and took their cars aboard the ship. The remaining passengers with round-trip tickets did not take their cars aboard, and they represent $0.6x$ (that is, 60 percent of the passengers with round-trip tickets). Thus, $0.6x + 20 = x$, from which it follows that $20 = 0.4x$, and so $x = 50$. The percent of passengers with round-trip tickets is, then, $\frac{50}{100} = 50\%$.

The correct answer is C.

147. If x and k are integers and $(12^x)(4^{2x+1}) = (2^k)(3^2)$, what is the value of k?

(A) 5
(B) 7
(C) 10
(D) 12
(E) 14

Arithmetic Exponents

Rewrite the expression on the left so that it is a product of powers of 2 and 3.

$$(12^x)(4^{2x+1}) = \left[(3 \cdot 2^2)^x\right]\left[(2^2)^{2x+1}\right]$$

$$= (3^x)\left[(2^2)^x\right]\left[2^{2(2x+1)}\right]$$

$$= (3^x)(2^{2x})(2^{4x+2})$$

$$= (3^x)(2^{6x+2})$$

Then, since $(12^x)(4^{2x+1}) = (2^k)(3^2)$, it follows that $(3^x)(2^{6x+2}) = (2^k)(3^2) = (3^2)(2^k)$, so $x = 2$ and $k = 6x + 2$. Substituting 2 for x gives $k = 6(2) + 2 = 14$.

The correct answer is E.

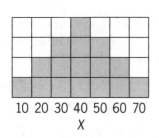

X

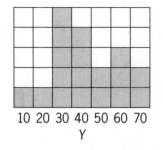

Y

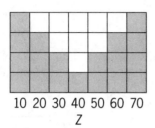

Z

148. If the variables, *X*, *Y*, and *Z* take on only the values 10, 20, 30, 40, 50, 60, or 70 with frequencies indicated by the shaded regions above, for which of the frequency distributions is the mean equal to the median?

(A) *X* only
(B) *Y* only
(C) *Z* only
(D) *X* and *Y*
(E) *X* and *Z*

Arithmetic Statistics

The frequency distributions for both X and Z are symmetric about 40, and thus both X and Z have mean = median = 40. Therefore, any answer choice that does not include both X and Z can be eliminated. This leaves only answer choice E.

The correct answer is E.

149. For every even positive integer *m*, *f*(*m*) represents the product of all even integers from 2 to *m*, inclusive. For example, $f(12) = 2 \times 4 \times 6 \times 8 \times 10 \times 12$. What is the greatest prime factor of *f*(24) ?

(A) 23
(B) 19
(C) 17
(D) 13
(E) 11

Arithmetic Properties of numbers

Rewriting $f(24) = 2 \times 4 \times 6 \times 8 \times 10 \times 12 \times 14 \times \ldots \times 20 \times 22 \times 24$ as $2 \times 4 \times 2(3) \times 8 \times 2(5) \times 12 \times 2(7) \times \ldots \times 20 \times 2(11) \times 24$ shows that all of the prime numbers from 2 through 11 are factors of $f(24)$. The next prime number is 13, but 13 is not a factor of $f(24)$ because none of the even integers from 2 through 24 has 13 as a factor. Therefore, the largest prime factor of $f(24)$ is 11.

The correct answer is E.

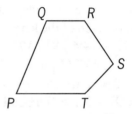

Note: Not drawn to scale.

150. In pentagon *PQRST*, $PQ = 3$, $QR = 2$, $RS = 4$, and $ST = 5$. Which of the lengths 5, 10, and 15 could be the value of *PT* ?

(A) 5 only
(B) 15 only
(C) 5 and 10 only
(D) 10 and 15 only
(E) 5, 10, and 15

Geometry Polygons; Triangles

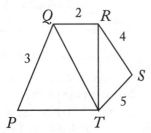

Note: Not drawn to scale.

In the figure above, diagonals $\overline{TQ}$ and $\overline{TR}$ have been drawn in to show ΔTRS and ΔTRQ. Because the length of any side of a triangle must be less than the sum of the lengths of the other two sides, $RT < 5 + 4 = 9$ in ΔTRS, and $QT < RT + 2$ in ΔTRQ. Since $RT < 9$, then $RT + 2 < 9 + 2 = 11$, which then implies $QT < 11$. Now, $PT < QT + 3$ in ΔTQP, and since $QT < 11$, $QT + 3 < 11 + 3 = 14$. It follows that $PT < 14$. Therefore, 15 cannot be the length of $\overline{PT}$ since $15 \not< 14$.

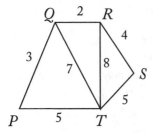

Note: Not drawn to scale.

To show that 5 can be the length of $\overline{PT}$, consider the figure above. For ΔTQP, the length of any side is less than the sum of the lengths of the other two sides as shown below.

$$QT = 7 < 8 = 5 + 3 = PT + PQ$$
$$PQ = 3 < 12 = 5 + 7 = PT + TQ$$
$$PT = 5 < 10 = 3 + 7 = PQ + TQ$$

For ΔRQT, the length of any side is less than the sum of the lengths of the other two sides as shown below.

$$RT = 8 < 9 = 7 + 2 = QT + QR$$
$$RQ = 2 < 15 = 7 + 8 = QT + RT$$
$$QT = 7 < 10 = 2 + 8 = QR + RT$$

For ΔRST, the length of any side is less than the sum of the lengths of the other two sides as shown below.

$$RS = 4 < 13 = 8 + 5 = TR + TS$$
$$RT = 8 < 9 = 5 + 4 = ST + SR$$
$$ST = 5 < 12 = 8 + 4 = TR + RS$$

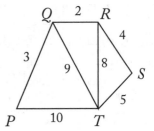

Note: Not drawn to scale.

To show that 10 can be the length of $\overline{PT}$, consider the figure above. For ΔTQP, the length of any side is less than the sum of the lengths of the other two sides as shown below.

$$QT = 9 < 13 = 10 + 3 = PT + PQ$$
$$PQ = 3 < 19 = 10 + 9 = PT + TQ$$
$$PT = 10 < 12 = 3 + 9 = PQ + TQ$$

For ΔRQT, the length of any side is less than the sum of the lengths of the other two sides as shown below.

$$RT = 8 < 11 = 9 + 2 = QT + QR$$
$$RQ = 2 < 17 = 9 + 8 = QT + RT$$
$$QT = 9 < 10 = 2 + 8 = QR + RT$$

For ΔRST, the length of any side is less than the sum of the lengths of the other two sides as shown below.

$$RS = 4 < 13 = 8 + 5 = TR + TS$$
$$RT = 8 < 9 = 5 + 4 = ST + SR$$
$$ST = 5 < 12 = 8 + 4 = TR + RS$$

Therefore, 5 and 10 can be the length of $\overline{PT}$, and 15 cannot be the length of $\overline{PT}$.

The correct answer is C.

151. A certain university will select 1 of 7 candidates eligible to fill a position in the mathematics department and 2 of 10 candidates eligible to fill 2 identical positions in the computer science department. If none of the candidates is eligible for a position in both departments, how many different sets of 3 candidates are there to fill the 3 positions?

    (A)   42
    (B)   70
    (C)   140
    (D)   165
    (E)   315

Arithmetic Elementary combinatorics

To fill the position in the math department, 1 candidate will be selected from a group of 7 eligible candidates, and so there are 7 sets of 1 candidate each to fill the position in the math department. To fill the positions in the computer science department, any one of the 10 eligible candidates can be chosen for the first position and any of the remaining 9 eligible candidates can be chosen for the second position, making a total of $10 \times 9 = 90$ sets of 2 candidates to fill the computer science positions. But, this number includes the set in which Candidate A was chosen to fill the first position and Candidate B was chosen to fill the second position as well as the set in which Candidate B was chosen for the first position and Candidate A was chosen for the second position. These sets are not different essentially since the positions are identical and in both sets Candidates A and B are chosen to fill the 2 positions. Therefore, there are $\dfrac{90}{2} = 45$ sets of 2 candidates to fill the computer science positions. Then, using the multiplication principle, there are $7 \times 45 = 315$ different sets of 3 candidates to fill the 3 positions.

The correct answer is E.

$$2x + y = 12$$
$$|y| \leq 12$$

152. For how many ordered pairs (x,y) that are solutions of the system above are x and y both integers?

    (A)   7
    (B)   10
    (C)   12
    (D)   13
    (E)   14

Algebra Absolute value

From $|y| \leq 12$, if y must be an integer, then y must be in the set $S = \{\pm 12, \pm 11, \pm 10, \ldots, \pm 3, \pm 2, \pm 1, 0\}$.

Since $2x + y = 12$, then $x = \dfrac{12 - y}{2}$. If x must be an integer, then $12 - y$ must be divisible by 2; that is, $12 - y$ must be even. Since 12 is even, $12 - y$ is even if and only if y is even. This eliminates all odd integers from S, leaving only the even integers $\pm 12, \pm 10, \pm 8, \pm 6, \pm 4, \pm 2$, and 0. Thus, there are 13 possible integer y-values, each with a corresponding integer x-value and, therefore, there are 13 ordered pairs (x,y), where x and y are both integers, that solve the system.

The correct answer is D.

153. The points R, T, and U lie on a circle that has radius 4. If the length of arc RTU is $\dfrac{4\pi}{3}$, what is the length of line segment RU?

    (A) $\dfrac{4}{3}$

    (B) $\dfrac{8}{3}$

    (C)   3
    (D)   4
    (E)   6

Geometry Circles; Triangles; Circumference

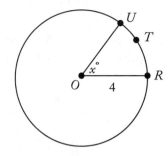

In the figure above, O is the center of the circle that contains R, T, and U and x is the degree measure of $\angle ROU$. Since the circumference of the circle is $2\pi(4) = 8\pi$ and there are $360°$ in the circle, the ratio of the length of arc RTU to the circumference of the circle is the same as the ratio of x to 360. Therefore, $\dfrac{\frac{4\pi}{3}}{8\pi} = \dfrac{x}{360}$. Then

$x = \dfrac{\frac{4\pi}{3}(360)}{8\pi} = \dfrac{480\pi}{8\pi} = 60$. This means that $\triangle ROU$ is an isosceles triangle with side lengths $OR = OU = 4$ and vertex angle measuring $60°$. The base angles of $\triangle ROU$ must have equal measures and the sum of their measures must be $180° - 60° = 120°$. Therefore, each base angle measures $60°$, $\triangle ROU$ is equilateral, and $RU = 4$.

The correct answer is D.

154. A survey of employers found that during 1993 employment costs rose 3.5 percent, where employment costs consist of salary costs and fringe-benefit costs. If salary costs rose 3 percent and fringe-benefit costs rose 5.5 percent during 1993, then fringe-benefit costs represented what percent of employment costs at the beginning of 1993 ?

    (A) 16.5%
    (B) 20%
    (C) 35%
    (D) 55%
    (E) 65%

Algebra; Arithmetic First-degree equations; Percents

Let E represent employment costs, S represent salary costs, and F represent fringe-benefit costs. Then $E = S + F$. An increase of 3 percent in salary costs and a 5.5 percent increase in fringe-benefit costs resulted in a 3.5 percent increase in employment costs. Therefore $1.03S + 1.055F = 1.035E$. But, $E = S + F$, so

$1.03S + 1.055F = 1.035(S + F) = 1.035S + 1.035F$.

Combining like terms gives

$(1.055 - 1.035)F = (1.035 - 1.03)S$ or

$0.02F = 0.005S$. Then, $S = \dfrac{0.02}{0.005}F = 4F$. Thus,

since $E = S + F$, it follows that $E = 4F + F = 5F$.

Then, F as a percent of E is $\dfrac{F}{E} = \dfrac{F}{5F} = \dfrac{1}{5} = 20\%$.

The correct answer is B.

155. A certain company that sells only cars and trucks reported that revenues from car sales in 1997 were down 11 percent from 1996 and revenues from truck sales in 1997 were up 7 percent from 1996. If total revenues from car sales and truck sales in 1997 were up 1 percent from 1996, what is the ratio of revenue from car sales in 1996 to revenue from truck sales in 1996 ?

    (A) 1:2
    (B) 4:5
    (C) 1:1
    (D) 3:2
    (E) 5:3

Algebra; Arithmetic First-degree equations; Percents

This problem is very similar to the preceding problem except that this problem involves both a percent decrease and a percent increase. Let C_{96} and C_{97} represent revenues from car sales in 1996 and 1997, respectively, and let T_{96} and T_{97} represent revenues from truck sales in 1996 and 1997, respectively. A decrease of 11 percent in revenue from car sales from 1996 to 1997 can be represented as $(1-0.11)C_{96} = C_{97}$, and a 7 percent increase in revenue from truck sales from 1996 to 1997 can be represented as $(1+0.07)T_{96} = T_{97}$. An overall increase of 1 percent in revenue from car and truck sales from 1996 to 1997 can be represented as $C_{97} + T_{97} = (1+0.01)(C_{96} + T_{96})$. Then, by substitution of expressions for C_{97} and T_{97} that were derived above,

$$(1-0.11)C_{96} + (1+0.07)T_{96} = (1+0.01)(C_{96} + T_{96})$$

and so $0.89C_{96} + 1.07T_{96} =$ $1.01(C_{96} + T_{96})$ or $0.89C_{96} + 1.07T_{96} =$ $1.01C_{96} + 1.01T_{96}$. Then, combining like terms gives $(1.07 - 1.01)T_{96} = (1.01 - 0.89)C_{96}$ or $0.06T_{96} = 0.12C_{96}$. Thus $\dfrac{C_{96}}{T_{96}} = \dfrac{0.06}{0.12} = \dfrac{1}{2}$. The ratio of revenue from car sales in 1996 to revenue from truck sales in 1996 is 1:2.

The correct answer is A.

156. If $4 < \dfrac{7-x}{3}$, which of the following must be true?

   I. $5 < x$

   II. $|x+3| > 2$

   III. $-(x+5)$ is positive.

(A)   II only
(B)   III only
(C)   I and II only
(D)   II and III only
(E)   I, II, and III

Algebra Inequalities

Given that $4 < \dfrac{7-x}{3}$, it follows that $12 < 7 - x$. Then, $5 < -x$ or, equivalently, $x < -5$.

I.   If $4 < \dfrac{7-x}{3}$, then $x < -5$. If $5 < x$ were true then, by combining $5 < x$ and $x < -5$, it would follow that $5 < -5$, which cannot be true. Therefore, it is not the case that, if $4 < \dfrac{7-x}{3}$, then Statement I must be true. In fact, Statement I is never true.

II.   If $4 < \dfrac{7-x}{3}$, then $x < -5$, and it follows that $x + 3 < -2$. Since $-2 < 0$, then $x + 3 < 0$ and $|x+3| = -(x+3)$. If $x + 3 < -2$, then $-(x+3) > 2$ and by substitution, $|x+3| > 2$. Therefore, Statement II must be true for every value of x such that $x < -5$. Therefore, Statement II must be true if $4 < \dfrac{7-x}{3}$.

III. If $4 < \dfrac{7-x}{3}$, then $x < -5$ and $x + 5 < 0$. But, if $x + 5 < 0$, then it follows that $-(x+5) > 0$ and so $-(x+5)$ is positive. Therefore Statement III must be true if $4 < \dfrac{7-x}{3}$.

The correct answer is D.

157. A certain right triangle has sides of length x, y, and z, where $x < y < z$. If the area of this triangular region is 1, which of the following indicates all of the possible values of y?

(A) $y > \sqrt{2}$

(B) $\dfrac{\sqrt{3}}{2} < y < \sqrt{2}$

(C) $\dfrac{\sqrt{2}}{3} < y < \dfrac{\sqrt{3}}{2}$

(D) $\dfrac{\sqrt{3}}{4} < y < \dfrac{\sqrt{2}}{3}$

(E) $y < \dfrac{\sqrt{3}}{4}$

Geometry; Algebra Triangles; Area; Inequalities

Since x, y, and z are the side lengths of a right triangle and $x < y < z$, it follows that x and y are the lengths of the legs of the triangle and so the area of the triangle is $\frac{1}{2}xy$. But, it is given that the area is 1 and so $\frac{1}{2}xy = 1$. Then, $xy = 2$ and $y = \frac{2}{x}$. Under the assumption that x, y, and z are all positive since they are the side lengths of a triangle, $x < y$ implies $\frac{1}{x} > \frac{1}{y}$ and then $\frac{2}{x} > \frac{2}{y}$. But, $y = \frac{2}{x}$, so by substitution, $y > \frac{2}{y}$, which implies that $y^2 > 2$ since y is positive. Thus, $y > \sqrt{2}$.

Alternatively, if $x < \sqrt{2}$ and $y < \sqrt{2}$, then $xy < 2$. If $x > \sqrt{2}$ and $y > \sqrt{2}$, then $xy > 2$. But, $xy = 2$ so one of x or y must be less than $\sqrt{2}$ and the other must be greater than $\sqrt{2}$. Since $x < y$, it follows that $x < \sqrt{2} < y$ and $y > \sqrt{2}$.

The correct answer is A.

158. A set of numbers has the property that for any number t in the set, $t + 2$ is in the set. If -1 is in the set, which of the following must also be in the set?

    I. -3
    II. 1
    III. 5

    (A)   I only
    (B)   II only
    (C)   I and II only
    (D)   II and III only
    (E)   I, II, and III

Arithmetic Properties of numbers

It is given that -1 is in the set and, if t is in the set, then $t + 2$ is in the set.

I.   Since $\{-1, 1, 3, 5, 7, 9, 11, \ldots\}$ contains -1 and satisfies the property that if t is in the set, then $t + 2$ is in the set, it is not true that -3 must be in the set.

II.   Since -1 is in the set, $-1 + 2 = 1$ is in the set. Therefore, it must be true that 1 is in the set.

III.   Since -1 is in the set, $-1 + 2 = 1$ is in the set. Since 1 is in the set, $1 + 2 = 3$ is in the set. Since 3 is in the set, $3 + 2 = 5$ is in the set. Therefore, it must be true that 5 is in the set.

The correct answer is D.

159. A group of store managers must assemble 280 displays for an upcoming sale. If they assemble 25 percent of the displays during the first hour and 40 percent of the remaining displays during the second hour, how many of the displays will <u>not</u> have been assembled by the end of the second hour?

    (A)   70
    (B)   98
    (C)   126
    (D)   168
    (E)   182

Arithmetic Percents

If, during the first hour, 25 percent of the total displays were assembled, then $280(0.25) = 70$ displays were assembled, leaving $280 - 70 = 210$ displays remaining to be assembled. Since 40 percent of the remaining displays were assembled during the second hour, $0.40(210) = 84$ displays were assembled during the second hour. Thus, $70 + 84 = 154$ displays were assembled during the first two hours and $280 - 154 = 126$ displays had not been assembled by the end of the second hour.

The correct answer is C.

160. A couple decides to have 4 children. If they succeed in having 4 children and each child is equally likely to be a boy or a girl, what is the probability that they will have exactly 2 girls and 2 boys?

    (A) $\frac{3}{8}$

    (B) $\frac{1}{4}$

    (C) $\frac{3}{16}$

    (D) $\frac{1}{8}$

    (E) $\frac{1}{16}$

Arithmetic Probability

Representing the birth order of the 4 children as a sequence of 4 letters, each of which is B for boy and G for girl, there are 2 possibilities (B or G) for the first letter, 2 for the second letter, 2 for the third letter, and 2 for the fourth letter, making a total of $2^4 = 16$ sequences. The table below categorizes some of these 16 sequences.

# of boys	# of girls	Sequences	# of sequences
0	4	GGGG	1
1	3	BGGG, GBGG, GGBG, GGGB	4
3	1	GBBB, BGBB, BBGB, BBBG	4
4	0	BBBB	1

The table accounts for $1 + 4 + 4 + 1 = 10$ sequences. The other 6 sequences will have 2Bs and 2Gs. Therefore the probability that the couple will have exactly 2 boys and 2 girls is $\frac{6}{16} = \frac{3}{8}$.

For the mathematically inclined, if it is assumed that a couple has a fixed number of children, that the probability of having a girl each time is p, and that the sex of each child is independent of the sex of the other children, then the number of girls, x, born to a couple with n children is a random variable having the binomial probability distribution. The probability of having exactly x girls born to a couple with n children is given by the formula $\binom{n}{x} p^x (1-p)^{n-x}$. For the problem at hand, it is given that each child is equally likely to be a boy or a girl, and so $p = \frac{1}{2}$. Thus, the probability of having exactly 2 girls born to a couple with 4 children is

$$\binom{4}{2}\left(\frac{1}{2}\right)^2\left(\frac{1}{2}\right)^2 = \frac{4!}{2!2!}\left(\frac{1}{2}\right)^2\left(\frac{1}{2}\right)^2 =$$

$$(6)\left(\frac{1}{4}\right)\left(\frac{1}{4}\right) = \frac{6}{16} = \frac{3}{8}.$$

The correct answer is A.

$$3, k, 2, 8, m, 3$$

161. The arithmetic mean of the list of numbers above is 4. If k and m are integers and $k \neq m$, what is the median of the list?

    (A) 2
    (B) 2.5
    (C) 3
    (D) 3.5
    (E) 4

Arithmetic Statistics

Since the arithmetic mean = $\frac{\text{sum of values}}{\text{number of values}}$, then $\frac{3 + k + 2 + 8 + m + 3}{6} = 4$, and so $\frac{16 + k + m}{6} = 4$, $16 + k + m = 24$, $k + m = 8$. Since $k \neq m$, then either $k < 4$ and $m > 4$ or $k > 4$ and $m < 4$. Because k and m are integers, either $k \leq 3$ and $5 \geq m$ or $k \geq 5$ and $m \leq 3$.

Case (i): If $k \leq 2$, then $m \geq 6$ and the six integers in ascending order are k, 2, 3, 3, m, 8 or k, 2, 3, 3, 8, m. The two middle integers are both 3 so the median is $\dfrac{3+3}{2} = 3$.

Case (ii): If $k = 3$, then $m = 5$ and the six integers in ascending order are 2, k, 3, 3, m, 8. The two middle integers are both 3 so the median is $\dfrac{3+3}{2} = 3$.

Case (iii): If $k = 5$, then $m = 3$ and the six integers in ascending order are 2, m, 3, 3, k, 8. The two middle integers are both 3 so the median is $\dfrac{3+3}{2} = 3$.

Case (iv): If $k \geq 6$, then $m \leq 2$ and the six integers in ascending order are m, 2, 3, 3, k, 8 or m, 2, 3, 3, 8, k. The two middle integers are both 3 so the median is $\dfrac{3+3}{2} = 3$.

The correct answer is C.

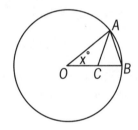

162. In the figure above, point O is the center of the circle and $OC = AC = AB$. What is the value of x?

(A) 40
(B) 36
(C) 34
(D) 32
(E) 30

Geometry Angles

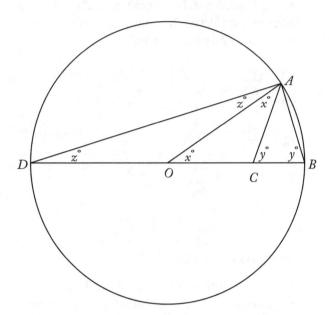

Consider the figure above, where $\overline{DB}$ is a diameter of the circle with center O and $\overline{AD}$ is a chord. Since $OC = AC$, $\triangle OCA$ is isosceles and so the base angles, $\angle AOC$ and $\angle OAC$, have the same degree measure. The measure of $\angle AOC$ is given as $x°$, so the measure of $\angle OAC$ is $x°$. Since $AC = AB$, $\triangle CAB$ is isosceles and so the base angles, $\angle ACB$ and $\angle ABC$, have the same degree measure. The measure of each is marked as $y°$. Likewise, since $\overline{OD}$ and $\overline{OA}$ are radii of the circle, $OD = OA$, and $\triangle DOA$ is isosceles with base angles, $\angle ADO$ and $\angle DAO$, each measuring $z°$. Each of the following statements is true:

(i) The measure of $\angle CAB$ is $180 - 2y$ since the sum of the measures of the angles of $\triangle CAB$ is 180.

(ii) $\angle DAB$ is a right angle (because $\overline{DB}$ is a diameter of the circle) and so $z + x + (180 - 2y) = 90$, or, equivalently, $2y - x - z = 90$.

(iii) $z + 90 + y = 180$ since the sum of the measures of the angles of right triangle $\triangle DAB$ is 180, or, equivalently, $z = 90 - y$.

(iv) $x = 2z$ because the measure of exterior angle $\angle AOC$ to $\triangle AOD$ is the sum of the measures of the two opposite interior angles, $\angle ODA$ and $\angle OAD$.

(v) $y = 2x$ because the measure of exterior angle $\angle ACB$ to $\triangle OCA$ is the sum of the measures of the two opposite interior angles, $\angle COA$ and $\angle CAO$.

Multiplying the final equation in (iii) by 2 gives $2z = 180 - 2y$. But, $x = 2z$ in (iv), so $x = 180 - 2y$. Finally, the sum of the measures of the angles of $\triangle CAB$ is 180 and so $y + y + x = 180$. Then from (v), $2x + 2x + x = 180$, $5x = 180$, and $x = 36$.

The correct answer is B.

163. $\dfrac{\left(8^2\right)\left(3^3\right)\left(2^4\right)}{96^2} =$

(A)   3
(B)   6
(C)   9
(D)   12
(E)   18

Arithmetic Operations on rational numbers

Simplify the expression.

$$\frac{\left(8^2\right)\left(3^3\right)\left(2^4\right)}{96^2} = \frac{\left(8^2\right)\left(3^3\right)\left(2^4\right)}{\left(8^2\right)\left(3^2\right)\left(2^4\right)} = 3$$

The correct answer is A.

164. When 10 is divided by the positive integer n, the remainder is $n - 4$. Which of the following could be the value of n?

(A)   3
(B)   4
(C)   7
(D)   8
(E)   12

Algebra Properties of numbers

If q is the quotient and $n - 4$ is the remainder when 10 is divided by the positive integer n, then $10 = qn + \left(n - 4\right)$. So, $14 = qn + n = n\left(q + 1\right)$. This means that n must be a factor of 14 and so $n = 1$, $n = 2$, $n = 7$, or $n = 14$ since n is a positive integer and the only positive integer factors of 14 are 1, 2, 7, and 14. The only positive integer factor of 14 given in the answer choices is 7.

The correct answer is C.

165. If $\frac{1}{2}$ of the money in a certain trust fund was invested in stocks, $\frac{1}{4}$ in bonds, $\frac{1}{5}$ in a mutual fund, and the remaining $10,000 in a government certificate, what was the total amount of the trust fund?

(A) $ 100,000
(B) $ 150,000
(C) $ 200,000
(D) $ 500,000
(E) $2,000,000

Arithmetic Operations on rational numbers

If T represents the total amount in the trust fund then the amount in stocks, bonds, and the mutual fund is $\frac{1}{2}T + \frac{1}{4}T + \frac{1}{5}T = \left(\frac{1}{2} + \frac{1}{4} + \frac{1}{5}\right)T =$ $\left(\frac{10 + 5 + 4}{20}\right)T = \frac{19}{20}T$. The remainder of the fund in the government certificate is then $T - \frac{19}{20}T = \frac{1}{20}T$ and this amount is $10,000. Therefore, $\frac{1}{20}T = \$10,000$ and $T = \$200,000$.

The correct answer is C.

166. If m is an integer such that $\left(-2\right)^{2m} = 2^{9-m}$, then $m =$

(A)   1
(B)   2
(C)   3
(D)   4
(E)   6

Algebra First-degree equations; Exponents

Because the exponent $2m$ is an even integer, $(-2)^{2m}$ will be positive and will have the same value as 2^{2m}. Therefore, $2^{2m} = \left(-2\right)^{2m} = 2^{9-m}$, so $2^{2m} = 2^{9-m}$, from which $2m = 9 - m$, $3m = 9$, and $m = 3$.

The correct answer is C.

167. In a mayoral election, Candidate X received $\frac{1}{3}$ more votes than Candidate Y, and Candidate Y received $\frac{1}{4}$ fewer votes than Candidate Z . If Candidate Z received 24,000 votes, how many votes did Candidate X receive?

 (A) 18,000
 (B) 22,000
 (C) 24,000
 (D) 26,000
 (E) 32,000

Algebra Applied problems

Let x, y, and z be the number of votes received by Candidates X, Y, and Z, respectively. Then

$$x = y + \frac{1}{3}y = \frac{4}{3}y,\ y = z - \frac{1}{4}z = \frac{3}{4}z,\text{ and}$$

$z = 24,000$. Substituting the value of z into the expression for y gives $y = \frac{3}{4}(24,000) = 18,000$, and substituting the value of y into the expression for x gives $x = \frac{4}{3}(18,000) = 24,000$. Alternatively, substituting the expression for y into the expression for x gives $x = \frac{4}{3}\left(\frac{3}{4}z\right) = z = 24,000$.

The correct answer is C.

168. An airline passenger is planning a trip that involves three connecting flights that leave from Airports A, B, and C, respectively. The first flight leaves Airport A every hour, beginning at 8:00 a.m., and arrives at Airport B $2\frac{1}{2}$ hours later. The second flight leaves Airport B every 20 minutes, beginning at 8:00 a.m., and arrives at Airport C $1\frac{1}{6}$ hours later. The third flight leaves Airport C every hour, beginning at 8:45 a.m. What is the least total amount of time the passenger must spend between flights if all flights keep to their schedules?

 (A) 25 min
 (B) 1 hr 5 min
 (C) 1 hr 15 min
 (D) 2 hr 20 min
 (E) 3 hr 40 min

Arithmetic Operations on rational numbers

Since the flight schedules at each of Airports A, B, and C are the same hour after hour, assume that the passenger leaves Airport A at 8:00 and arrives at Airport B at 10:30. Since flights from Airport B leave at 20-minute intervals beginning on the hour, the passenger must wait 10 minutes at Airport B for the flight that leaves at 10:40 and arrives at Airport C $1\frac{1}{6}$ hours or 1 hour 10 minutes later. Thus, the passenger arrives at Airport C at 11:50. Having arrived too late for the 11:45 flight from Airport C, the passenger must wait 55 minutes for the 12:45 flight. Thus, the least total amount of time the passenger must spend waiting between flights is $10 + 55 = 65$ minutes, or 1 hour 5 minutes.

The correct answer is B.

169. If n is a positive integer and n^2 is divisible by 72, then the largest positive integer that must divide n is

 (A) 6
 (B) 12
 (C) 24
 (D) 36
 (E) 48

Arithmetic Properties of numbers

Since n^2 is divisible by 72, $n^2 = 72k$ for some positive integer k. Since $n^2 = 72k$, then $72k$ must be a perfect square. Since $72k = (2^3)(3^2)k$, then $k = 2m^2$ for some positive integer m in order for $72k$ to be a perfect square. Then,

$$n^2 = 72k = (2^3)(3^2)(2m^2) = (2^4)(3^2)m^2$$
$$= \left[(2^2)(3)(m)\right]^2,\text{ and } n = (2^2)(3)(m).\text{ The positive}$$

integers that MUST divide n are 1, 2, 3, 4, 6, and 12. Therefore, the largest positive integer that must divide n is 12.

The correct answer is B.

170. If n is a positive integer and $k + 2 = 3^n$, which of the following could NOT be a value of k?

(A) 1
(B) 4
(C) 7
(D) 25
(E) 79

Arithmetic Operations on rational numbers

For a number to equal 3^n, the number must be a power of 3. Substitute the answer choices for k in the equation given, and determine which one does not yield a power of 3.

A $1 + 2 = 3$ power of 3 (3^1)

B $4 + 2 = 6$ multiple of 3, but NOT a power of 3

C $7 + 2 = 9$ power of 3 (3^2)

D $25 + 2 = 27$ power of 3 (3^3)

E $79 + 2 = 81$ power of 3 (3^4)

The correct answer is B.

171. A certain grocery purchased x pounds of produce for p dollars per pound. If y pounds of the produce had to be discarded due to spoilage and the grocery sold the rest for s dollars per pound, which of the following represents the gross profit on the sale of the produce?

(A) $(x - y)s - xp$
(B) $(x - y)p - ys$
(C) $(s - p)y - xp$
(D) $xp - ys$
(E) $(x - y)(s - p)$

Algebra Simplifying algebraic expressions; Applied problems

Since the grocery bought x pounds of produce for p dollars per pound, the total cost of the produce was xp dollars. Since y pounds of the produce was discarded, the grocery sold $x - y$ pounds of produce at the price of s dollars per pound, yielding a total revenue of $(x - y)s$ dollars. Then, the grocery's gross profit on the sale of the produce is its total revenue minus its total cost or $(x - y)s - xp$ dollars.

The correct answer is A.

172. If x, y, and z are positive integers such that x is a factor of y, and x is a multiple of z, which of the following is NOT necessarily an integer?

(A) $\dfrac{x + z}{z}$

(B) $\dfrac{y + z}{x}$

(C) $\dfrac{x + y}{z}$

(D) $\dfrac{xy}{z}$

(E) $\dfrac{yz}{x}$

Arithmetic Properties of numbers

Since the positive integer x is a factor of y, then $y = kx$ for some positive integer k. Since x is a multiple of the positive integer z, then $x = mz$ for some positive integer m.

Substitute these expressions for x and/or y into each answer choice to find the one expression that is NOT necessarily an integer.

A $\dfrac{x + z}{z} = \dfrac{mz + z}{z} = \dfrac{(m + 1)z}{z} = m + 1$, which MUST be an integer

B $\dfrac{y + z}{x} = \dfrac{y}{x} + \dfrac{z}{x} = \dfrac{kx}{x} + \dfrac{z}{mz} = k + \dfrac{1}{m}$, which NEED NOT be an integer

Because only one of the five expressions need not be an integer, the expressions given in C, D, and E need not be tested. However, for completeness,

C $\dfrac{x + y}{z} = \dfrac{mz + kx}{z} = \dfrac{mz + k(mz)}{z} = \dfrac{mz(1 + k)}{z}$ $= m(1 + k)$, which MUST be an integer

D $\dfrac{xy}{z} = \dfrac{(mz)y}{z} = my$, which MUST be an integer

E $\dfrac{yz}{x} = \dfrac{(kx)(z)}{x} = kz$, which MUST be an integer

The correct answer is B.

173. Running at their respective constant rates, Machine X takes 2 days longer to produce w widgets than Machine Y. At these rates, if the two machines together produce $\frac{5}{4}w$ widgets in 3 days, how many days would it take Machine X alone to produce $2w$ widgets?

    (A)   4
    (B)   6
    (C)   8
    (D)   10
    (E)   12

Algebra; Applied problems

If x, where $x > 2$, represents the number of days Machine X takes to produce w widgets, then Machine Y takes $x - 2$ days to produce w widgets. It follows that Machines X and Y can produce $\frac{w}{x}$ and $\frac{w}{x-2}$ widgets, respectively, in 1 day and together they can produce $\frac{w}{x} + \frac{w}{x-2}$ widgets in 1 day. Since it is given that, together, they can produce $\frac{5}{4}w$ widgets in 3 days, it follows that, together, they can produce $\frac{1}{3}\left(\frac{5}{4}w\right) = \frac{5}{12}w$ widgets in 1 day. Thus,

$$\frac{w}{x} + \frac{w}{x-2} = \frac{5}{12}w$$

$$\left(\frac{1}{x} + \frac{1}{x-2}\right)w = \frac{5}{12}w$$

$$\left(\frac{1}{x} + \frac{1}{x-2}\right) = \frac{5}{12}$$

$$12x(x-2)\left(\frac{1}{x} + \frac{1}{x-2}\right) = 12x(x-2)\left(\frac{5}{12}\right)$$

$$12[(x-2)+x] = 5x(x-2)$$

$$12(2x-2) = 5x(x-2)$$

$$24x - 24 = 5x^2 - 10x$$

$$0 = 5x^2 - 34x + 24$$

$$0 = (5x-4)(x-6)$$

$$x = \frac{4}{5} \text{ or } 6$$

Therefore, since $x > 2$, it follows that $x = 6$. Machine X takes 6 days to produce w widgets and $2(6) = 12$ days to produce $2w$ widgets.

The correct answer is E.

$$\frac{\square\triangle}{\times\ \triangle\square}$$

174. The product of the two-digit numbers above is the three-digit number $\square\diamond\square$, where $\square$, $\triangle$, and $\diamond$, are three different nonzero digits. If $\square \times \triangle < 10$, what is the two-digit number $\square\triangle$?

    (A)   11
    (B)   12
    (C)   13
    (D)   21
    (E)   31

Arithmetic Operations on rational numbers

Since it is given that $\square \diamond \square$ is a three-digit number, $\square \neq 0$ because "three-digit number" is used to characterize a number between 100 and 999, inclusive. Since $\square \neq 0$, $\square \times \triangle < 10$, and the units digit of the three-digit number $\square \diamond \square$ is $\square$, then $\square \times \triangle = \square$, which implies $\triangle = 1$. Then the problem simplifies to

$$\begin{array}{r} \square 1 \\ \times\ 1\square \\ \hline \square^2\square \\ \square 1 \\ \hline \square\diamond\square \end{array}$$

Notice that the hundreds digit in the solution is the same as the hundreds digit of the second partial product, so there is no carrying over from the tens column. This means that $\diamond < 10$ and since $\diamond = \square^2 + 1$, then $\square^2 + 1 < 10$, $\square^2 < 9$, and $\square < 3$. Since $\triangle = 1$ and $\square$ is different from $\triangle$, it follows that $\square = 2$. Thus, the value of $\square\triangle$ is 21.

The correct answer is D.

175. A square wooden plaque has a square brass inlay in the center, leaving a wooden strip of uniform width around the brass square. If the ratio of the brass area to the wooden area is 25 to 39, which of the following could be the width, in inches, of the wooden strip?

   I.   1
   II.   3
   III. 4

   (A)   I only
   (B)   II only
   (C)   I and II only
   (D)   I and III only
   (E)   I, II, and III

Geometry Area

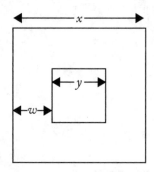

Note: Not drawn to scale.

Let x represent the side length of the entire plaque, let y represent the side length of the brass inlay, and w represent the uniform width of the wooden strip around the brass inlay, as shown in the figure above. Since the ratio of the area of the brass inlay to the area of the wooden strip is 25 to 39, the ratio of the area of the brass inlay to the area of the entire plaque is $\dfrac{y^2}{x^2} = \dfrac{25}{25+39} = \dfrac{25}{64}$.

Then, $\dfrac{y}{x} = \sqrt{\dfrac{25}{64}} = \dfrac{5}{8}$ and $y = \dfrac{5}{8}x$. Also, $x = y + 2w$ and $w = \dfrac{x-y}{2}$. Substituting $\dfrac{5}{8}x$ for y into this expression for w gives $w = \dfrac{x - \frac{5}{8}x}{2} = \dfrac{\frac{3}{8}x}{2} = \dfrac{3}{16}x$.
Thus,

   I.   If the plaque were $\dfrac{16}{3}$ inches on a side, then the width of the wooden strip would be 1 inch, and so 1 inch is a possible width for the wooden strip.

   II. If the plaque were 16 inches on a side, then the width of the wooden strip would be 3 inches, and so 3 inches is a possible width for the wooden strip.

   III. If the plaque were $\dfrac{64}{3}$ inches on a side, then the width of the wooden strip would be 4 inches, and so 4 inches is a possible width for the wooden strip.

The correct answer is E.

176. $\dfrac{2\frac{3}{5} - 1\frac{2}{3}}{\frac{2}{3} - \frac{3}{5}} =$

   (A)   16
   (B)   14
   (C)   3
   (D)   1
   (E)   −1

Arithmetic Operations on rational numbers

Work the problem:

$$\dfrac{2\frac{3}{5} - 1\frac{2}{3}}{\frac{2}{3} - \frac{3}{5}} =$$

$$\dfrac{\frac{13}{5} - \frac{5}{3}}{\frac{2}{3} - \frac{3}{5}} = \dfrac{\frac{39-25}{15}}{\frac{10-9}{15}} = \dfrac{\frac{14}{15}}{\frac{1}{15}} = \dfrac{14}{15} \times \dfrac{15}{1} = 14$$

The correct answer is B.

5.0 Data Sufficiency

5.0 Data Sufficiency

Data sufficiency questions appear in the Quantitative section of the GMAT® test. Multiple-choice data sufficiency questions are intermingled with problem solving questions throughout the section. You will have 75 minutes to complete the Quantitative section of the GMAT test, or about 2 minutes to answer each question. These questions require knowledge of the following topics:

- Arithmetic
- Elementary algebra
- Commonly known concepts of geometry

Data sufficiency questions are designed to measure your ability to analyze a quantitative problem, recognize which given information is relevant, and determine at what point there is sufficient information to solve a problem. In these questions, you are to classify each problem according to the five fixed answer choices, rather than find a solution to the problem.

Each data sufficiency question consists of a question, often accompanied by some initial information, and two statements, labeled (1) and (2), which contain additional information. You must decide whether the information in each statement is sufficient to answer the question or— if neither statement provides enough information—whether the information in the two statements together is sufficient. It is also possible that the statements in combination do not give enough information to answer the question.

Begin by reading the initial information and the question carefully. Next, consider the first statement. Does the information provided by the first statement enable you to answer the question? Go on to the second statement. Try to ignore the information given in the first statement when you consider whether the second statement provides information that, by itself, allows you to answer the question. Now you should be able to say, for each statement, whether it is sufficient to determine the answer.

Next, consider the two statements in tandem. Do they, together, enable you to answer the question?

Look again at your answer choices. Select the one that most accurately reflects whether the statements provide the information required to answer the question.

5.1 Test-Taking Strategies

1. **Do not waste valuable time solving a problem.**
   You only need to determine whether sufficient information is given to solve it.

2. **Consider each statement separately.**
   First, decide whether each statement alone gives sufficient information to solve the problem. Be sure to disregard the information given in statement (1) when you evaluate the information given in statement (2). If either, or both, of the statements give(s) sufficient information to solve the problem, select the answer corresponding to the description of which statement(s) give(s) sufficient information to solve the problem.

3. **Judge the statements in tandem if neither statement is sufficient by itself.**
   It is possible that the two statements together do not provide sufficient information. Once you decide, select the answer corresponding to the description of whether the statements together give sufficient information to solve the problem.

4. **Answer the question asked.**
   For example, if the question asks, "What is the value of y ?" for an answer statement to be sufficient, you must be able to find one and only one value for y. Being able to determine minimum or maximum values for an answer (e.g., $y = x + 2$) is not sufficient, because such answers constitute a range of values rather than the specific value of y.

5. **Be very careful not to make unwarranted assumptions based on the images represented.**
   Figures are not necessarily drawn to scale; they are generalized figures showing little more than intersecting line segments and the relationships of points, angles, and regions. So, for example, if a figure described as a rectangle looks like a square, do *not* conclude that it is, in fact, a square just by looking at the figure.

If statement 1 is sufficient, then the answer must be **A or D.**

If statement 2 is not sufficient, then the answer must be **A.**

If statement 2 is sufficient, then the answer must be **D.**

If statement 1 is not sufficient, then the answer must be **B, C, or E.**

If statement 2 is sufficient, then the answer must be **B.**

If statement 2 is not sufficient, then the answer must be **C or E.**

If both statements together are sufficient, then the answer must be **C.**

If both statements together are still not sufficient, then the answer must be **E.**

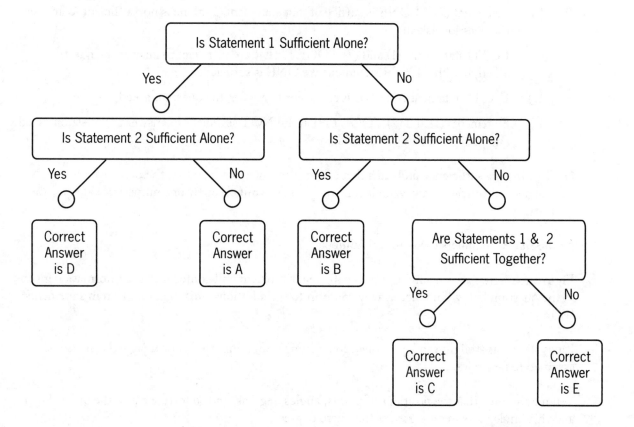

5.2 The Directions

These directions are similar to those you will see for data sufficiency questions when you take the GMAT test. If you read the directions carefully and understand them clearly before going to sit for the test, you will not need to spend much time reviewing them when you take the GMAT test.

Each data sufficiency problem consists of a question and two statements, labeled (1) and (2), that give data. You have to decide whether the data given in the statements are *sufficient* for answering the question. Using the data given in the statements *plus* your knowledge of mathematics and everyday facts (such as the number of days in July or the meaning of *counterclockwise*), you must indicate whether the data given in the statements are sufficient for answering the questions and then indicate one of the following answer choices:

(A)   Statement (1) ALONE is sufficient, but statement (2) alone is not sufficient to answer the question asked;

(B)   Statement (2) ALONE is sufficient, but statement (1) alone is not sufficient to answer the question asked;

(C)   BOTH statements (1) and (2) TOGETHER are sufficient to answer the question asked, but NEITHER statement ALONE is sufficient;

(D)   EACH statement ALONE is sufficient to answer the question asked;

(E)   Statements (1) and (2) TOGETHER are NOT sufficient to answer the question asked, and additional data are needed.

NOTE: In data sufficiency problems that ask for the value of a quantity, the data given in the statements are sufficient only when it is possible to determine exactly one numerical value for the quantity.

Numbers: All numbers used are real numbers.

Figures: A figure accompanying a data sufficiency problem will conform to the information given in the question but will not necessarily conform to the additional information given in statements (1) and (2).

Lines shown as straight can be assumed to be straight and lines that appear jagged can also be assumed to be straight.

You may assume that the positions of points, angles, regions, and so forth exist in the order shown and that angle measures are greater than zero degrees.

All figures lie in a plane unless otherwise indicated.

5.3 Sample Questions

Each <u>data sufficiency</u> problem consists of a question and two statements, labeled (1) and (2), which contain certain data. Using these data and your knowledge of mathematics and everyday facts (such as the number of days in July or the meaning of the word *counterclockwise*), decide whether the data given are sufficient for answering the question and then indicate one of the following answer choices:

A   Statement (1) ALONE is sufficient, but statement (2) alone is not sufficient.
B   Statement (2) ALONE is sufficient, but statement (1) alone is not sufficient.
C   BOTH statements TOGETHER are sufficient, but NEITHER statement ALONE is sufficient.
D   EACH statement ALONE is sufficient.
E   Statements (1) and (2) TOGETHER are not sufficient.

<u>Note:</u> In data sufficiency problems that ask for the value of a quantity, the data given in the statements are sufficient only when it is possible to determine exactly one numerical value for the quantity.
<u>Example:</u>

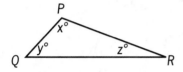

In $\triangle PQR$, what is the value of x ?

(1) $PQ = PR$
(2) $y = 40$

<u>Explanation:</u> According to statement (1) $PQ = PR$; therefore, $\triangle PQR$ is isosceles and $y = z$. Since $x + y + z = 180$, it follows that $x + 2y = 180$. Since statement (1) does not give a value for y, you cannot answer the question using statement (1) alone. According to statement (2), $y = 40$; therefore, $x + z = 140$. Since statement (2) does not give a value for z, you cannot answer the question using statement (2) alone. Using both statements together, since $x + 2y = 180$ and the value of y is given, you can find the value of x. Therefore, BOTH statements (1) and (2) TOGETHER are sufficient to answer the questions, but NEITHER statement ALONE is sufficient.

<u>Numbers:</u> All numbers used are real numbers.

<u>Figures:</u>
- Figures conform to the information given in the question, but will not necessarily conform to the additional information given in statements (1) and (2).
- Lines shown as straight are straight, and lines that appear jagged are also straight.
- The positions of points, angles, regions, etc., exist in the order shown, and angle measures are greater than zero.
- All figures lie in a plane unless otherwise indicated.

1. What is the average (arithmetic mean) of x and y?

    (1) The average of x and $2y$ is 10.
    (2) The average of $2x$ and $7y$ is 32.

2. What is the value of $\frac{r}{2} + \frac{s}{2}$?

    (1) $\frac{r+s}{2} = 5$
    (2) $r + s = 10$

3. If n is an integer, then n is divisible by how many positive integers?

    (1) n is the product of two different prime numbers.
    (2) n and 2^3 are each divisible by the same number of positive integers.

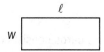

4. If ℓ and w represent the length and width, respectively, of the rectangle above, what is the perimeter?

    (1) $2\ell + w = 40$
    (2) $\ell + w = 25$

5. A retailer purchased a television set for x percent less than its list price, and then sold it for y percent less than its list price. What was the list price of the television set?

    (1) $x = 15$
    (2) $x - y = 5$

6. If Ann saves x dollars each week and Beth saves y dollars each week, what is the total amount that they save per week?

    (1) Beth saves $5 more per week than Ann saves per week.
    (2) It takes Ann 6 weeks to save the same amount that Beth saves in 5 weeks.

7. A certain dealership has a number of cars to be sold by its salespeople. How many cars are to be sold?

    (1) If each of the salespeople sells 4 of the cars, 23 cars will remain unsold.
    (2) If each of the salespeople sells 6 of the cars, 5 cars will remain unsold.

8. Committee member W wants to schedule a one-hour meeting on Thursday for himself and three other committee members, X, Y, and Z. Is there a one-hour period on Thursday that is open for all four members?

    (1) On Thursday W and X have an open period from 9:00 a.m. to 12:00 noon.
    (2) On Thursday Y has an open period from 10:00 a.m. to 1:00 p.m. and Z has an open period from 8:00 a.m. to 11:00 a.m.

9. Some computers at a certain company are Brand X and the rest are Brand Y. If the ratio of the number of Brand Y computers to the number of Brand X computers at the company is 5 to 6, how many of the computers are Brand Y?

    (1) There are 80 more Brand X computers than Brand Y computers at the company.
    (2) There is a total of 880 computers at the company.

10. Of the 230 single-family homes built in City X last year, how many were occupied at the end of the year?

    (1) Of all single-family homes in City X, 90 percent were occupied at the end of last year.
    (2) A total of 7,200 single-family homes in City X were occupied at the end of last year.

11. If J, S, and V are points on the number line, what is the distance between S and V?

    (1) The distance between J and S is 20.
    (2) The distance between J and V is 25.

12. What were the gross revenues from ticket sales for a certain film during the second week in which it was shown?

    (1) Gross revenues during the second week were $1.5 million less than during the first week.
    (2) Gross revenues during the third week were $2.0 million less than during the first week.

13. The total cost of an office dinner was shared equally by k of the n employees who attended the dinner. What was the total cost of the dinner?

   (1) Each of the k employees who shared the cost of the dinner paid $19.
   (2) If the total cost of the dinner had been shared equally by $k+1$ of the n employees who attended the dinner, each of the $k+1$ employees would have paid $18.

14. For a recent play performance, the ticket prices were $25 per adult and $15 per child. A total of 500 tickets were sold for the performance. How many of the tickets sold were for adults?

   (1) Revenue from ticket sales for this performance totaled $10,500.
   (2) The average (arithmetic mean) price per ticket sold was $21.

15. What is the value of x ?

   (1) $x+1=2-3x$
   (2) $\dfrac{1}{2x}=2$

16. If x and y are positive integers, what is the remainder when $10^x + y$ is divided by 3 ?

   (1) $x=5$
   (2) $y=2$

17. What was the amount of money donated to a certain charity?

   (1) Of the amount donated, 40 percent came from corporate donations.
   (2) Of the amount donated, $1.5 million came from noncorporate donations.

18. What is the value of the positive integer n ?

   (1) $n^4 < 25$
   (2) $n \neq n^2$

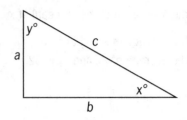

19. In the triangle above, does $a^2 + b^2 = c^2$?

   (1) $x+y=90$
   (2) $x=y$

20. If x, y, and z are three integers, are they consecutive integers?

   (1) $z-x=2$
   (2) $x<y<z$

21. A collection of 36 cards consists of 4 sets of 9 cards each. The 9 cards in each set are numbered 1 through 9. If one card has been removed from the collection, what is the number on that card?

   (1) The units digit of the sum of the numbers on the remaining 35 cards is 6.
   (2) The sum of the numbers on the remaining 35 cards is 176.

22. In the xy-plane, point (r,s) lies on a circle with center at the origin. What is the value of $r^2 + s^2$?

   (1) The circle has radius 2.
   (2) The point $\left(\sqrt{2},-\sqrt{2}\right)$ lies on the circle.

23. What is the value of x ?

   (1) $-(x+y)=x-y$
   (2) $x+y=2$

24. If r, s, and t are nonzero integers, is $r^5 s^3 t^4$ negative?

   (1) rt is negative.
   (2) s is negative.

25. If x and y are integers, what is the value of y ?

   (1) $xy=27$
   (2) $x=y^2$

26. How many newspapers were sold at a certain newsstand today?

    (1) A total of 100 newspapers were sold at the newsstand yesterday, 10 fewer than twice the number sold today.
    (2) The number of newspapers sold at the newsstand yesterday was 45 more than the number sold today.

27. What is Ricky's age now?

    (1) Ricky is now twice as old as he was exactly 8 years ago.
    (2) Ricky's sister Teresa is now 3 times as old as Ricky was exactly 8 years ago.

28. If both x and y are nonzero numbers, what is the value of $\frac{y}{x}$?

    (1) $x = 6$
    (2) $y^2 = x^2$

29. John took a test that had 60 questions numbered from 1 to 60. How many of the questions did he answer correctly?

    (1) The number of questions he answered correctly in the first half of the test was 7 more than the number he answered correctly in the second half of the test.
    (2) He answered $\frac{5}{6}$ of the odd-numbered questions correctly and $\frac{4}{5}$ of the even-numbered questions correctly.

30. If $x = 0.rstu$, where r, s, t, and u each represent a nonzero digit of x, what is the value of x?

    (1) $r = 3s = 2t = 6u$
    (2) The product of r and u is equal to the product of s and t.

31. If x is a positive integer, is $\sqrt{x}$ an integer?

    (1) $\sqrt{4x}$ is an integer.
    (2) $\sqrt{3x}$ is not an integer.

32. Is the value of n closer to 50 than to 75?

    (1) $75 - n > n - 50$
    (2) $n > 60$

33. Last year, if Elena spent a total of $720 on newspapers, magazines, and books, what amount did she spend on newspapers?

    (1) Last year, the amount that Elena spent on magazines was 80 percent of the amount that she spent on books.
    (2) Last year, the amount that Elena spent on newspapers was 60 percent of the total amount that she spent on magazines and books.

34. If p, q, x, y, and z are different positive integers, which of the five integers is the median?

    (1) $p + x < q$
    (2) $y < z$

35. If $w + z = 28$, what is the value of wz?

    (1) w and z are positive integers.
    (2) w and z are consecutive odd integers.

36. Elena receives a salary plus a commission that is equal to a fixed percentage of her sales revenue. What was the total of Elena's salary and commission last month?

    (1) Elena's monthly salary is $1,000.
    (2) Elena's commission is 5 percent of her sales revenue.

37. What is the value of $a - b$?

    (1) $a = b + 4$
    (2) $(a - b)^2 = 16$

38. Machine X runs at a constant rate and produces a lot consisting of 100 cans in 2 hours. How much less time would it take to produce the lot of cans if both Machines X and Y were run simultaneously?

    (1) Both Machines X and Y produce the same number of cans per hour.
    (2) It takes Machine X twice as long to produce the lot of cans as it takes Machines X and Y running simultaneously to produce the lot.

39. Can the positive integer p be expressed as the product of two integers, each of which is greater than 1?

    (1) $31 < p < 37$
    (2) p is odd.

40. Is $x < y$?

    (1) $z < y$
    (2) $z < x$

41. If S is a set of four numbers w, x, y, and z, is the range of the numbers in S greater than 2 ?

    (1) $w - z > 2$
    (2) z is the least number in S.

42. If y is greater than 110 percent of x, is y greater than 75 ?

    (1) $x > 75$
    (2) $y - x = 10$

43. What is the area of rectangular region R ?

    (1) Each diagonal of R has length 5.
    (2) The perimeter of R is 14.

44. If Q is an integer between 10 and 100, what is the value of Q ?

    (1) One of Q's digits is 3 more than the other, and the sum of its digits is 9.
    (2) $Q < 50$

45. If p and q are positive integers and $pq = 24$, what is the value of p ?

    (1) $\frac{q}{6}$ is an integer.
    (2) $\frac{p}{2}$ is an integer.

46. What is the value of $x^2 - y^2$?

    (1) $x - y = y + 2$
    (2) $x - y = \frac{1}{x + y}$

47. Hoses X and Y simultaneously fill an empty swimming pool that has a capacity of 50,000 liters. If the flow in each hose is independent of the flow in the other hose, how many hours will it take to fill the pool?

    (1) Hose X alone would take 28 hours to fill the pool.
    (2) Hose Y alone would take 36 hours to fill the pool.

48. If $abc \neq 0$, is $\dfrac{\frac{a}{b}}{c} = \dfrac{a}{\frac{b}{c}}$?

    (1) $a = 1$
    (2) $c = 1$

49. How many integers n are there such that $r < n < s$?

    (1) $s - r = 5$
    (2) r and s are not integers.

50. If the total price of n equally priced shares of a certain stock was $12,000, what was the price per share of the stock?

    (1) If the price per share of the stock had been $1 more, the total price of the n shares would have been $300 more.
    (2) If the price per share of the stock had been $2 less, the total price of the n shares would have been 5 percent less.

51. If n is positive, is $\sqrt{n} > 100$?

    (1) $\sqrt{n-1} > 99$
    (2) $\sqrt{n+1} > 101$

52. Is $xy > 5$?

    (1) $1 \le x \le 3$ and $2 \le y \le 4$.
    (2) $x + y = 5$

53. In Year X, 8.7 percent of the men in the labor force were unemployed in June compared with 8.4 percent in May. If the number of men in the labor force was the same for both months, how many men were unemployed in June of that year?

    (1) In May of Year X, the number of unemployed men in the labor force was 3.36 million.
    (2) In Year X, 120,000 more men in the labor force were unemployed in June than in May.

54. If $x \neq 0$, what is the value of $\left(\dfrac{x^p}{x^q}\right)^4$?

    (1) $p = q$
    (2) $x = 3$

55. On Monday morning a certain machine ran continuously at a uniform rate to fill a production order. At what time did it completely fill the order that morning?

    (1) The machine began filling the order at 9:30 a.m.

    (2) The machine had filled $\frac{1}{2}$ of the order by 10:30 a.m. and $\frac{5}{6}$ of the order by 11:10 a.m.

56. If $xy < 3$, is $x < 1$?

    (1) $y > 3$
    (2) $x < 3$

57. If $\frac{m}{n} = \frac{5}{3}$, what is the value of $m + n$?

    (1) $m > 0$
    (2) $2m + n = 26$

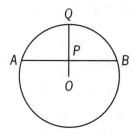

58. What is the radius of the circle above with center O?

    (1) The ratio of OP to PQ is 1 to 2.
    (2) P is the midpoint of chord AB.

59. What is the number of 360-degree rotations that a bicycle wheel made while rolling 100 meters in a straight line without slipping?

    (1) The diameter of the bicycle wheel, including the tire, was 0.5 meter.

    (2) The wheel made twenty 360-degree rotations per minute.

60. The perimeter of a rectangular garden is 360 feet. What is the length of the garden?

    (1) The length of the garden is twice the width.
    (2) The difference between the length and width of the garden is 60 feet.

61. If $2x(5n) = t$, what is the value of t?

    (1) $x = n + 3$
    (2) $2x = 32$

62. In the equation $x^2 + bx + 12 = 0$, x is a variable and b is a constant. What is the value of b?

    (1) $x - 3$ is a factor of $x^2 + bx + 12$.
    (2) 4 is a root of the equation $x^2 + bx + 12 = 0$.

63. A Town T has 20,000 residents, 60 percent of whom are female. What percent of the residents were born in Town T?

    (1) The number of female residents who were born in Town T is twice the number of male residents who were <u>not</u> born in Town T.

    (2) The number of female residents who were <u>not</u> born in Town T is twice the number of female residents who were born in Town T.

64. If y is an integer, is y^3 divisible by 9?

    (1) y is divisible by 4.
    (2) y is divisible by 6.

65. In $\triangle XYZ$, what is the length of YZ?

    (1) The length of XY is 3.
    (2) The length of XZ is 5.

66. If the average (arithmetic mean) of n consecutive odd integers is 10, what is the least of the integers?

    (1) The range of the n integers is 14.
    (2) The greatest of the n integers is 17.

67. What was the ratio of the number of cars to the number of trucks produced by Company X last year?

    (1) Last year, if the number of cars produced by Company X had been 8 percent greater, the number of cars produced would have been 150 percent of the number of trucks produced by Company X.

    (2) Last year Company X produced 565,000 cars and 406,800 trucks.

68. Is $xy < 6$?

    (1) $x < 3$ and $y < 2$.
    (2) $\frac{1}{2} < x < \frac{2}{3}$ and $y^2 < 64$.

69. If x, y, and z are positive numbers, is $x > y > z$?

    (1) $xz > yz$
    (2) $yx > yz$

70. K is a set of numbers such that

    (i)   if x is in K, then $-x$ is in K, and
    (ii) if each of x and y is in K, then xy is in K.

    Is 12 in K ?

    (1) 2 is in K.
    (2) 3 is in K.

71. How long did it take Betty to drive nonstop on a trip from her home to Denver, Colorado?

    (1) If Betty's average speed for the trip had been $1\frac{1}{2}$ times as fast, the trip would have taken 2 hours.
    (2) Betty's average speed for the trip was 50 miles per hour.

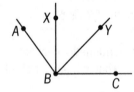

72. In the figure above, what is the measure of $\angle ABC$?

    (1) BX bisects $\angle ABY$ and BY bisects $\angle XBC$.
    (2) The measure of $\angle ABX$ is 40°.

73. If $x^2 + y^2 = 29$, what is the value of $(x - y)^2$?

    (1) $xy = 10$
    (2) $x = 5$

74. If x, y, and z are numbers, is $z = 18$?

    (1) The average (arithmetic mean) of x, y, and z is 6.
    (2) $x = -y$

75. After winning 50 percent of the first 20 games it played, Team A won all of the remaining games it played. What was the total number of games that Team A won?

    (1) Team A played 25 games altogether.
    (2) Team A won 60 percent of all the games it played.

76. Is x between 0 and 1 ?

    (1) x^2 is less than x.
    (2) x^3 is positive.

77. A jar contains 30 marbles, of which 20 are red and 10 are blue. If 9 of the marbles are removed, how many of the marbles left in the jar are red?

    (1) Of the marbles removed, the ratio of the number of red ones to the number of blue ones is 2:1.
    (2) Of the first 6 marbles removed, 4 are red.

78. Is p^2 an odd integer?

    (1) p is an odd integer.
    (2) $\sqrt{p}$ is an odd integer.

79. If m and n are nonzero integers, is m^n an integer?

    (1) n^m is positive.
    (2) n^m is an integer.

80. What is the value of xy ?

    (1) $x + y = 10$
    (2) $x - y = 6$

81. Is x^2 greater than x ?

    (1) x^2 is greater than 1.
    (2) x is greater than -1.

82. Michael arranged all his books in a bookcase with 10 books on each shelf and no books left over. After Michael acquired 10 additional books, he arranged all his books in a new bookcase with 12 books on each shelf and no books left over. How many books did Michael have before he acquired the 10 additional books?

    (1) Before Michael acquired the 10 additional books, he had fewer than 96 books.
    (2) Before Michael acquired the 10 additional books, he had more than 24 books.

83. If $xy > 0$, does $(x - 1)(y - 1) = 1$?

    (1) $x + y = xy$
    (2) $x = y$

84. The only contents of a parcel are 25 photographs and 30 negatives. What is the total weight, in ounces, of the parcel's contents?

    (1) The weight of each photograph is 3 times the weight of each negative.
    (2) The total weight of 1 of the photographs and 2 of the negatives is $\frac{1}{3}$ ounce.

85. Last year in a group of 30 businesses, 21 reported a net profit and 15 had investments in foreign markets. How many of the businesses did not report a net profit nor invest in foreign markets last year?

    (1) Last year 12 of the 30 businesses reported a net profit and had investments in foreign markets.
    (2) Last year 24 of the 30 businesses reported a net profit or invested in foreign markets, or both.

86. If m and n are consecutive positive integers, is m greater than n?

    (1) $m-1$ and $n+1$ are consecutive positive integers.
    (2) m is an even integer.

87. If k and n are integers, is n divisible by 7?

    (1) $n-3=2k$
    (2) $2k-4$ is divisible by 7.

88. Is the perimeter of square S greater than the perimeter of equilateral triangle T?

    (1) The ratio of the length of a side of S to the length of a side of T is 4:5.
    (2) The sum of the lengths of a side of S and a side of T is 18.

89. If $x+y+z>0$, is $z>1$?

    (1) $z>x+y+1$
    (2) $x+y+1<0$

90. Can the positive integer n be written as the sum of two different positive prime numbers?

    (1) n is greater than 3.
    (2) n is odd.

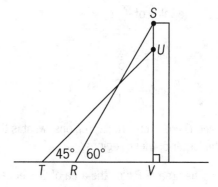

91. In the figure above, segments RS and TU represent two positions of the same ladder leaning against the side SV of a wall. The length of TV is how much greater than the length of RV?

    (1) The length of TU is 10 meters.
    (2) The length of RV is 5 meters.

92. Is the integer x divisible by 36?

    (1) x is divisible by 12.
    (2) x is divisible by 9.

Cancellation Fees	
Days Prior to Departure	Percent of Package Price
46 or more	10%
45–31	35%
30–16	50%
15–5	65%
4 or fewer	100%

93. The table above shows the cancellation fee schedule that a travel agency uses to determine the fee charged to a tourist who cancels a trip prior to departure. If a tourist canceled a trip with a package price of $1,700 and a departure date of September 4, on what day was the trip canceled?

    (1) The cancellation fee was $595.
    (2) If the trip had been canceled one day later, the cancellation fee would have been $255 more.

94. What is the value of $\dfrac{x}{yz}$?

    (1) $x = \dfrac{y}{2}$ and $z = \dfrac{2x}{5}$.

    (2) $\dfrac{x}{z} = \dfrac{5}{2}$ and $\dfrac{1}{y} = \dfrac{1}{10}$.

95. If P and Q are each circular regions, what is the radius of the larger of these regions?

    (1)   The area of P plus the area of Q is equal to 90π.

    (2)   The larger circular region has a radius that is 3 times the radius of the smaller circular region.

96. For all z, $\lceil z \rceil$ denotes the least integer greater than or equal to z. Is $\lceil x \rceil = 0$?

    (1) $-1 < x < -0.1$

    (2) $\lceil x + 0.5 \rceil = 1$

97. If Aaron, Lee, and Tony have a total of $36, how much money does Tony have?

    (1)   Tony has twice as much money as Lee and $\dfrac{1}{3}$ as much as Aaron.

    (2)   The sum of the amounts of money that Tony and Lee have is half the amount that Aaron has.

98. Is z less than 0 ?

    (1) $xy > 0$ and $yz < 0$.

    (2) $x > 0$

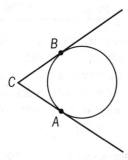

99. The circular base of an above-ground swimming pool lies in a level yard and just touches two straight sides of a fence at points A and B, as shown in the figure above. Point C is on the ground where the two sides of the fence meet. How far from the center of the pool's base is point A ?

    (1)   The base has area 250 square feet.

    (2)   The center of the base is 20 feet from point C.

100. If $xy = -6$, what is the value of $xy(x+y)$?

    (1) $x - y = 5$

    (2) $xy^2 = 18$

101. If the average (arithmetic mean) of 4 numbers is 50, how many of the numbers are greater than 50 ?

    (1)   None of the four numbers is equal to 50.

    (2)   Two of the numbers are equal to 25.

102. $[y]$ denotes the greatest integer less than or equal to y. Is $d < 1$?

    (1) $d = y - [y]$

    (2) $[d] = 0$

103. If x is a positive number less than 10, is z greater than the average (arithmetic mean) of x and 10 ?

    (1)   On the number line, z is closer to 10 than it is to x.

    (2) $z = 5x$

104. If m is a positive integer, then m^3 has how many digits?

    (1) m has 3 digits.

    (2) m^2 has 5 digits.

105. If $t \neq 0$, is r greater than zero?

    (1) $rt = 12$

    (2) $r + t = 7$

106. If $kmn \neq 0$, is $\dfrac{x}{m}(m^2 + n^2 + k^2) = xm + yn + zk$?

    (1) $\dfrac{z}{k} = \dfrac{x}{m}$

    (2) $\dfrac{x}{m} = \dfrac{y}{n}$

107. The sequence $s_1, s_2, s_3, \ldots, s_n, \ldots$ is such that $s_n = \dfrac{1}{n} - \dfrac{1}{n+1}$ for all integers $n \geq 1$. If k is a positive integer, is the sum of the first k terms of the sequence greater than $\dfrac{9}{10}$?

    (1) $k > 10$

    (2) $k < 19$

108. A bookstore that sells used books sells each of its paperback books for a certain price and each of its hardcover books for a certain price. If Joe, Maria, and Paul bought books in this store, how much did Maria pay for 1 paperback book and 1 hardcover book?

    (1) Joe bought 2 paperback books and 3 hardcover books for $12.50.
    (2) Paul bought 4 paperback books and 6 hardcover books for $25.00.

109. If x, y, and z are positive, is $x = \dfrac{y}{z^2}$?

    (1) $z = \dfrac{y}{xz}$
    (2) $z = \sqrt{\dfrac{y}{x}}$

110. If n is an integer between 2 and 100 and if n is also the square of an integer, what is the value of n ?

    (1) n is even.
    (2) The cube root of n is an integer.

111. In the sequence S of numbers, each term after the first two terms is the sum of the two immediately preceding terms. What is the 5th term of S ?

    (1) The 6th term of S minus the 4th term equals 5.
    (2) The 6th term of S plus the 7th term equals 21.

112. For a certain set of n numbers, where $n > 1$, is the average (arithmetic mean) equal to the median?

    (1) If the n numbers in the set are listed in increasing order, then the difference between any pair of successive numbers in the set is 2.
    (2) The range of the n numbers in the set is $2(n-1)$.

113. If d is a positive integer, is $\sqrt{d}$ an integer?

    (1) d is the square of an integer.
    (2) $\sqrt{d}$ is the square of an integer.

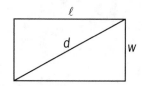

114. What is the area of the rectangular region above?

    (1) $\ell + w = 6$
    (2) $d^2 = 20$

115. Is the positive integer n a multiple of 24 ?

    (1) n is a multiple of 4.
    (2) n is a multiple of 6.

116. If 75 percent of the guests at a certain banquet ordered dessert, what percent of the guests ordered coffee?

    (1) 60 percent of the guests who ordered dessert also ordered coffee.
    (2) 90 percent of the guests who ordered coffee also ordered dessert.

117. A tank containing water started to leak. Did the tank contain more than 30 gallons of water when it started to leak? (Note: 1 gallon = 128 ounces)

    (1) The water leaked from the tank at a constant rate of 6.4 ounces per minute.
    (2) The tank became empty less than 12 hours after it started to leak.

118. If x is an integer, is y an integer?

    (1) The average (arithmetic mean) of x, y, and $y - 2$ is x.
    (2) The average (arithmetic mean) of x and y is **not** an integer.

119. In the fraction $\dfrac{x}{y}$, where x and y are positive integers, what is the value of y ?

    (1) The least common denominator of $\dfrac{x}{y}$ and $\dfrac{1}{3}$ is 6.
    (2) $x = 1$

120. Is $\dfrac{1}{a-b} < b - a$?

    (1) $a < b$
    (2) $1 < |a - b|$

121. If x and y are nonzero integers, is $x^y < y^x$?

    (1) $x = y^2$
    (2) $y > 2$

122. If 2 different representatives are to be selected at random from a group of 10 employees and if p is the probability that both representatives selected will be women, is $p > \frac{1}{2}$?

    (1) More than $\frac{1}{2}$ of the 10 employees are women.

    (2) The probability that both representatives selected will be men is less than $\frac{1}{10}$.

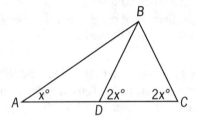

123. In triangle *ABC* above, what is the length of side *BC* ?

    (1) Line segment *AD* has length 6.
    (2) $x = 36$

124. If $rs \neq 0$, is $\frac{1}{r} + \frac{1}{s} = 4$?

    (1) $r + s = 4rs$
    (2) $r = s$

5.4 Answer Key

1.	C	32.	A	63.	C	94.	B
2.	D	33.	B	64.	B	95.	C
3.	D	34.	E	65.	E	96.	A
4.	B	35.	B	66.	D	97.	A
5.	E	36.	E	67.	D	98.	C
6.	C	37.	A	68.	B	99.	A
7.	C	38.	D	69.	E	100.	B
8.	C	39.	A	70.	C	101.	E
9.	D	40.	E	71.	A	102.	D
10.	E	41.	A	72.	C	103.	A
11.	E	42.	A	73.	A	104.	E
12.	E	43.	C	74.	C	105.	C
13.	C	44.	C	75.	D	106.	C
14.	D	45.	E	76.	A	107.	A
15.	D	46.	B	77.	A	108.	E
16.	B	47.	C	78.	D	109.	D
17.	C	48.	B	79.	E	110.	B
18.	C	49.	C	80.	C	111.	A
19.	A	50.	D	81.	A	112.	A
20.	C	51.	B	82.	A	113.	D
21.	D	52.	E	83.	A	114.	C
22.	D	53.	D	84.	C	115.	E
23.	A	54.	A	85.	D	116.	C
24.	E	55.	B	86.	A	117.	E
25.	C	56.	A	87.	C	118.	A
26.	A	57.	B	88.	A	119.	E
27.	A	58.	E	89.	B	120.	A
28.	E	59.	A	90.	E	121.	C
29.	B	60.	D	91.	D	122.	E
30.	A	61.	C	92.	C	123.	A
31.	A	62.	D	93.	C	124.	A

5.5 Answer Explanations

The following discussion of data sufficiency is intended to familiarize you with the most efficient and effective approaches to the kinds of problems common to data sufficiency. The particular questions in this chapter are generally representative of the kinds of data sufficiency questions you will encounter on the GMAT. Remember that it is the problem solving strategy that is important, not the specific details of a particular question.

1. What is the average (arithmetic mean) of x and y ?

    (1)   The average of x and 2y is 10.
    (2)   The average of 2x and 7y is 32.

    Algebra Statistics

    The average of x and y is $\dfrac{x+y}{2}$, which can be determined if and only if the value of $x + y$ can be determined.

    (1)   It is given that the average of x and $2y$ is 10. Therefore, $\dfrac{x+2y}{2} = 10$, or $x + 2y = 20$. Because the value of $x + y$ is desired, rewrite the last equation as $(x+y)+y = 20$, or $x + y = 20 - y$. This shows that the value of $x + y$ can vary. For example, if $x = 20$ and $y = 0$, then $x + 2y = 20$ and $x + y = 20$. However, if $x = 18$ and $y = 1$, then $x + 2y = 20$ and $x + y = 19$; NOT sufficient.

    (2)   It is given that the average of $2x$ and $7y$ is 32. Therefore, $\dfrac{2x+7y}{2} = 32$, or $2x + 7y = 64$. Because the value of $x + y$ is desired, rewrite the last equation as $2(x+y)+5y = 64$, or $x + y = \dfrac{64-5y}{2}$. This shows that the value of $x + y$ can vary. For example, if $x = 32$ and $y = 0$, then $2x + 7y = 64$ and $x + y = 32$. However, if $x = 4$ and $y = 8$, then $2x + 7y = 64$ and $x + y = 12$; NOT sufficient.

    Given (1) and (2), it follows that $x + 2y = 20$ and $2x + 7y = 64$. These two equations can be solved simultaneously to obtain the individual values of x and y, which can then be used to determine the average of x and y. From $x + 2y = 20$ it follows that $x = 20 - 2y$. Substituting $20 - 2y$ for x in $2x + 7y = 64$ gives $2(20-2y)+7y = 64$, or $40 - 4y + 7y = 64$, or $3y = 24$, or $y = 8$. Thus, using $x = 20 - 2y$, the value of x is $20 - 2(8) = 4$. Alternatively, it can be seen that unique values for x and y are determined from (1) and (2) by the fact that the equations $x + 2y = 20$ and $2x + 7y = 64$ represent two nonparallel lines in the standard (x,y) coordinate plane, which have a unique point in common.

    The correct answer is C; both statements together are sufficient.

2. What is the value of $\dfrac{r}{2} + \dfrac{s}{2}$?

    (1) $\dfrac{r+s}{2} = 5$

    (2) $r + s = 10$

    Arithmetic Operations with rational numbers

    Since $\dfrac{r}{2} + \dfrac{s}{2} = \dfrac{r+s}{2} = \dfrac{1}{2}(r+s)$, the value of $\dfrac{r}{2} + \dfrac{s}{2}$ can be determined exactly when either the value of $\dfrac{r+s}{2}$ can be determined or the value of $r + s$ can be determined.

    (1)   It is given that $\dfrac{r+s}{2} = 5$. Therefore, $\dfrac{r}{2} + \dfrac{s}{2} = 5$; SUFFICIENT.

    (2)   It is given that $r + s = 10$. Therefore, $\dfrac{r}{2} + \dfrac{s}{2} = \dfrac{1}{2}(r+s) = \dfrac{1}{2}(10) = 5$; SUFFICIENT.

    The correct answer is D; each statement alone is sufficient.

3. If n is an integer, then n is divisible by how many positive integers?

   (1) n is the product of two different prime numbers.
   (2) n and 2^3 are each divisible by the same number of positive integers.

   Arithmetic Properties of numbers

   (1) $n = pq$, where both p and q are prime numbers and $p \neq q$. Thus, n is divisible by the positive integers 1, p, q, pq, and no others; SUFFICIENT.
   (2) Given $2^3 = 8$, the number of positive divisors of 8 (and thus of n) can be determined; SUFFICIENT.

   **The correct answer is D;
   each statement alone is sufficient.**

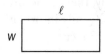

4. If ℓ and w represent the length and width, respectively, of the rectangle above, what is the perimeter?

   (1) $2\ell + w = 40$
   (2) $\ell + w = 25$

   Geometry Perimeter

   The perimeter of the rectangle is $2(\ell + w)$, which can be determined exactly when the value of $\ell + w$ can be determined.

   (1) It is given that $2\ell + w = 40$. Therefore, $(2\ell + w) - \ell = 40 - \ell$, or $\ell + w = 40 - \ell$.

   Therefore, different values of $\ell + w$ can be obtained by choosing different values of ℓ. For example, if $\ell = 10$ and $w = 40 - 2\ell = 20$, then $\ell + w = 30$. However, if $\ell = 15$ and $w = 40 - 2\ell = 10$, then $\ell + w = 25$; NOT sufficient.

   (2) It is given that $\ell + w = 25$; SUFFICIENT.

   **The correct answer is B;
   statement 2 alone is sufficient.**

5. A retailer purchased a television set for x percent less than its list price, and then sold it for y percent less than its list price. What was the list price of the television set?

   (1) $x = 15$
   (2) $x - y = 5$

   Arithmetic Percents

   (1) This provides information only about the value of x. The list price cannot be determined using x because no dollar value for the purchase price is given; NOT sufficient.
   (2) This provides information about the relationship between x and y but does not provide dollar values for either of these variables; NOT sufficient.

   The list price cannot be determined without a dollar value for either the retailer's purchase price or the retailer's selling price. Even though the values for x and y are given or can be determined, taking (1) and (2) together provides no dollar value for either.

   **The correct answer is E;
   both statements together are still not sufficient.**

6. If Ann saves x dollars each week and Beth saves y dollars each week, what is the total amount that they save per week?

   (1) Beth saves $5 more per week than Ann saves per week.
   (2) It takes Ann 6 weeks to save the same amount that Beth saves in 5 weeks.

   Algebra Simultaneous equations

   Determine the value of $x + y$.

   (1) It is given that $y = 5 + x$. Therefore, $x + y = x + (5 + x) = 2x + 5$, which can vary in value. For example, if $x = 5$ and $y = 10$, then $y = 5 + x$ and $x + y = 15$. However, if $x = 10$ and $y = 15$, then $y = 5 + x$ and $x + y = 25$; NOT sufficient.

(2)　It is given that $6x = 5y$, or $y = \frac{6}{5}x$.

Therefore, $x + y = x + \frac{6}{5}x = \frac{11}{5}x$, which can vary in value. For example, if $x = 5$ and $y = 6$, then $y = \frac{6}{5}x$ and $x + y = 11$. However, if $x = 10$ and $y = 12$, then $y = \frac{6}{5}x$ and $x + y = 22$; NOT sufficient.

Given (1) and (2), it follows that $y = 5 + x$ and $y = \frac{6}{5}x$. These two equations can be solved simultaneously to obtain the individual values of x and y, which can then be used to determine $x + y$. Equating the two expressions for y gives $5 + x = \frac{6}{5}x$, or $25 + 5x = 6x$, or $25 = x$. Therefore, $y = 5 + 25 = 30$ and $x + y = 55$.

**The correct answer is C;
both statements together are sufficient.**

7.　A certain dealership has a number of cars to be sold by its salespeople. How many cars are to be sold?

(1)　If each of the salespeople sells 4 of the cars, 23 cars will remain unsold.

(2)　If each of the salespeople sells 6 of the cars, 5 cars will remain unsold.

Algebra Simultaneous equations

Let T be the total number of cars to be sold and S be the number of salespeople. Determine the value of T.

(1)　Given that $T = 4S + 23$, it follows that the positive integer value of T can vary, since the positive integer value of S cannot be determined; NOT sufficient.

(2)　Given that $T = 6S + 5$, it follows that the positive integer value of T can vary, since the positive integer value of S cannot be determined; NOT sufficient.

(1) and (2) together give a system of two equations in two unknowns. Equating the two expressions for T gives $4S + 23 = 6S + 5$, or $18 = 2S$, or $S = 9$. From this the value of T can be determined by $4(9) + 23$ or $6(9) + 5$.

**The correct answer is C;
both statements together are sufficient.**

8.　Committee member W wants to schedule a one-hour meeting on Thursday for himself and three other committee members, X, Y, and Z. Is there a one-hour period on Thursday that is open for all four members?

(1)　On Thursday W and X have an open period from 9:00 a.m. to 12:00 noon.

(2)　On Thursday Y has an open period from 10:00 a.m. to 1:00 p.m. and Z has an open period from 8:00 a.m. to 11:00 a.m.

Arithmetic Sets

(1)　There is no information about Y and Z, only information about W and X; NOT sufficient.

(2)　Similarly, there is no information about W and X, only information about Y and Z; NOT sufficient.

Together, (1) and (2) detail information about all four committee members, and it can be determined that on Thursday all four members have an open one-hour period from 10:00 a.m. to 11:00 a.m.

**The correct answer is C;
both statements together are sufficient.**

9.　Some computers at a certain company are Brand X and the rest are Brand Y. If the ratio of the number of Brand Y computers to the number of Brand X computers at the company is 5 to 6, how many of the computers are Brand Y?

(1)　There are 80 more Brand X computers than Brand Y computers at the company.

(2)　There is a total of 880 computers at the company.

Algebra Simultaneous equations

Let x and y be the numbers of Brand X computers and Brand Y computers, respectively, at the company. Then $\frac{y}{x} = \frac{5}{6}$, or after cross multiplying, $6y = 5x$. Determine the value of y.

(1) Given that $x = 80 + y$, it follows that $5x = 5(80 + y) = 400 + 5y$. Substituting $6y$ for $5x$ on the left side of the last equation gives $6y = 400 + 5y$, or $y = 400$. Alternatively, it can be seen that unique values for x and y are determined by the fact that $6y = 5x$ and $x = 80 + y$ represent the equations of two nonparallel lines in the standard (x,y) coordinate plane, which have a unique point in common; SUFFICIENT.

(2) Given that $x + y = 880$, it follows that $5x + 5y = 5(880)$. Substituting $6y$ for $5x$ on the left side of the last equation gives $6y + 5y = 5(880)$, or $11y = 5(880)$, or $y = 5(80) = 400$. Alternatively, it can be seen that unique values for x and y are determined by the fact that $6y = 5x$ and $x + y = 880$ represent the equations of two nonparallel lines in the standard (x,y) coordinate plane, which have a unique point in common; SUFFICIENT.

The correct answer is D; each statement alone is sufficient.

10. Of the 230 single-family homes built in City X last year, how many were occupied at the end of the year?

    (1) Of all single-family homes in City X, 90 percent were occupied at the end of last year.
    (2) A total of 7,200 single-family homes in City X were occupied at the end of last year.

Arithmetic Percents

(1) The percentage of the occupied single-family homes that were *built* last year is not given, and so the number occupied cannot be found; NOT sufficient.

(2) Again, there is no information about the occupancy of the single-family homes that were *built* last year; NOT sufficient.

Together (1) and (2) yield only the total number of the single-family homes that were occupied. Neither statement offers the needed information as to how many of the single-family homes *built* last year were occupied at the end of last year.

The correct answer is E; both statements together are still not sufficient.

11. If J, S, and V are points on the number line, what is the distance between S and V?

    (1) The distance between J and S is 20.
    (2) The distance between J and V is 25.

Arithmetic Properties of numbers

(1) Since no restriction is placed on the location of V, the distance between S and V could be any positive real number; NOT sufficient.

(2) Since no restriction is placed on the location of S, the distance between S and V could be any positive real number; NOT sufficient.

Given (1) and (2) together, it follows that $JS = 20$ and $JV = 25$. However, V could be on the left side of S or V could be on the right side of S. For example, suppose J is located at 0 and S is located at 20. If V were on the left side of S, then V would be located at -25, and thus SV would be $25 + 20 = 45$, as shown below.

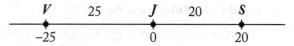

However, if V were on the right side of S, then V would be located at 25, and thus SV would be $25 - 20 = 5$, as shown below.

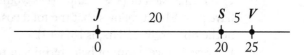

The correct answer is E; both statements together are still not sufficient.

12. What were the gross revenues from ticket sales for a certain film during the second week in which it was shown?

    (1) Gross revenues during the second week were $1.5 million less than during the first week.
    (2) Gross revenues during the third week were $2.0 million less than during the first week.

Arithmetic Arithmetic operations

(1) Since the amount of gross revenues during the first week is not given, the gross revenues during the second week cannot be determined; NOT sufficient.

(2) No information is provided, directly or indirectly, about gross revenues during the second week; NOT sufficient.

With (1) and (2) taken together, additional information, such as the amount of gross revenues during either the first or the third week, is still needed.

**The correct answer is E;
both statements together are still not sufficient.**

13. The total cost of an office dinner was shared equally by *k* of the *n* employees who attended the dinner. What was the total cost of the dinner?

(1) Each of the *k* employees who shared the cost of the dinner paid $19.
(2) If the total cost of the dinner had been shared equally by *k* + 1 of the *n* employees who attended the dinner, each of the *k* + 1 employees would have paid $18.

Algebra Simultaneous equations

(1) Given that each of the *k* employees paid $19, it follows that the total cost of the dinner, in dollars, is 19*k*. However, since *k* cannot be determined, the value of 19*k* cannot be determined; NOT sufficient.

(2) Given that each of $(k+1)$ employees would have paid $18, it follows that the total cost of the dinner, in dollars, is $18(k+1)$. However, since *k* cannot be determined, the value of $18(k+1)$ cannot be determined; NOT sufficient.

Given (1) and (2) together, it follows that $19k = 18(k+1)$, or $19k = 18k + 18$, or $k = 18$. Therefore, the total cost of the dinner is $(\$19)k = (\$19)(18)$.

**The correct answer is C;
both statements together are sufficient.**

14. For a recent play performance, the ticket prices were $25 per adult and $15 per child. A total of 500 tickets were sold for the performance. How many of the tickets sold were for adults?

(1) Revenue from ticket sales for this performance totaled $10,500.
(2) The average (arithmetic mean) price per ticket sold was $21.

Algebra Simultaneous equations

Let *A* and *C* be the numbers of adult and child tickets sold, respectively. Given that $A + C = 500$, or $C = 500 - A$, determine the value of *A*.

(1) Given that $25A + 15C = 10,500$, or $5A + 3C = 2,100$, it follows by substituting $500 - A$ for *C* that $5A + 3(500 - A) = 2,100$, which can be solved to obtain a unique value for *A*. Alternatively, it can be seen that unique values for *A* and *C* are determined by the fact that $A + C = 500$ and $5A + 3C = 2,100$ represent the equations of two nonparallel lines in the standard (x,y) coordinate plane, which have a unique point in common; SUFFICIENT.

(2) It is given that $\frac{25A+15C}{500} = 21$, or $25A + 15C = (21)(500) = 10,500$, which is the same information given in (1). Therefore, *A* can be determined, as shown in (1) above; SUFFICIENT.

**The correct answer is D;
each statement alone is sufficient.**

15. What is the value of *x* ?

(1) $x + 1 = 2 - 3x$
(2) $\frac{1}{2x} = 2$

Algebra First- and second-degree equations

(1) Transposing terms gives the equivalent equation $4x = 1$, or $x = \frac{1}{4}$; SUFFICIENT.

(2) Multiplying both sides by 2*x* gives the equivalent equation $1 = 4x$, or $x = \frac{1}{4}$; SUFFICIENT.

**The correct answer is D;
each statement alone is sufficient.**

16. If x and y are positive integers, what is the remainder when $10^x + y$ is divided by 3 ?

    (1) $x = 5$
    (2) $y = 2$

Arithmetic Properties of numbers

(1)   Given that $x = 5$, then $10^x + y = 100,000 + y$. More than one remainder is possible when $100,000 + y$ is divided by 3. For example, by long division, or by using the fact that $100,000 + y = 99,999 + (1 + y)$ $= 3(33,333) + (1 + y)$, the remainder is 2 when $y = 1$ and the remainder is 0 when $y = 2$; NOT sufficient.

(2)   Given that $y = 2$, then $10^x + y = 10^x + 2$. Since the sum of the digits of $10^x + 2$ is 3, which is divisible by 3, it follows that $10^x + 2$ is divisible by 3, and hence has remainder 0 when divided by 3. This can also be seen by writing $10^x + 2$ as $(10^x - 1 + 1) + 2$ $= (10^x - 1) + 1 + 2 = 999\ldots99,999 + 3$ $= 3(333\ldots33,333 + 1)$, which is divisible by 3; SUFFICIENT.

The correct answer is B; statement 2 alone is sufficient.

17. What was the amount of money donated to a certain charity?

    (1)   Of the amount donated, 40 percent came from corporate donations.
    (2)   Of the amount donated, $1.5 million came from noncorporate donations.

Arithmetic Percents

The statements suggest considering the amount of money donated to be the total of the corporate donations and the noncorporate donations.

(1)   From this, only the portion that represented corporate donations is known, with no means of determining the total amount donated; NOT sufficient.

(2)   From this, only the dollar amount that represented noncorporate donations is known, with no means of determining the portion of the total donations that it represents; NOT sufficient.

Letting x represent the total dollar amount donated, it follows from (1) that the amount donated from corporate sources can be represented as $0.40x$. Combining the information from (1) and (2) yields the equation $0.40x + \$1,500,000 = x$, which can be solved to obtain exactly one solution for x.

The correct answer is C; both statements together are sufficient.

18. What is the value of the positive integer n ?

    (1) $n^4 < 25$
    (2) $n \neq n^2$

Arithmetic Arithmetic operations

(1)   If n is a positive integer and $n^4 < 25$, then n can be either 1 or 2, since $1^4 = 1 \times 1 \times 1 \times 1 = 1$ and $2^4 = 2 \times 2 \times 2 \times 2 = 16$; NOT sufficient.

(2)   Since the only positive integer equal to its square is 1, each positive integer that is not equal to 1 satisfies (2); NOT sufficient.

Using (1) and (2) together, it follows from (1) that $n = 1$ or $n = 2$, and it follows from (2) that $n \neq 1$, and hence the value of n must be 2.

The correct answer is C; both statements together are sufficient.

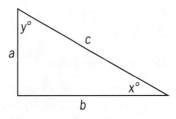

19. In the triangle above, does $a^2 + b^2 = c^2$?

    (1) $x + y = 90$
    (2) $x = y$

Geometry Triangles

The Pythagorean theorem states that $a^2 + b^2 = c^2$ for any right triangle with legs of lengths a and b and hypotenuse of length c. A right triangle is a triangle whose largest angle has measure $90°$. The converse of the Pythagorean theorem also holds: If $a^2 + b^2 = c^2$, then the triangle is a right triangle.

(1) The sum of the degree measures of the three interior angles of a triangle is $180°$. It is given that $x + y = 90$. Thus, the remaining interior angle (not labeled) has degree measure $180° - 90° = 90°$. Therefore, the triangle is a right triangle, and hence it follows from the Pythagorean theorem that $a^2 + b^2 = c^2$; SUFFICIENT.

(2) Given that $x = y$, the triangle could be a right triangle (for example, $x = y = 45$) or fail to be a right triangle (for example, $x = y = 40$), and hence $a^2 + b^2 = c^2$ can be true (this follows from the Pythagorean theorem) or $a^2 + b^2 = c^2$ can be false (this follows from the converse of the Pythagorean theorem); NOT sufficient.

**The correct answer is A;
statement 1 alone is sufficient.**

20. If x, y, and z are three integers, are they consecutive integers?

(1) $z - x = 2$
(2) $x < y < z$

Arithmetic Properties of numbers

(1) Given $z - x = 2$, it is possible to choose y so that x, y, and z are consecutive integers (for example, $x = 1$, $y = 2$, and $z = 3$) and it is possible to choose y so that x, y, and z are not consecutive integers (for example, $x = 1$, $y = 4$, and $z = 3$); NOT sufficient.

(2) Given that $x < y < z$, the three integers can be consecutive (for example, $x = 1$, $y = 2$, and $z = 3$) and the three integers can fail to be consecutive (for example, $x = 1$, $y = 3$, and $z = 4$); NOT sufficient.

Using (1) and (2) together, it follows that y is the unique integer between x and z and hence the three integers are consecutive.

**The correct answer is C;
both statements together are sufficient.**

21. A collection of 36 cards consists of 4 sets of 9 cards each. The 9 cards in each set are numbered 1 through 9. If one card has been removed from the collection, what is the number on that card?

(1) The units digit of the sum of the numbers on the remaining 35 cards is 6.
(2) The sum of the numbers on the remaining 35 cards is 176.

Arithmetic Properties of numbers

The sum $1 + 2 + \ldots + 9$ can be evaluated quickly by several methods. One method is to group the terms as $(1 + 9) + (2 + 8) + (3 + 7) + (4 + 6) + 5$, and therefore the sum is $(4)(10) + 5 = 45$. Thus, the sum of the numbers on all 36 cards is $(4)(45) = 180$.

(1) It is given that the units digit of the sum of the numbers on the remaining 35 cards is 6. Since the sum of the numbers on all 36 cards is 180, the sum of the numbers on the remaining 35 cards must be 179, 178, 177, …, 171, and of these values, only 176 has a units digit of 6. Therefore, the number on the card removed must be $180 - 176 = 4$; SUFFICIENT.

(2) It is given that the sum of the numbers on the remaining 35 cards is 176. Since the sum of the numbers on all 36 cards is 180, it follows that the number on the card removed must be $180 - 176 = 4$; SUFFICIENT.

**The correct answer is D;
each statement alone is sufficient.**

22. In the xy-plane, point (r,s) lies on a circle with center at the origin. What is the value of $r^2 + s^2$?

(1) The circle has radius 2.
(2) The point $\left(\sqrt{2}, -\sqrt{2}\right)$ lies on the circle.

Geometry Simple coordinate geometry

Let R be the radius of the circle. A right triangle with legs of lengths $|r|$ and $|s|$ can be formed so that the line segment with endpoints (r,s) and $(0,0)$ is the hypotenuse. Since the length of the hypotenuse is R, the Pythagorean theorem for this right triangle gives $R^2 = r^2 + s^2$. Therefore, to determine the value of $r^2 + s^2$, it is sufficient to determine the value of R.

(1) It is given that $R = 2$; SUFFICIENT.

(2) It is given that $\left(\sqrt{2}, -\sqrt{2}\right)$ lies on the circle. A right triangle with legs each of length $\sqrt{2}$ can be formed so that the line segment with endpoints $\left(\sqrt{2}, -\sqrt{2}\right)$ and $(0,0)$ is the hypotenuse. Since the length of the hypotenuse is the radius of the circle, which is R, where $R^2 = r^2 + s^2$, the Pythagorean theorem for this right triangle gives $R^2 = \left(\sqrt{2}\right)^2 + \left(\sqrt{2}\right)^2 = 2 + 2 = 4$. Therefore, $r^2 + s^2 = 4$; SUFFICIENT.

**The correct answer is D;
each statement alone is sufficient.**

23. What is the value of x ?

(1) $-(x + y) = x - y$

(2) $x + y = 2$

Algebra First- and second-degree equations

(1) The equation is equivalent to $2x = 0$, or $x = 0$; SUFFICIENT.

(2) Since no other information is given about the value of y, more than one value of x can be found to satisfy $x + y = 2$. For example, $x = 1$ is possible (use $y = 1$) and $x = 0$ is possible (use $y = 2$); NOT sufficient.

**The correct answer is A;
statement 1 alone is sufficient.**

24. If r, s, and t are nonzero integers, is $r^5 s^3 t^4$ negative?

(1) rt is negative.

(2) s is negative.

Arithmetic Properties of numbers

Since $r^5 s^3 t^4 = (rt)^4 rs^3$ and $(rt)^4$ is positive, $r^5 s^3 t^4$ will be negative if and only if rs^3 is negative, or if and only if r and s have opposite signs.

(1) It is given that rt is negative, but nothing can be determined about the sign of s. If the sign of s is the opposite of the sign of r, then $r^5 s^3 t^4 = (rt)^4 rs^3$ will be negative. However, if the sign of s is the same as the sign of r, then $r^5 s^3 t^4 = (rt)^4 rs^3$ will be positive; NOT sufficient.

(2) It is given that s is negative, but nothing can be determined about the sign of r. If r is positive, then $r^5 s^3 t^4 = (rt)^4 rs^3$ will be negative. However, if r is negative, then $r^5 s^3 t^4 = (rt)^4 rs^3$ will be positive; NOT sufficient.

Given (1) and (2), it is still not possible to determine whether r and s have opposite signs. For example, (1) and (2) hold if r is positive, s is negative, and t is negative, and in this case r and s have opposite signs. However, (1) and (2) hold if r is negative, s is negative, and t is positive, and in this case r and s have the same sign.

**The correct answer is E;
both statements together are still not sufficient.**

25. If x and y are integers, what is the value of y ?

(1) $xy = 27$

(2) $x = y^2$

Arithmetic Arithmetic operations

(1) Many different pairs of integers have the product 27, for example, $(-3)(-9)$ and $(1)(27)$. There is no way to determine which pair of integers is intended, and there is also no way to determine which member of a pair is x and which member of a pair is y; NOT sufficient.

(2) Given that $x = y^2$, more than one integer value for y is possible. For example, y could be 1 (with the value of x being 1) or y could be 2 (with the value of x being 4); NOT sufficient.

Using both (1) and (2), y^2 can be substituted for the value of x in (1) to give $y^3 = 27$, which has exactly one solution, $y = 3$.

The correct answer is C;
both statements together are sufficient.

26. How many newspapers were sold at a certain newsstand today?

    (1) A total of 100 newspapers were sold at the newsstand yesterday, 10 fewer than twice the number sold today.

    (2) The number of newspapers sold at the newsstand yesterday was 45 more than the number sold today.

    Algebra First- and second-degree equations

    Let t be the number of newspapers sold today.

    (1) The given information can be expressed as $100 = 2t - 10$, which can be solved for a unique value of t; SUFFICIENT.

    (2) It is given that $45 + t$ newspapers were sold at the newsstand yesterday. Since the number sold yesterday is unknown, t cannot be determined; NOT sufficient.

    The correct answer is A;
    statement 1 alone is sufficient.

27. What is Ricky's age now?

    (1) Ricky is now twice as old as he was exactly 8 years ago.

    (2) Ricky's sister Teresa is now 3 times as old as Ricky was exactly 8 years ago.

    Algebra Translation into equations

    Let r represent Ricky's age now and let t represent Teresa's age now.

    (1) The information given can be represented as $r = 2(r - 8)$, which can be solved for a unique value of r; SUFFICIENT.

    (2) The information given can be represented as $t = 3(r - 8)$, which has more than one solution in which r and t are integers greater than 8. For example, r could be 12 (with the value of t being 12) and r could be 18 (with the value of t being 30); NOT sufficient.

    The correct answer is A;
    statement 1 alone is sufficient.

28. If both x and y are nonzero numbers, what is the value of $\frac{y}{x}$?

    (1) $x = 6$

    (2) $y^2 = x^2$

    Arithmetic Powers of numbers

    (1) This states only the value of x, with the value of y not determined and no means for it to be determined; NOT sufficient.

    (2) Although the squares of x and y are equal, the values of x and y are not necessarily equal. For example, if $x = 6$ and $y = 6$, then $x^2 = y^2$ and $\frac{y}{x} = 1$, but if $x = 6$ and $y = -6$, then $x^2 = y^2$ and $\frac{y}{x} = -1$; NOT sufficient.

    The two statements together are not sufficient, which follows from the examples given in (2).

    The correct answer is E;
    both statements together are still not sufficient.

29. John took a test that had 60 questions numbered from 1 to 60. How many of the questions did he answer correctly?

    (1) The number of questions he answered correctly in the first half of the test was 7 more than the number he answered correctly in the second half of the test.

    (2) He answered $\frac{5}{6}$ of the odd-numbered questions correctly and $\frac{4}{5}$ of the even-numbered questions correctly.

Arithmetic Fractions

(1) Let f represent the number of questions answered correctly in the first half of the test and let s represent the number of questions answered correctly in the second half of the test. Then the given information can be expressed as $f = 7 + s$, which has several solutions in which f and s are integers between 1 and 60, leading to different values of $f + s$. For example, f could be 10 and s could be 3, which gives $f + s = 13$, or f could be 11 and s could be 4, which gives $f + s = 15$; NOT sufficient.

(2) Since there are 30 odd-numbered questions and 30 even-numbered questions in a 60-question test, from the information given it follows that the number of questions answered correctly was equal to $\frac{5}{6}(30) + \frac{4}{5}(30)$; SUFFICIENT.

**The correct answer is B;
statement 2 alone is sufficient.**

30. If $x = 0.rstu$, where r, s, t, and u each represent a nonzero digit of x, what is the value of x ?

(1) $r = 3s = 2t = 6u$
(2) The product of r and u is equal to the product of s and t.

Arithmetic Decimals; Properties of numbers

(1) Since $r = 6u$ and r and u must be nonzero digits, it must be true that $u = 1$ and $r = 6$. This is because if u were greater than 1, then r would be greater than or equal to 12, and hence r could not be a nonzero digit (i.e., r could not be 1, 2, 3, 4, 5, 6, 7, 8, or 9). From $u = 1$ and $2t = 6u$, it follows that $2t = 6$, and hence $t = 3$. From $3s = 6u$, it follows that $3s = 6$, and hence $s = 2$. With the values established for r, s, t, and u, $x = 0.6231$; SUFFICIENT.

(2) There is more than one assignment of nonzero digits to r, s, t, and u such that $r = s$ and $u = t$, so the value of x is not uniquely determined from the given information. For example, x could be 0.3366, 0.2299, or 0.1188; NOT sufficient.

**The correct answer is A;
statement 1 alone is sufficient.**

31. If x is a positive integer, is $\sqrt{x}$ an integer?

(1) $\sqrt{4x}$ is an integer.
(2) $\sqrt{3x}$ is not an integer.

Algebra Radicals

(1) It is given that $\sqrt{4x} = n$, or $4x = n^2$, for some positive integer n. Since $4x$ is the square of an integer, it follows that in the prime factorization of $4x$, each distinct prime factor is repeated an even number of times. Therefore, the same must be true for the prime factorization of x, since the prime factorization of x only differs from the prime factorization of $4x$ by two factors of 2, and hence by an even number of factors of 2; SUFFICIENT.

(2) Given that $\sqrt{3x}$ is not an integer, it is possible for $\sqrt{x}$ to be an integer (for example, $x = 1$) and it is possible for $\sqrt{x}$ to not be an integer (for example, $x = 2$); NOT sufficient.

**The correct answer is A;
statement 1 alone is sufficient.**

32. Is the value of n closer to 50 than to 75 ?

(1) $75 - n > n - 50$
(2) $n > 60$

Algebra Inequalities

Begin by considering the value of n when it is at the exact same distance from both 50 and 75. The value of n is equidistant between 50 and 75 when n is the midpoint between 75 and 50, that is, when $n = \frac{50 + 75}{2} = 62.5$. Alternatively stated, n is equidistant between 50 and 75 when the distance that n is below 75 is equal to the distance that n is above 50, i.e., when $75 - n = n - 50$, as indicated on the number line below.

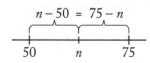

(1) Since here $75 - n > n - 50$, it follows that the value of n is closer to 50 than to 75; SUFFICIENT.

(2) Although n is greater than 60, for all values of n between 60 and 62.5, n is closer to 50, and for all values of n greater than 62.5, n is closer to 75. Without further information, the value of n relative to 50 and 75 cannot be determined; NOT sufficient.

The correct answer is A;
statement 1 alone is sufficient.

33. Last year, if Elena spent a total of $720 on newspapers, magazines, and books, what amount did she spend on newspapers?

(1) Last year, the amount that Elena spent on magazines was 80 percent of the amount that she spent on books.

(2) Last year, the amount that Elena spent on newspapers was 60 percent of the total amount that she spent on magazines and books.

Arithmetic Percents

Let n, m, and b be the amounts, in dollars, that Elena spent last year on newspapers, magazines, and books, respectively. Given that $n + m + b = 720$, determine the value of n.

(1) Given that m is 80% of b, or $m = \frac{4}{5}b$, it follows from $n + m + b = 720$ that $n + \frac{4}{5}b + b = 720$, or $n = -\frac{9}{5}b + 720$. Since more than one positive value of b is possible, the value of n cannot be determined; NOT sufficient.

(2) Given that n is 60% of the sum of m and b, or $n = \frac{3}{5}(m + b)$, or $\frac{5}{3}n = m + b$, it follows from $n + m + b = 720$ that $n + \frac{5}{3}n = 720$, which can be solved to obtain a unique value of n; SUFFICIENT.

The correct answer is B;
statement 2 alone is sufficient.

34. If p, q, x, y, and z are different positive integers, which of the five integers is the median?

(1) $p + x < q$

(2) $y < z$

Arithmetic Statistics

Since there are five different integers, there are two integers greater and two integers less than the median, which is the middle number.

(1) No information is given about the order of y and z with respect to the other three numbers; NOT sufficient.

(2) This statement does not relate y and z to the other three integers; NOT sufficient.

Because (1) and (2) taken together do not relate p, x, and q to y and z, it is impossible to tell which is the median. For example, if $p = 3$, $x = 4$, $q = 8$, $y = 9$, and $z = 10$, then the median is 8, but if $p = 3$, $x = 4$, $q = 8$, $y = 1$, and $z = 2$, then the median is 3.

The correct answer is E;
both statements together are still not sufficient.

35. If $w + z = 28$, what is the value of wz ?

(1) w and z are positive integers.

(2) w and z are consecutive odd integers.

Arithmetic Arithmetic operations

(1) The fact that w and z are both positive integers does not allow the values of w and z to be determined because, for example, if $w = 20$ and $z = 8$, then $wz = 160$, and if $w = 10$ and $z = 18$, then $wz = 180$; NOT sufficient.

(2)   Since w and z are consecutive odd integers whose sum is 28, it is reasonable to consider the possibilities for the sum of consecutive odd integers: $\ldots, (-5)+(-3)=-8,$

$(-3)+(-1)=-4, (-1)+1=0, 1+3=4, \ldots,$

$9+11=20, 11+13=24, 13+15=28,$

$15+17=32, \ldots.$ From this list it follows that only one pair of consecutive odd integers has 28 for its sum, and hence there is exactly one possible value for wz.

This problem can also be solved algebraically by letting the consecutive odd integers w and z be represented by $2n+1$ and $2n+3$, where n can be any integer. Since $28 = w+z$, it follows that

$28 = (2n+1)+(2n+3)$

$28 = 4n+4$ simplify

$24 = 4n$ subtract 4 from both sides

$6 = n$ divide both sides by 4

Thus, $w = 2(6)+1 = 13$, $z = 2(6)+3 = 15$, and hence exactly one value can be determined for wz; SUFFICIENT.

The correct answer is B; statement 2 alone is sufficient.

36.   Elena receives a salary plus a commission that is equal to a fixed percentage of her sales revenue. What was the total of Elena's salary and commission last month?

(1)   Elena's monthly salary is $1,000.
(2)   Elena's commission is 5 percent of her sales revenue.

Arithmetic Percents

The total of Elena's salary and commission last month can be determined if each of the following can be determined: her monthly salary, her sales revenue last month, and the percent of her sales revenue that is her commission. Also, if at least one of these quantities can vary independent of the other two, then the total of Elena's salary and commission last month cannot be determined.

(1)   Elena's monthly salary is given, but there is no information about the other components that made up her salary last month; NOT sufficient.

(2)   The percent of Elena's sales revenue that is her commission is given, but there is no information about her sales revenue for the month or her monthly salary; NOT sufficient.

Using both (1) and (2) still yields no information about Elena's sales revenue from last month, and thus the total of her salary and commission last month cannot be determined.

The correct answer is E; both statements together are still not sufficient.

37.   What is the value of $a-b$?

(1) $a = b+4$
(2) $(a-b)^2 = 16$

Algebra First- and second-degree equations

(1)   If $a = b+4$ then, when b is subtracted from both sides, the resultant equation is $a-b = 4$; SUFFICIENT.

(2)   Since $(a-b)^2 = 16$, either $a-b = 4$ or $a-b = -4$. There is no further information available to determine a single numerical value of $a-b$; NOT sufficient.

The correct answer is A; statement 1 alone is sufficient.

38.   Machine X runs at a constant rate and produces a lot consisting of 100 cans in 2 hours. How much less time would it take to produce the lot of cans if both Machines X and Y were run simultaneously?

(1)   Both Machines X and Y produce the same number of cans per hour.
(2)   It takes Machine X twice as long to produce the lot of cans as it takes Machines X and Y running simultaneously to produce the lot.

Arithmetic Rate problems

The problem states that the job is to produce 100 cans and that Machine X can do the job in 2 hours. Thus, to determine how much less time it would take for both of them running simultaneously to do the job, it is sufficient to know the rate for Machine Y or the time that Machines X and Y together take to complete the job.

(1)　This states that the rate for Y is the same as the rate for X, which is given; SUFFICIENT.

(2)　Since double the time corresponds to half the rate, the rate for X is $\frac{1}{2}$ the combined rate for X and Y running simultaneously, it can be determined that X and Y together would take $\frac{1}{2}$ the time, or 1 hour, to do the job; SUFFICIENT.

**The correct answer is D;
each statement alone is sufficient.**

39.　Can the positive integer p be expressed as the product of two integers, each of which is greater than 1 ?

　(1)　$31 < p < 37$
　(2)　p is odd.

Arithmetic Properties of numbers

(1)　This statement implies that p can be only among the integers 32, 33, 34, 35, and 36. Because each of these integers can be expressed as the product of two integers, each of which is greater than 1 (e.g., $32 = 4 \times 8, 33 = 3 \times 11$, etc.), the question can be answered even though the specific value of p is not known; SUFFICIENT.

(2)　If $p = 3$, then p cannot be expressed as the product of two integers, each of which is greater than 1. However, if $p = 9$, then p can be expressed as the product of two integers, each of which is greater than 1; NOT sufficient.

**The correct answer is A;
statement 1 alone is sufficient.**

40.　Is $x < y$?

　(1)　$z < y$
　(2)　$z < x$

Algebra Inequalities

(1)　This gives no information about x and its relationship to y; NOT sufficient.

(2)　This gives no information about y and its relationship to x; NOT sufficient.

From (1) and (2) together, it can be determined only that z is less than both x and y. It is still not possible to determine the relationship of x and y, and x might be greater than, equal to, or less than y.

**The correct answer is E;
both statements together are still not sufficient.**

41.　If S is a set of four numbers w, x, y, and z, is the range of the numbers in S greater than 2 ?

　(1)　$w - z > 2$
　(2)　z is the least number in S.

Arithmetic Statistics

The range of the numbers w, x, y, and z is equal to the greatest of those numbers minus the least of those numbers.

(1)　This reveals that the difference between two of the numbers in the set is greater than 2, which means that the range of the four numbers must also be greater than 2; SUFFICIENT.

(2)　The information that z is the least number gives no information regarding the other numbers or their range; NOT sufficient.

**The correct answer is A;
statement 1 alone is sufficient.**

42.　If y is greater than 110 percent of x, is y greater than 75 ?

　(1)　$x > 75$
　(2)　$y - x = 10$

Arithmetic; Algebra Percents; Inequalities

(1) It is given that $y > (110\%)x = 1.1x$ and $x > 75$. Therefore, $y > (1.1)(75)$, and so y is greater than 75; SUFFICIENT.

(2) Although it is given that $y - x = 10$, more information is needed to determine if y is greater than 75. For example, if $x = 80$ and $y = 90$, then y is greater than 110 percent of x, $y - x = 10$, and y is greater than 75. However, if $x = 20$ and $y = 30$, then y is greater than 110 percent of x, $y - x = 10$, and y is not greater than 75; NOT sufficient.

The correct answer is A;
statement 1 alone is sufficient.

43. What is the area of rectangular region R?

(1) Each diagonal of R has length 5.
(2) The perimeter of R is 14.

Geometry Rectangles

Let L and W be the length and width of the rectangle, respectively. Determine the value of LW.

(1) It is given that a diagonal's length is 5. Thus, by the Pythagorean theorem, it follows that $L^2 + W^2 = 5^2 = 25$. The value of LW cannot be determined, however, because $L = \sqrt{15}$ and $W = \sqrt{10}$ satisfy $L^2 + W^2 = 25$ with $LW = \sqrt{150}$, and $L = \sqrt{5}$ and $W = \sqrt{20}$ satisfy $L^2 + W^2 = 25$ with $LW = \sqrt{100}$; NOT sufficient.

(2) It is given that $2L + 2W = 14$, or $L + W = 7$, or $L = 7 - W$. Therefore, $LW = (7 - W)W$, which can vary in value. For example, if $L = 3$ and $W = 4$, then $L + W = 7$ and $LW = 12$. However, if $L = 2$ and $W = 5$, then $L + W = 7$ and $LW = 10$; NOT sufficient.

Given (1) and (2) together, it follows from (2) that $(L + W)^2 = 7^2 = 49$, or $L^2 + W^2 + 2LW = 49$. Using (1), 25 can be substituted for $L^2 + W^2$ to obtain $25 + 2LW = 49$, or $2LW = 24$, or $LW = 12$. Alternatively, $7 - W$ can be substituted for L in $L^2 + W^2 = 25$ to obtain the quadratic equation $(7 - W)^2 + W^2 = 25$, or $49 - 14W + W^2 + W^2 = 25$, or $2W^2 - 14W + 24 = 0$, or $W^2 - 7W + 12 = 0$. The left side of the last equation can be factored to give $(W - 4)(W - 3) = 0$. Therefore, $W = 4$, which gives $L = 7 - W = 7 - 4 = 3$ and $LW = (3)(4) = 12$, or $W = 3$, which gives $L = 7 - W = 7 - 3 = 4$ and $LW = (4)(3) = 12$. Since $LW = 12$ in either case, a unique value for LW can be determined.

The correct answer is C;
both statements together are sufficient.

44. If Q is an integer between 10 and 100, what is the value of Q?

(1) One of Q's digits is 3 more than the other, and the sum of its digits is 9.
(2) $Q < 50$

Algebra Properties of numbers

(1) While it is quite possible to guess that the two integers satisfying these stipulations are 36 and 63, these two integers can also be determined algebraically. Letting x and y be the digits of Q, the given information can be expressed as $x = y + 3$ and $x + y = 9$. These equations can be solved simultaneously to obtain the digits 3 and 6, leading to the integers 36 and 63. However, it is unknown which of these two integers is the value of Q; NOT sufficient.

(2) There is more than one integer between 10 and 49; NOT sufficient.

When the information from (1) and (2) is combined, the value of Q can be uniquely determined, because, of the two possible values for Q, only 36 is between 10 and 49.

The correct answer is C;
both statements together are sufficient.

45. If p and q are positive integers and $pq = 24$, what is the value of p ?

(1)　$\dfrac{q}{6}$ is an integer.

(2)　$\dfrac{p}{2}$ is an integer.

Arithmetic Arithmetic operations

There are four pairs of positive integers whose product is 24: 1 and 24, 2 and 12, 3 and 8, and 4 and 6.

(1)　The possible values of q are therefore 6, 12, and 24, and for each of these there is a different value of p (4, 2, and 1); NOT sufficient.

(2)　The possible values of p are therefore 2, 4, 6, 8, 12, and 24; NOT sufficient.

From (1) and (2) together, the possible values of q can only be narrowed down to 6 or 12, with corresponding values of p being either 4 or 2.

**The correct answer is E;
both statements together are still not sufficient.**

46. What is the value of $x^2 - y^2$?

(1)　$x - y = y + 2$

(2)　$x - y = \dfrac{1}{x + y}$

Algebra First- and second-degree equations

(1)　If $x - y = y + 2$, then $x = 2y + 2$. When this expression for x is substituted in $x^2 - y^2$, the result is $\left(2y + 2\right)^2 - y^2$, which can vary in value. For example, if $y = 0$ (and hence, $x = 2$), then $\left(2y + 2\right)^2 - y^2 = 4$. However, if $y = 1$ (and hence, $x = 4$), then $\left(2y + 2\right)^2 - y^2 = 15$; NOT sufficient.

(2)　Since $x - y = \dfrac{1}{x + y}$, $\left(x - y\right)\left(x + y\right) = 1$, or $x^2 - y^2 = 1$. Thus, the value of $x^2 - y^2$ is 1; SUFFICIENT.

**The correct answer is B;
statement 2 alone is sufficient.**

47. Hoses X and Y simultaneously fill an empty swimming pool that has a capacity of 50,000 liters. If the flow in each hose is independent of the flow in the other hose, how many hours will it take to fill the pool?

(1)　Hose X alone would take 28 hours to fill the pool.

(2)　Hose Y alone would take 36 hours to fill the pool.

Arithmetic Arithmetic operations

In order to answer this problem about *two* hoses being used *simultaneously* to fill a pool, information about the filling rate for *both* hoses is needed.

(1)　Only the filling rate for Hose X is given; NOT sufficient.

(2)　Only the filling rate for Hose Y is given; NOT sufficient.

Using both (1) and (2) the filling rates for both hoses are known, and thus the time needed to fill the pool can be determined. Since Hose X fills the pool in 28 hours, Hose X fills $\dfrac{1}{28}$ of the pool in 1 hour. Since Hose Y fills the pool in 36 hours, Hose Y fills $\dfrac{1}{36}$ of the pool in 1 hour. Therefore, together they fill $\dfrac{1}{28} + \dfrac{1}{36} = \dfrac{9}{252} + \dfrac{7}{252} = \dfrac{16}{252} = \dfrac{4}{63}$ of the pool in 1 hour. The time (t) that it will take them to fill the pool together can be found by solving for t in $\dfrac{4}{63}\left(t\right) = 1$. Remember in answering that it is enough to establish the sufficiency of the data; it is not actually necessary to do the computations.

**The correct answer is C;
both statements together are sufficient.**

48. If $abc \neq 0$, is $\dfrac{\frac{a}{b}}{c} = \dfrac{a}{\frac{b}{c}}$?

(1)　$a = 1$

(2)　$c = 1$

Algebra Fractions

Since $\dfrac{\frac{a}{b}}{c} = \dfrac{a}{b} \div c = \dfrac{a}{b} \times \dfrac{1}{c} = \dfrac{a}{bc}$ and

$\dfrac{a}{\frac{b}{c}} = a \div \dfrac{b}{c} = a \times \dfrac{c}{b} = \dfrac{ac}{b}$, it is to be determined

whether $\dfrac{a}{bc} = \dfrac{ac}{b}$.

(1) Given that $a = 1$, the equation to be investigated, $\dfrac{a}{bc} = \dfrac{ac}{b}$, is $\dfrac{1}{bc} = \dfrac{c}{b}$. This equation can be true for some nonzero values of b and c (for example, $b = c = 1$) and false for other nonzero values of b and c (for example, $b = 1$ and $c = 2$); NOT sufficient.

(2) Given that $c = 1$, the equation to be investigated, $\dfrac{a}{bc} = \dfrac{ac}{b}$, is $\dfrac{a}{b} = \dfrac{a}{b}$. This equation is true for all nonzero values of a and b; SUFFICIENT.

**The correct answer is B;
statement 2 alone is sufficient.**

49. How many integers n are there such that $r < n < s$?

(1) $s - r = 5$
(2) r and s are not integers.

Arithmetic Properties of numbers

(1) The difference between s and r is 5. If r and s are integers (e.g., 7 and 12), the number of integers between them (i.e., n could be 8, 9, 10, or 11) is 4. If r and s are not integers (e.g., 6.5 and 11.5), then the number of integers between them (i.e., n could be 7, 8, 9, 10, or 11) is 5. No information is given that allows a determination of whether s and r are integers; NOT sufficient.

(2) No information is given about the difference between r and s. If $r = 0.4$ and $s = 0.5$, then r and s have no integers between them. However, if $r = 0.4$ and $s = 5.5$, then r and s have 3 integers between them; NOT sufficient.

Using the information from both (1) and (2), it can be determined that, because r and s are not integers, there are 5 integers between them.

**The correct answer is C;
both statements together are sufficient.**

50. If the total price of n equally priced shares of a certain stock was $12,000, what was the price per share of the stock?

(1) If the price per share of the stock had been $1 more, the total price of the n shares would have been $300 more.
(2) If the price per share of the stock had been $2 less, the total price of the n shares would have been 5 percent less.

Arithmetic Arithmetic operations; Percents

Since the price per share of the stock can be expressed as $\dfrac{\$12,000}{n}$, determining the value of n is sufficient to answer this question.

(1) A per-share increase of $1 and a total increase of $300 for n shares of stock mean together that $n\bigl(\$1\bigr) = \$300$. It follows that $n = 300$; SUFFICIENT.

(2) If the price of each of the n shares had been reduced by $2, the total reduction in price would have been 5 percent less or $0.05(\$12,000)$. The equation $2n = 0.05\bigl(\$12,000\bigr)$ expresses this relationship. The value of n can be determined to be 300 from this equation; SUFFICIENT.

**The correct answer is D;
each statement alone is sufficient.**

51. If n is positive, is $\sqrt{n} > 100$?

(1) $\sqrt{n-1} > 99$
(2) $\sqrt{n+1} > 101$

Algebra Radicals

Determine if $\sqrt{n} > 100$, or equivalently, if
$n > (100)(100) = 10,000$.

(1) Given that $\sqrt{n-1} > 99$, or equivalently,
$n - 1 > (99)(99)$, it follows from

$$(99)(99) = 99(100 - 1)$$

$$= 9,900 - 99$$

$$= 9,801$$

that $\sqrt{n-1} > 99$ is equivalent to $n - 1 > 9,801$,
or $n > 9,802$. Since $n > 9,802$ allows for
values of n that are greater than 10,000
and $n > 9,802$ allows for values of n that
are not greater than 10,000, it cannot be
determined if $n > 10,000$; NOT sufficient.

(2) Given that $\sqrt{n+1} > 101$, or equivalently,
$n + 1 > (101)(101)$, it follows from

$$(101)(101) = 101(100 + 1)$$

$$= 10,100 + 101$$

$$= 10,201$$

that $\sqrt{n+1} > 101$ is equivalent to
$n + 1 > 10,201$, or $n > 10,200$. Since
$10,200 > 10,000$, it can be determined
that $n > 10,000$; SUFFICIENT.

**The correct answer is B;
statement 2 alone is sufficient.**

52. Is $xy > 5$?

(1) $1 \le x \le 3$ and $2 \le y \le 4$.
(2) $x + y = 5$

Algebra Inequalities

(1) While it is known that $1 \le x \le 3$ and
$2 \le y \le 4$, xy could be $(3)(4) = 12$, which is
greater than 5, or xy could be $(1)(2) = 2$,
which is not greater than 5; NOT sufficient.

(2) Given that $x + y = 5$, xy could be 6 (when
$x = 2$ and $y = 3$), which is greater than 5, and
xy could be 4 (when $x = 1$ and $y = 4$), which
is not greater than 5; NOT sufficient.

Both (1) and (2) together are not sufficient since
the two examples given in (2) are consistent with
both statements.

**The correct answer is E;
both statements together are still not sufficient.**

53. In Year X, 8.7 percent of the men in the labor force
were unemployed in June compared with 8.4 percent
in May. If the number of men in the labor force was the
same for both months, how many men were
unemployed in June of that year?

(1) In May of Year X, the number of unemployed
men in the labor force was 3.36 million.
(2) In Year X, 120,000 more men in the labor force
were unemployed in June than in May.

Arithmetic Percents

Since 8.7 percent of the men in the labor force were
unemployed in June, the number of unemployed
men could be calculated if the total number of
men in the labor force was known. Let t represent
the total number of men in the labor force.

(1) This implies that for May
$(8.4\%)t = 3,360,000$, from which the value
of t can be determined; SUFFICIENT.

(2) This implies that $(8.7\% - 8.4\%)t = 120,000$
or $(0.3\%)t = 120,000$. This equation can be
solved for t; SUFFICIENT.

**The correct answer is D;
each statement alone is sufficient.**

54. If $x \ne 0$, what is the value of $\left(\dfrac{x^p}{x^q}\right)^4$?

(1) $p = q$
(2) $x = 3$

Arithmetic; Algebra Arithmetic operations;
Simplifying expressions

(1) Since $p = q$, it follows that
$$\left(\frac{x^p}{x^q}\right)^4 = \left(\frac{x^p}{x^p}\right)^4 = (1)^4; \text{SUFFICIENT.}$$

(2) Since $x = 3$ (and, therefore, $x \neq 1$) and the values of p or q are unknown, the value of the expression $\left(\dfrac{x^p}{x^q}\right)^4$ cannot be determined; NOT sufficient.

The correct answer is A; statement 1 alone is sufficient.

55. On Monday morning a certain machine ran continuously at a uniform rate to fill a production order. At what time did it completely fill the order that morning?

(1) The machine began filling the order at 9:30 a.m.

(2) The machine had filled $\dfrac{1}{2}$ of the order by 10:30 a.m. and $\dfrac{5}{6}$ of the order by 11:10 a.m.

Arithmetic Arithmetic operations

(1) This merely states what time the machine began filling the order; NOT sufficient.

(2) In the 40 minutes between 10:30 a.m. and 11:10 a.m., $\dfrac{5}{6} - \dfrac{1}{2} = \dfrac{1}{3}$ of the order was filled. Therefore, the entire order was completely filled in $3 \times 40 = 120$ minutes, or 2 hours. Since half the order took 1 hour and was filled by 10:30 a.m., the second half of the order, and thus the entire order, was filled by 11:30 a.m.; SUFFICIENT.

The correct answer is B; statement 2 alone is sufficient.

56. If $xy < 3$, is $x < 1$?

(1) $y > 3$

(2) $x < 3$

Algebra Inequalities

(1) If $y > 3$, then it follows that $x < 1$ cannot be false. Otherwise, if $x < 1$ were false, then $x \geq 1$, and hence $xy \geq y > 3$, which contradicts the given condition $xy < 3$. Therefore, it can be concluded that $x < 1$. Alternatively, divide both sides of $xy < 3$ by y to get $\dfrac{xy}{y} < \dfrac{3}{y}$ and use $y > 3$, or equivalently $\dfrac{1}{y} < \dfrac{1}{3}$, to obtain $\dfrac{3}{y} < \dfrac{3}{3}$, from which it follows that $\dfrac{xy}{y} < \dfrac{3}{3}$, or $x < 1$; SUFFICIENT.

(2) The information that $x < 3$ is not enough to determine whether $x < 1$, since x could be 0 ($x < 1$ is true) and x could be 2 ($x < 1$ is not true); NOT sufficient.

The correct answer is A; statement 1 alone is sufficient.

57. If $\dfrac{m}{n} = \dfrac{5}{3}$, what is the value of $m + n$?

(1) $m > 0$

(2) $2m + n = 26$

Algebra Simultaneous equations

(1) Given $\dfrac{m}{n} = \dfrac{5}{3}$, it follows from $\dfrac{5}{3} = \dfrac{10}{6}$ that $m + n$ could be 8 ($m = 5$ and $n = 3$) and $m + n$ could be 16 ($m = 10$ and $n = 6$); NOT sufficient.

(2) The given equation $\dfrac{m}{n} = \dfrac{5}{3}$, or $3m = 5n$ (by cross multiplying), and the equation $2m + n = 26$ can be solved simultaneously for unique values of m and n, from which a unique value of $m + n$ can be determined. Alternatively, when graphed the two equations correspond to two nonparallel lines that have exactly one point of intersection, from which unique values of m and n, and hence a unique value of $m + n$, can be determined; SUFFICIENT.

The correct answer is B; statement 2 alone is sufficient.

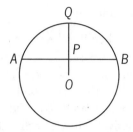

58. What is the radius of the circle above with center O?

(1) The ratio of OP to PQ is 1 to 2.
(2) P is the midpoint of chord AB.

Geometry Circles

(1) It can be concluded only that the radius is 3 times the length of OP, which is unknown; NOT sufficient.

(2) It can be concluded only that AP = PB, and the chord is irrelevant to the radius; NOT sufficient.

Together, (1) and (2) do not give the length of any line segment shown in the circle. In fact, if the circle and all the line segments were uniformly expanded by a factor of, say, 5, the resulting circle and line segments would still satisfy both (1) and (2). Therefore, the radius of the circle cannot be determined from (1) and (2) together.

The correct answer is E; both statements together are still not sufficient.

59. What is the number of 360-degree rotations that a bicycle wheel made while rolling 100 meters in a straight line without slipping?

(1) The diameter of the bicycle wheel, including the tire, was 0.5 meter.
(2) The wheel made twenty 360-degree rotations per minute.

Geometry Circles

For each 360-degree rotation, the wheel has traveled a distance equal to its circumference. Given either the circumference of the wheel or the means to calculate its circumference, it is thus possible to determine the number of times the circumference of the wheel was laid out along the straight-line path of 100 meters.

(1) The circumference of the bicycle wheel can be determined from the given diameter using the equation $C = \pi d$, where d = the diameter; SUFFICIENT.

(2) The speed of the rotations is irrelevant, and no dimensions of the wheel are given; NOT sufficient.

The correct answer is A; statement 1 alone is sufficient.

60. The perimeter of a rectangular garden is 360 feet. What is the length of the garden?

(1) The length of the garden is twice the width.
(2) The difference between the length and width of the garden is 60 feet.

Geometry; Algebra Perimeter; Simultaneous Equations

If ℓ and w denote the length and width of the garden, respectively, then it is given that the perimeter is $2(\ell + w) = 360$. When both sides of the equation are divided by 2, the result is $\ell + w = 180$.

(1) This can be represented as $\ell = 2w$, or $w = \dfrac{\ell}{2}$. By substituting $\dfrac{\ell}{2}$ for w in the equation $\ell + w = 180$, the resulting equation of $\ell + \dfrac{\ell}{2} = 180$ can be solved for exactly one value of ℓ; SUFFICIENT.

(2) This can be represented as $\ell - w = 60$. The length can then be determined by solving the two equations, $\ell - w = 60$ and $\ell + w = 180$, simultaneously. Adding the two equations yields $2\ell - w + w = 240$ or $\ell = 120$; SUFFICIENT.

The correct answer is D; each statement alone is sufficient.

61. If $2x(5n) = t$, what is the value of t?

(1) $x = n + 3$
(2) $2x = 32$

Algebra First- and second-degree equations

Because $t = 10xn$, the value of t can be determined exactly when the value of xn can be determined.

(1)   Given that $x = n + 3$, more than one value of xn is possible. For example, xn could be 0 (if $x = 3$ and $n = 0$) and xn could be 4 (if $x = 4$ and $n = 1$); NOT sufficient.

(2)   Given that $2x = 32$, or $x = 16$, more than one value of xn is possible, since $xn = 16n$, which will vary in value when n varies in value; NOT sufficient.

The value of x determined from equation (2) can be substituted in equation (1) to obtain $16 = n + 3$, or $n = 13$. Therefore, $xn = (16)(13)$.

**The correct answer is C;
both statements together are sufficient.**

62.   In the equation $x^2 + bx + 12 = 0$, x is a variable and b is a constant. What is the value of b ?

(1) $x - 3$ is a factor of $x^2 + bx + 12$.

(2)   4 is a root of the equation $x^2 + bx + 12 = 0$.

Algebra First- and second-degree equations

(1)   Method 1: If $x - 3$ is a factor, then $x^2 + bx + 12 = (x - 3)(x + c)$ for some constant c. Equating the constant terms (or substituting $x = 0$), it follows that $12 = -3c$, or $c = -4$. Therefore, the quadratic polynomial is $(x - 3)(x - 4)$, which is equal to $x^2 - 7x + 12$, and hence $b = -7$.

Method 2: If $x - 3$ is a factor of $x^2 + bx + 12$, then 3 is a root of $x^2 + bx + 12 = 0$. Therefore, $3^2 + 3b + 12 = 0$, which can be solved to get $b = -7$.

Method 3: The value of b can be found by long division:

$$x - 3 \overline{\smash{\big)}\, x^2 + bx + 12} \quad \genfrac{}{}{0pt}{}{x + (b + 3)}{}$$

$$\begin{array}{r} x + (b+3) \\ x - 3 \overline{\smash{\big)}\, x^2 + bx + 12} \\ \underline{x^2 - 3x} \\ (b+3)x + 12 \\ \underline{(b+3)x - 3b - 9} \\ 3b + 21 \end{array}$$

These calculations show that the remainder is $3b + 21$. Since the remainder must be 0, it follows that $3b + 21 = 0$, or $b = -7$; SUFFICIENT.

(2)   If 4 is a root of the equation, then 4 can be substituted for x in the equation $x^2 + bx + 12 = 0$, yielding $4^2 + 4b + 12 = 0$. This last equation can be solved to obtain a unique value for b; SUFFICIENT.

**The correct answer is D;
each statement alone is sufficient.**

63.   A Town T has 20,000 residents, 60 percent of whom are female. What percent of the residents were born in Town T ?

(1)   The number of female residents who were born in Town T is twice the number of male residents who were <u>not</u> born in Town T.

(2)   The number of female residents who were <u>not</u> born in Town T is twice the number of female residents who were born in Town T.

Arithmetic Percents

Since 60 percent of the residents are female, there are $0.6(20,000) = 12,000$ female residents. The remaining residents are male, so there are $20,000 - 12,000 = 8,000$ male residents. Let N be the number of residents who were born in Town T. The percent of the residents who were born in Town T is $\dfrac{N}{20,000}$, which can be determined exactly when N can be determined.

This information is displayed in the following table:

Table 1			
	Male	Female	Total
Born in Town T			N
Not Born in Town T			
Total	8,000	12,000	20,000

(1)   Let x represent the number of male residents who were not born in Town T. Then the number of female residents who were born in Town T is $2x$. Adding this information to Table 1 gives

Table 2			
	Male	Female	Total
Born in Town T		$2x$	N
Not Born in Town T	x		
Total	8,000	12,000	20,000

Other cells in the table can then be filled in as shown below.

Table 3			
	Male	Female	Total
Born in Town T	$8,000 - x$	$2x$	N
Not Born in Town T	x	$12,000 - 2x$	$12,000 - x$
Total	8,000	12,000	20,000

Then, it can be seen from Table 3 that $N = (8,000 - x) + 2x = 8,000 + x$ and also that $N = 20,000 - (12,000 - x) = 8,000 + x$. However, without a value for x, the value of N cannot be determined; NOT sufficient.

(2)   Let y represent the number of female residents who were born in Town T. Then the number of female residents who were not born in Town T is $2y$. Adding this information to Table 1 gives

Table 4			
	Male	Female	Total
Born in Town T		y	N
Not Born in Town T		$2y$	
Total	8,000	12,000	20,000

From Table 4 it can be seen that $y + 2y = 12,000$, so $3y = 12,000$ and $y = 4,000$. With this value, the table can be expanded to

Table 5			
	Male	Female	Total
Born in Town T		4,000	N
Not Born in Town T		8,000	
Total	8,000	12,000	20,000

However, there is not enough information to determine the value of N; NOT sufficient.

Given (1) and (2) together, the information from Table 3, which uses the information given in (1), can be combined with Table 5, which uses the information given in (2), to obtain $2x = 4,000$. Therefore, $x = 2,000$ and thus $N = 8,000 + 2,000 = 10,000$.

The correct answer is C; both statements together are sufficient.

64.   If y is an integer, is y^3 divisible by 9 ?

(1) y is divisible by 4.
(2) y is divisible by 6.

Arithmetic Properties of numbers

The integers y and $y^3 = (y)(y)(y)$ have the same prime factors. Also, each of these prime factors appears 3 times as often in y^3 as in y. Therefore, y is divisible by 3 if and only if y^3 is divisible by 3. Also, when y is divisible by 3, then y^3 is actually divisible by $(3)(3)(3) = 27$, and hence y^3 is divisible by 9.

(1) Some multiples of 4 are divisible by 3, such as 12 ($y = 12$ is divisible by 3, hence $y^3 = 12^3$ is divisible by 27, and so $y^3 = 12^3$ is divisible by 9), and some multiples of 4 are not divisible by 3 ($y = 8$ is not divisible by 3, hence $y^3 = 8^3$ is not divisible by 3, and so $y^3 = 8^3$ certainly cannot be divisible by 9); NOT sufficient.

(2) Any number divisible by 6 is also divisible by 3, and hence the cube of this number is divisible by 9; SUFFICIENT.

The correct answer is B; statement 2 alone is sufficient.

65. In $\triangle XYZ$, what is the length of YZ?

(1) The length of XY is 3.
(2) The length of XZ is 5.

Geometry Triangles

Given the length of one side of a triangle, it is known that the sum of the lengths of the other two sides is greater than that given length. The length of either of the other two sides, however, can be any positive number.

(1) Only the length of one side, XY, is given, and that is not enough to determine the length of YZ; NOT sufficient.

(2) Again, only the length of one side, XZ, is given and that is not enough to determine the length of YZ; NOT sufficient.

Even by using the triangle inequality stated above, only a range of values for YZ can be determined from (1) and (2). If the length of side YZ is represented by k, then it is known both that $3 + 5 > k$ and that $3 + k > 5$, or $k > 2$. Combining these inequalities to determine the length of k yields only that $8 > k > 2$.

The correct answer is E; both statements together are still not sufficient.

66. If the average (arithmetic mean) of n consecutive odd integers is 10, what is the least of the integers?

(1) The range of the n integers is 14.
(2) The greatest of the n integers is 17.

Arithmetic Statistics

Let k be the least of the n consecutive odd integers. Then the n consecutive odd integers are $k, k+2, k+4, ..., k+2(n-1)$, where $k+2(n-1)$ is the greatest of the n consecutive odd integers and $[k+2(n-1)] - k = 2(n-1)$ is the range of the n consecutive odd integers. Determine the value of k.

(1) Given that the range of the odd integers is 14, it follows that $2(n-1) = 14$, or $n-1 = 7$, or $n = 8$. It is also given that the average of the 8 consecutive odd integers is 10, and so $\frac{k+(k+2)+(k+4)+...+(k+14)}{8} = 10$, from which a unique value for k can be determined; SUFFICIENT.

(2) Given that the greatest of the odd integers is 17, it follows that the n consecutive odd integers can be expressed as $17, 17-2, 17-4, ..., 17-2(n-1)$. Since the average of the n consecutive odd integers is 10, then $\frac{17+(17-2)+(17-4)+...+[17-2(n-1)]}{n} = 10,$ or

$$17+(17-2)+(17-4)+...+[17-2(n-1)] = 10n \text{ (i)}$$

The n consecutive odd integers can also be expressed as $k, k+2, k+4, ..., k+2(n-1)$. Since the average of the n consecutive odd integers is 10, then

$$\frac{k+(k+2)+(k+4)+...+[k+2(n-1)]}{n}=10,$$

or

$$k+(k+2)+(k+4)+...+[k+2(n-1)]=10n \text{ (ii)}$$

Adding equations (i) and (ii) gives

$$(17+k)+(17+k)+(17+k)+...+(17+k)=20n$$
$$n(17+k)=20n$$
$$17+k=20$$
$$k=3$$

Alternatively, because the numbers are consecutive odd integers, they form a data set that is symmetric about its average, and so the average of the numbers is the average of the least and greatest numbers. Therefore, $10=\frac{k+17}{2}$, from which a unique value for k can be determined; SUFFICIENT.

The correct answer is D; each statement alone is sufficient.

67. What was the ratio of the number of cars to the number of trucks produced by Company X last year?

(1) Last year, if the number of cars produced by Company X had been 8 percent greater, the number of cars produced would have been 150 percent of the number of trucks produced by Company X.
(2) Last year Company X produced 565,000 cars and 406,800 trucks.

Arithmetic Ratio; Percents

Let c equal the number of cars and t the number of trucks produced by Company X last year. The ratio of cars to trucks produced last year can be expressed as $\frac{c}{t}$.

(1) An 8 percent increase in the number of cars produced can be expressed as 108 percent of c, or $1.08c$. Similarly, 150 percent of the number of trucks produced can be expressed as $1.5t$. The relationship between the two can be expressed in the equation $1.08c=1.5t$. From this:

$$\frac{1.08c}{t}=1.5 \quad \text{divide both sides by } t$$
$$\frac{c}{t}=\frac{1.5}{1.08} \quad \text{divide both sides by 1.08}$$

Thus the ratio of cars to trucks produced last year can be determined; SUFFICIENT.

(2) The values of c and t are given; so the ratio $\frac{c}{t}$ can be determined; SUFFICIENT.

The correct answer is D; each statement alone is sufficient.

68. Is $xy<6$?

(1) $x<3$ and $y<2$.
(2) $\frac{1}{2}<x<\frac{2}{3}$ and $y^2<64$.

Algebra Inequalities

(1) For some values of $x<3$ and $y<2$, $xy<6$, but for other values, $xy>6$. If x and y were restricted to nonnegative values, then $xy<6$. However, if x and y were both negative and sufficiently large, xy would not be less than 6. For example, if $x=y=-3$, then xy would be $(-3)^2$, or 9, which is clearly greater than 6; NOT sufficient.

(2) This restricts x to the interval $\frac{1}{2}<x<\frac{2}{3}$ and y to the interval $-8<y<8$. Thus, the largest value possible for xy is less than $\left(\frac{2}{3}\right)(8)$, or less than $5\frac{1}{3}$, which is clearly less than 6; SUFFICIENT.

The correct answer is B; statement 2 alone is sufficient.

69. If x, y, and z are positive numbers, is $x > y > z$?

    (1) $xz > yz$
    (2) $yx > yz$

Algebra Inequalities

(1) Dividing both sides of the inequality by z yields $x > y$. However, there is no information relating z to either x or y; NOT sufficient.

(2) Dividing both sides of the inequality by y yields only that $x > z$, with no further information relating y to either x or z; NOT sufficient.

From (1) and (2) it can be determined that x is greater than both y and z. Since it still cannot be determined which of y or z is the least, the correct ordering of the three numbers also cannot be determined.

**The correct answer is E;
both statements together are still not sufficient.**

70. K is a set of numbers such that

    (i)   if x is in K, then $-x$ is in K, and
    (ii) if each of x and y is in K, then xy is in K.

    Is 12 in K ?

    (1) 2 is in K.
    (2) 3 is in K.

Arithmetic Properties of numbers

(1) Given that 2 is in K, it follows that K could be the set of all real numbers, which contains 12. However, if K is the set $\{..., -16, -8, -4, -2, 2, 4, 8, 16, ...\}$, then K contains 2 and K satisfies both (i) and (ii), but K does not contain 12. To see that K satisfies (ii), note that K can be written as $\{..., -2^4, -2^3, -2^2, -2^1, 2^1, 2^2, 2^3, 2^4, ...\}$, and thus a verification of (ii) can reduce to verifying that the sum of two positive integer exponents is a positive integer exponent; NOT sufficient.

(2) Given that 3 is in K, it follows that K could be the set of all real numbers, which contains 12. However, if K is the set $\{..., -81, -27, -9, -3, 3, 9, 27, 81, ...\}$, then K contains 3 and K satisfies both (i) and (ii), but K does not contain 12. To see that K satisfies (ii), note that K can be written as $\{..., -3^4, -3^3, -3^2, -3^1, 3^1, 3^2, 3^3, 3^4, ...\}$, and thus a verification of (ii) can reduce to verifying that the sum of two positive integer exponents is a positive integer exponent; NOT sufficient.

Given (1) and (2), it follows that both 2 and 3 are in K. Thus, by (ii), $(2)(3) = 6$ is in K. Therefore, by (ii), $(2)(6) = 12$ is in K.

**The correct answer is C;
both statements together are sufficient.**

71. How long did it take Betty to drive nonstop on a trip from her home to Denver, Colorado?

    (1) If Betty's average speed for the trip had been $1\frac{1}{2}$ times as fast, the trip would have taken 2 hours.
    (2) Betty's average speed for the trip was 50 miles per hour.

Arithmetic Distance/rate problems

The formula for calculating distance is $d = rt$, where d is the distance in miles, r is the rate (or speed) in miles per hour, and t is the time in hours.

(1) If Betty had driven $1\frac{1}{2}$ times as fast, then her driving rate would be $\frac{3}{2}r$. Thus, the distance as calculated by the faster rate is $d = \left(\frac{3}{2}r\right)(2) = 3r$. Since this is the same distance as calculated using Betty's actual driving rate, $d = rt$, it follows that $rt = 3r$. Dividing both sides of this last equation by r gives $t = 3$; SUFFICIENT.

(2) Only Betty's driving rate is given, so Betty could have driven a total of 5 minutes or a total of 3 hours; NOT sufficient.

**The correct answer is A;
statement 1 alone is sufficient.**

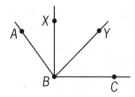

72. In the figure above, what is the measure of ∠ABC ?

    (1) BX bisects ∠ABY and BY bisects ∠XBC.
    (2) The measure of ∠ABX is 40°.

Geometry Angles

(1) From this, it can be determined that the measure of ∠ABX = the measure of ∠XBY, and the measure of ∠XBY = the measure of ∠YBC so that all three angles are equal in measure. The measure of ∠ABC cannot be determined without information on the measure of any one of the three angles; NOT sufficient.

(2) The measure of part of ∠ABC is given, but there is no information about the measure of ∠XBC; NOT sufficient.

From (1) and (2) together, it can be determined that the measure of ∠ABX = the measure of ∠XBY = the measure of ∠YBC = 40°, so ∠ABC measures $3(40) = 120°$.

The correct answer is C; both statements together are sufficient.

73. If $x^2 + y^2 = 29$, what is the value of $(x - y)^2$?

    (1) $xy = 10$
    (2) $x = 5$

Algebra Simplifying algebraic expressions

Since $(x - y)^2 = (x^2 + y^2) - 2xy$ and it is given that $x^2 + y^2 = 29$, it follows that $(x - y)^2 = 29 - 2xy$.

Therefore, the value of $(x - y)^2$ can be determined if and only if the value of xy can be determined.

(1) Since the value of xy is given, the value of $(x - y)^2$ can be determined; SUFFICIENT.

(2) Given only that $x = 5$, it is not possible to determine the value of xy. Therefore, the value of $(x - y)^2$ cannot be determined; NOT sufficient.

The correct answer is A; statement 1 alone is sufficient.

74. If x, y, and z are numbers, is $z = 18$?

    (1) The average (arithmetic mean) of x, y, and z is 6.
    (2) $x = -y$

Arithmetic Statistics

(1) From this, it is known that $\frac{x + y + z}{3} = 6$ or, when both sides are multiplied by 3, $x + y + z = 18$.

Since nothing is known about the value of $x + y$, no conclusion can be drawn about the value of z; NOT sufficient.

(2) This implies that $x + y = 0$ but gives no further information about the values of x, y, and z; NOT sufficient.

Taking (1) and (2) together is sufficient since 0 can be substituted for $x + y$ in the equation $x + y + z = 18$ to yield $z = 18$.

The correct answer is C; both statements together are sufficient.

75. After winning 50 percent of the first 20 games it played, Team A won all of the remaining games it played. What was the total number of games that Team A won?

    (1) Team A played 25 games altogether.
    (2) Team A won 60 percent of all the games it played.

Arithmetic Percents

Let r be the number of the remaining games played, all of which the team won. Since the team won $(50\%)(20) = 10$ of the first 20 games and the r remaining games, the total number of games the team won is $10 + r$. Also, the total number of games the team played is $20 + r$. Determine the value of r.

(1) Given that the total number of games played is 25, it follows that $20 + r = 25$, or $r = 5$; SUFFICIENT.

(2) It is given that the total number of games won is $(60\%)(20 + r)$, which can be expanded as $12 + 0.6r$. Since it is also known that the number of games won is $10 + r$, it follows that $12 + 0.6r = 10 + r$. Solving this equation gives $12 - 10 = r - 0.6r$, or $2 = 0.4r$, or $r = 5$; SUFFICIENT.

**The correct answer is D;
each statement alone is sufficient.**

76. Is x between 0 and 1?

(1) x^2 is less than x.
(2) x^3 is positive.

Arithmetic Arithmetic operations

(1) Since x^2 is always positive, it follows that here x must also be positive, that is, greater than 0. Furthermore, if x is greater than 1, then x^2 is greater than x. If $x = 0$ or 1, then $x^2 = x$. Therefore, x must be between 0 and 1; SUFFICIENT.

(2) If x^3 is positive, then x is positive, but x can be any positive number; NOT sufficient.

**The correct answer is A;
statement 1 alone is sufficient.**

77. A jar contains 30 marbles, of which 20 are red and 10 are blue. If 9 of the marbles are removed, how many of the marbles left in the jar are red?

(1) Of the marbles removed, the ratio of the number of red ones to the number of blue ones is 2:1.
(2) Of the first 6 marbles removed, 4 are red.

Arithmetic Discrete probability

(1) Of the 9 marbles removed, the ratio of red to blue was 2 to 1; thus 6 red and 3 blue marbles were removed. Since there were originally 20 red marbles in the jar, the number of red marbles remaining in the jar is $20 - 6 = 14$; SUFFICIENT.

(2) Knowing that 4 of the first 6 marbles removed were red does not tell us how many of the other 3 marbles removed were red. It cannot be determined how many red marbles were left in the jar; NOT sufficient.

**The correct answer is A;
statement 1 alone is sufficient.**

78. Is p^2 an odd integer?

(1) p is an odd integer.
(2) $\sqrt{p}$ is an odd integer.

Arithmetic Properties of numbers

The product of two or more odd integers is always odd.

(1) Since p is an odd integer, $p \times p = p^2$ is an odd integer; SUFFICIENT.

(2) If $\sqrt{p}$ is an odd integer, then $\sqrt{p} \times \sqrt{p} = p$ is an odd integer. Therefore, $p \times p = p^2$ is also an odd integer; SUFFICIENT.

**The correct answer is D;
each statement alone is sufficient.**

79. If m and n are nonzero integers, is m^n an integer?

(1) n^m is positive.
(2) n^m is an integer.

Arithmetic Properties of numbers

It is useful to note that if $m > 1$ and $n < 0$, then $0 < m^n < 1$, and therefore m^n will not be an integer. For example, if $m = 3$ and $n = -2$, then $m^n = 3^{-2} = \frac{1}{3^2} = \frac{1}{9}$.

(1) Although it is given that n^m is positive, m^n can be an integer or m^n can fail to be an integer. For example, if $m = 2$ and $n = 2$, then $n^m = 2^2 = 4$ is positive and $m^n = 2^2 = 4$ is an integer. However, if $m = 2$ and $n = -2$, then $n^m = (-2)^2 = 4$ is positive and $m^n = 2^{-2} = \frac{1}{2^2} = \frac{1}{4}$ is not an integer; NOT sufficient.

(2) Although it is given that n^m is an integer, m^n can be an integer or m^n can fail to be an integer. For example, if $m = 2$ and $n = 2$, then $n^m = 2^2 = 4$ is an integer and $m^n = 2^2 = 4$ is an integer. However, if $m = 2$ and $n = -2$, then $n^m = (-2)^2 = 4$ is an integer and $m^n = 2^{-2} = \frac{1}{2^2} = \frac{1}{4}$ is not an integer; NOT sufficient.

Taking (1) and (2) together, it is still not possible to determine if m^n is an integer, since the same examples are used in both (1) and (2) above.

**The correct answer is E;
both statements together are still not sufficient.**

80. What is the value of xy?

   (1) $x + y = 10$
   (2) $x - y = 6$

**Algebra First- and second-degree equations;
Simultaneous equations**

(1) Given $x + y = 10$, or $y = 10 - x$, it follows that $xy = x(10 - x)$, which does not have a unique value. For example, if $x = 0$, then $xy = (0)(10) = 0$, but if $x = 1$, then $xy = (1)(9) = 9$; NOT sufficient.

(2) Given $x - y = 6$, or $y = x - 6$, it follows that $xy = x(x - 6)$, which does not have a unique value. For example, if $x = 0$, then $xy = (0)(-6) = 0$, but if $x = 1$, then $xy = (1)(-5) = -5$; NOT sufficient.

Using (1) and (2) together, the two equations can be solved simultaneously for x and y. One way to do this is by adding the two equations, $x + y = 10$ and $x - y = 6$, to get $2x = 16$, or $x = 8$. Then substitute $x = 8$ into either of the equations to obtain an equation that can be solved to get $y = 2$. Thus, xy can be determined to have the value $(8)(2) = 16$. Alternatively, the two equations correspond to a pair of nonparallel lines in the (x,y) coordinate plane, which have a unique point in common.

**The correct answer is C;
both statements together are sufficient.**

81. Is x^2 greater than x?

   (1) x^2 is greater than 1.
   (2) x is greater than -1.

Arithmetic; Algebra Exponents; Inequalities

(1) Given $x^2 > 1$, it follows that either $x > 1$ or $x < -1$. If $x > 1$, then multiplying both sides of the inequality by the positive number x gives $x^2 > x$. On the other hand, if $x < -1$, then x is negative and x^2 is positive (because $x^2 > 1$), which also gives $x^2 > x$; SUFFICIENT.

(2) Given $x > -1$, x^2 can be greater than x (for example, $x = 2$) and x^2 can fail to be greater than x (for example, $x = 0$); NOT sufficient.

**The correct answer is A;
statement 1 alone is sufficient.**

82. Michael arranged all his books in a bookcase with 10 books on each shelf and no books left over. After Michael acquired 10 additional books, he arranged all his books in a new bookcase with 12 books on each shelf and no books left over. How many books did Michael have before he acquired the 10 additional books?

   (1)   Before Michael acquired the 10 additional books, he had fewer than 96 books.
   (2)   Before Michael acquired the 10 additional books, he had more than 24 books.

Arithmetic Properties of numbers

If x is the number of books Michael had before he acquired the 10 additional books, then x is a multiple of 10. After Michael acquired the 10 additional books, he had $x + 10$ books and $x + 10$ is a multiple of 12.

(1) If $x < 96$, where x is a multiple of 10, then $x = 10, 20, 30, 40, 50, 60, 70, 80,$ or 90 and $x + 10 = 20, 30, 40, 50, 60, 70, 80, 90,$ or 100. Since $x + 10$ is a multiple of 12, then $x + 10 = 60$ and $x = 50$; SUFFICIENT.

(2)   If $x > 24$, where x is a multiple of 10, then x must be one of the numbers 30, 40, 50, 60, 70, 80, 90, 100, 110, …, and $x + 10$ must be one of the numbers 40, 50, 60, 70, 80, 90, 100, 110, 120, …. Since there is more than one multiple of 12 among these numbers (for example, 60 and 120), the value of $x + 10$, and therefore the value of x, cannot be determined; NOT sufficient.

**The correct answer is A;
statement 1 alone is sufficient.**

83.   If $xy > 0$, does $(x-1)(y-1) = 1$?

(1) $x + y = xy$
(2) $x = y$

Algebra First- and second-degree equations

By expanding the product $(x-1)(y-1)$, the question is equivalent to whether $xy - y - x + 1 = 1$, or $xy - y - x = 0$, when $xy > 0$.

(1)   If $x + y = xy$, then $xy - y - x = 0$, and hence by the remarks above, $(x-1)(y-1) = 1$; SUFFICIENT.

(2)   If $x = y$, then $(x-1)(y-1) = 1$ can be true $(x = y = 2)$ and $(x-1)(y-1) = 1$ can be false $(x = y = 1)$; NOT sufficient.

**The correct answer is A;
statement 1 alone is sufficient.**

84.   The only contents of a parcel are 25 photographs and 30 negatives. What is the total weight, in ounces, of the parcel's contents?

(1)   The weight of each photograph is 3 times the weight of each negative.
(2)   The total weight of 1 of the photographs and 2 of the negatives is $\frac{1}{3}$ ounce.

Algebra Simultaneous equations

Let p and n denote the weight, in ounces, of a photograph and a negative, respectively, and let W denote the total weight of the parcel's contents in ounces. Then the total weight of the parcel's contents can be expressed as $W = 25p + 30n$.

(1)   This information can be written as $p = 3n$. When $3n$ is substituted for p in the above equation, $W = 25(3n) + 30n$, the equation cannot be solved for W because there is no way to discover the value of n; NOT sufficient.

(2)   This information can be written as $p + 2n = \frac{1}{3}$, or $p = \frac{1}{3} - 2n$. After substituting for p, the equation $W = 25\left(\frac{1}{3} - 2n\right) + 30n$ cannot be solved for W because again there is no way to discover the value of n. Similarly, the equation $p + 2n = \frac{1}{3}$ is also equivalent to $2n = \frac{1}{3} - p$, or $n = \frac{1}{6} - \frac{p}{2}$. After substituting for n, the equation $W = 25p + 30\left(\frac{1}{6} - \frac{p}{2}\right)$ cannot be solved for W because there is no way to discover the value of p; NOT sufficient.

The two linear equations from (1) and (2) can be solved simultaneously for p and n, since $p = 3n$ and $p + 2n = \frac{1}{3}$, where $3n$ can be substituted for p. Thus, by substitution $(3n) + 2n = \frac{1}{3}$, by simplification $5n = \frac{1}{3}$, and by division of both sides by 5 then $n = \frac{1}{15}$. This value of n, $\frac{1}{15}$, can in turn be substituted in $p = 3n$, and a value of $\frac{1}{5}$ can be determined for p. Using these values of n and p, it is possible to solve the equation $W = 25p + 30n$ and answer the original question about the total weight of the parcel's contents.

**The correct answer is C;
both statements together are sufficient.**

85.   Last year in a group of 30 businesses, 21 reported a net profit and 15 had investments in foreign markets. How many of the businesses did not report a net profit nor invest in foreign markets last year?

(1)   Last year 12 of the 30 businesses reported a net profit and had investments in foreign markets.
(2)   Last year 24 of the 30 businesses reported a net profit or invested in foreign markets, or both.

Arithmetic Statistics

Consider the Venn diagram below in which x represents the number of businesses that reported a net profit and had investments in foreign markets. Since 21 businesses reported a net profit, $21 - x$ businesses reported a net profit only. Since 15 businesses had investments in foreign markets, $15 - x$ businesses had investments in foreign markets only. Finally, since there is a total of 30 businesses, the number of businesses that did not report a net profit and did not invest in foreign markets is $30 - (21 - x + x + 15 - x) = x - 6$. Determine the value of $x - 6$, or equivalently, the value of x.

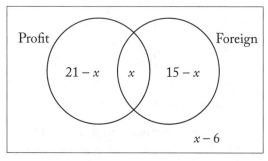

(1) It is given that $12 = x$; SUFFICIENT.

(2) It is given that $24 = (21 - x) + x + (15 - x)$. Therefore, $24 = 36 - x$, or $x = 12$.

   Alternatively, the information given is exactly the number of businesses that are not among those to be counted in answering the question posed in the problem, and therefore the number of businesses that are to be counted is $30 - 24 = 6$; SUFFICIENT.

**The correct answer is D;
each statement alone is sufficient.**

86. If m and n are consecutive positive integers, is m greater than n?

   (1) $m - 1$ and $n + 1$ are consecutive positive integers.
   (2) m is an even integer.

Arithmetic Properties of numbers

For two integers x and y to be consecutive, it is both necessary and sufficient that $|x - y| = 1$.

(1) Given that $m - 1$ and $n + 1$ are consecutive integers, it follows that $|(m - 1) - (n + 1)| = 1$, or $|m - n - 2| = 1$. Therefore, $m - n - 2 = 1$ or $m - n - 2 = -1$. The former equation implies that $m - n = 3$, which contradicts the fact that m and n are consecutive integers. Therefore, $m - n - 2 = -1$, or $m = n + 1$, and hence $m > n$; SUFFICIENT.

(2) If $m = 2$ and $n = 1$, then m is greater than n. However, if $m = 2$ and $n = 3$, then m is not greater than n; NOT sufficient.

**The correct answer is A;
statement 1 alone is sufficient.**

87. If k and n are integers, is n divisible by 7?

   (1) $n - 3 = 2k$
   (2) $2k - 4$ is divisible by 7.

Arithmetic Properties of numbers

(1) This is equivalent to the equation $n = 2k + 3$. By picking various integers to be the value of k, it can be shown that for some values of k (e.g., $k = 2$), $2k + 3$ is divisible by 7, and for some other values of k (e.g., $k = 1$), $2k + 3$ is not divisible by 7; NOT sufficient.

(2) While $2k - 4$ is divisible by 7, this imposes no constraints on the integer n, and therefore n could be divisible by 7 (e.g., $n = 7$) and n could be not divisible by 7 (e.g., $n = 8$); NOT sufficient.

Applying both (1) and (2), it is possible to answer the question. From (1), it follows that $n - 3$ can be substituted for $2k$. Carrying this out in (2), it follows that $(n - 3) - 4$, or $n - 7$, is divisible by 7. This means that $n - 7 = 7q$ for some integer q. It follows that $n = 7q + 7 = 7(q + 1)$, and so n is divisible by 7.

**The correct answer is C;
both statements together are sufficient.**

88. Is the perimeter of square S greater than the perimeter of equilateral triangle T?

    (1) The ratio of the length of a side of S to the length of a side of T is 4:5.
    (2) The sum of the lengths of a side of S and a side of T is 18.

Geometry Perimeter

Letting s and t be the side lengths of square S and triangle T, respectively, the task is to determine if $4s > 3t$, which is equivalent (divide both sides by $4t$) to determining if $\dfrac{s}{t} > \dfrac{3}{4}$.

(1) It is given that $\dfrac{s}{t} = \dfrac{4}{5}$. Since $\dfrac{4}{5} > \dfrac{3}{4}$, it follows that $\dfrac{s}{t} > \dfrac{3}{4}$; SUFFICIENT.

(2) Many possible pairs of numbers have the sum of 18. For some of these (s,t) pairs it is the case that $\dfrac{s}{t} > \dfrac{3}{4}$ (for example, $s = t = 9$), and for others of these pairs it is not the case that $\dfrac{s}{t} > \dfrac{3}{4}$ (for example, $s = 1$ and $t = 17$); NOT sufficient.

The correct answer is A; statement 1 alone is sufficient.

89. If $x + y + z > 0$, is $z > 1$?

    (1) $z > x + y + 1$
    (2) $x + y + 1 < 0$

Algebra Inequalities

(1) The inequality $x + y + z > 0$ gives $z > -x - y$. Adding this last inequality to the given inequality, $z > x + y + 1$, gives $2z > 1$, or $z > \dfrac{1}{2}$, which suggests that (1) is not sufficient. Indeed, z could be 2 ($x = y = 0$ and $z = 2$ satisfy both $x + y + z > 0$ and $z > x + y + 1$), which is greater than 1, and z could be $\dfrac{3}{4}$ ($x = y = -\dfrac{1}{4}$ and $z = \dfrac{3}{4}$ satisfy both $x + y + z > 0$ and $z > x + y + 1$), which is not greater than 1; NOT sufficient.

(2) It follows from the inequality $x + y + z > 0$ that $z > -(x + y)$. It is given that $x + y + 1 < 0$, or $(x + y) < -1$, or $-(x + y) > 1$. Therefore, $z > -(x + y)$ and $-(x + y) > 1$, from which it follows that $z > 1$; SUFFICIENT.

The correct answer is B; statement 2 alone is sufficient.

90. Can the positive integer n be written as the sum of two different positive prime numbers?

    (1) n is greater than 3.
    (2) n is odd.

Arithmetic Properties of numbers

The prime numbers are 2, 3, 5, 7, 11, 13, 17, 19, etc., that is, those integers $p > 1$ whose only positive factors are 1 and p.

(1) If $n = 5$, then n can be written as the sum of two different primes $(5 = 2 + 3)$. If $n = 4$, however, then n cannot be written as the sum of two different primes. (Note that while $4 = 1 + 3 = 2 + 2$, neither of these sums satisfies both requirements of the question.) This value of n does not allow an answer to be determined; NOT sufficient.

(2) While some odd integers can be written as the sum of two different primes (e.g., $5 = 2 + 3$), others cannot (e.g., 11). This value of n does not allow an answer to be determined; NOT sufficient.

Since the sum of two odd integers is always even, for an odd integer greater than 3 to be the sum of two prime numbers, one of those prime numbers must be an even number. The only even prime number is 2. Thus, the only odd integers that can be expressed as the sum of two different prime numbers are those for which $n - 2$ is an odd prime number. Using the example of 11 (an odd integer greater than 3), $11 - 2 = 9$, which is not a prime number. Statements (1) and (2) together do not define n well enough to determine the answer.

The correct answer is E; both statements together are still not sufficient.

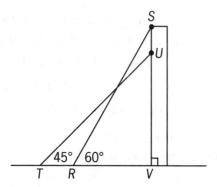

91. In the figure above, segments *RS* and *TU* represent two positions of the same ladder leaning against the side *SV* of a wall. The length of *TV* is how much greater than the length of *RV*?

    (1) The length of *TU* is 10 meters.
    (2) The length of *RV* is 5 meters.

Geometry Triangles

The Pythagorean theorem $\left(a^2 + b^2 = c^2\right)$ can be applied here. Since the triangle *TUV* is a $45° - 45° - 90°$ triangle, the lengths of the sides are in the ratio $1:1:\sqrt{2}$; so the length of any one side determines the length of the other two sides. Similarly, the triangle *RSV* is a $30° - 60° - 90°$ triangle with the lengths of the sides in the ratio $1:\sqrt{3}:2$; so the length of any one side determines the length of the other two sides. Also, the length of the hypotenuse is the same in both triangles, because it is the length of the ladder. Hence, the length of any one side of either triangle determines the lengths of all sides of both triangles.

(1) Since the length of one side of triangle *TUV* is given, the length of any side of either triangle can be found. Therefore, the difference between *TV* and *RV* can also be found; SUFFICIENT.

(2) Since the length of one side of triangle *RSV* is given, the length of any side of either triangle can be found. Therefore, the difference between *TV* and *RV* can also be found; SUFFICIENT.

**The correct answer is D;
both statements alone are sufficient.**

92. Is the integer *x* divisible by 36 ?

    (1) *x* is divisible by 12.
    (2) *x* is divisible by 9.

Arithmetic Properties of numbers

When discussing divisibility, it is helpful to express a number as the product of prime factors. The integer 36 can be expressed as the product of prime numbers, i.e., $36 = 2 \times 2 \times 3 \times 3$. If *x* is divisible by 36, it would follow that when *x* is expressed as a product of prime numbers, this product would contain at least two 2s and two 3s (from the prime factorization of 36).

(1) The prime factorization of 12 is $12 = 2 \times 2 \times 3$, which implies that the prime factorization of *x* contains at least two 2s and at least one 3. This does not contain at least two 2s and two 3s, but does not exclude these factors, either; NOT sufficient.

(2) The prime factorization of 9 is $9 = 3 \times 3$, which implies that the prime factorization of *x* contains at least two 3s. Again, this does not contain at least two 2s and two 3s, but does not exclude these factors, either; NOT sufficient.

However, both (1) and (2) together imply that the prime factorization of *x* contains at least two 2s (1) and two 3s (2), so *x* must be divisible by 36.

**The correct answer is C;
both statements together are sufficient.**

Cancellation Fees	
Days Prior to Departure	Percent of Package Price
46 or more	10%
45–31	35%
30–16	50%
15–5	65%
4 or fewer	100%

93. The table above shows the cancellation fee schedule that a travel agency uses to determine the fee charged to a tourist who cancels a trip prior to departure. If a tourist canceled a trip with a package price of $1,700 and a departure date of September 4, on what day was the trip canceled?

    (1) The cancellation fee was $595.
    (2) If the trip had been canceled one day later, the cancellation fee would have been $255 more.

Arithmetic Percents

(1) The cancellation fee given is $\frac{\$595}{\$1,700} = 35\%$ of the package price, which is the percent charged for cancellation 45–31 days prior to the departure date of September 4. However, there is no further information to determine exactly when within this interval the trip was cancelled; NOT sufficient.

(2) This implies that the increase in the cancellation fee for canceling one day later would have been $\frac{\$255}{\$1,700} = 15\%$ of the package price. The cancellation could thus have occurred either 31 days or 16 days prior to the departure date of September 4 because the cancellation fee would have increased by that percentage either 30 days before departure or 15 days before departure. However, there is no further information to establish whether the interval before departure was 31 days or 16 days; NOT sufficient.

Taking (1) and (2) together establishes that the trip was canceled 31 days prior to September 4.

The correct answer is C; both statements together are sufficient.

94. What is the value of $\frac{x}{yz}$?

    (1) $x = \frac{y}{2}$ and $z = \frac{2x}{5}$.
    (2) $\frac{x}{z} = \frac{5}{2}$ and $\frac{1}{y} = \frac{1}{10}$.

Algebra Evaluating expressions

(1) From this, z can be expressed in terms of y by substituting $\frac{y}{2}$ for x in the equation $z = \frac{2x}{5}$, which gives $z = \frac{2\left(\frac{y}{2}\right)}{5} = \frac{y}{5}$. The value of $\frac{x}{yz}$ in terms of y is then $\frac{\frac{y}{2}}{y\left(\frac{y}{5}\right)} = \frac{y}{2}\left(\frac{5}{y^2}\right) = \frac{5}{2y}$. This expression cannot be evaluated further since no information is given about the value of y; NOT sufficient.

(2) Because $\frac{x}{yz} = \left(\frac{1}{y}\right)\left(\frac{x}{z}\right)$ by substitution the given information can be stated as $\left(\frac{1}{10}\right)\left(\frac{5}{2}\right)$ or $\frac{1}{4}$; SUFFICIENT.

The correct answer is B; statement 2 alone is sufficient.

95. If P and Q are each circular regions, what is the radius of the larger of these regions?

    (1) The area of P plus the area of Q is equal to 90π.
    (2) The larger circular region has a radius that is 3 times the radius of the smaller circular region.

Geometry Circles

The area of a circle with a radius of r is equal to πr^2. For this problem, let r represent the radius of the smaller circular region, and let R represent the radius of the larger circular region.

(1) This can be expressed as $\pi r^2 + \pi R^2 = 90\pi$. Dividing both sides of the equation by π gives $r^2 + R^2 = 90$, but this is not nough information to determine R; NOT sufficient.

(2)   This can be expressed as $R = 3r$, which by itself is not enough to determine R; NOT sufficient.

Using (1) and (2), the value of R, or the radius of the larger circular region, can be determined. In (2), $R = 3r$, and thus $r = \dfrac{R}{3}$. Therefore, $\dfrac{R}{3}$ can be substituted for r in the equation $\pi r^2 + \pi R^2 = 90\pi$ from (1). The result is the equation $\pi\left(\dfrac{R}{3}\right)^2 + \pi R^2 = 90\pi$ that can be solved for a unique value of R^2, and thus for a unique positive value of R. Remember that it is only necessary to establish the sufficiency of the data; there is no need to actually find the value of R.

The correct answer is C; both statements together are sufficient.

96.   For all z, $\lceil z \rceil$ denotes the least integer greater than or equal to z. Is $\lceil x \rceil = 0$?

(1) $-1 < x < -0.1$
(2) $\lceil x + 0.5 \rceil = 1$

Algebra Operations with real numbers

Determining if $\lceil x \rceil = 0$ is equivalent to determining if $-1 < x \le 0$. This can be inferred by examining a few representative examples, such as $\lceil -1.1 \rceil = -1$, $\lceil -1 \rceil = -1$, $\lceil -0.9 \rceil = 0$, $\lceil -0.1 \rceil = 0$, $\lceil 0 \rceil = 0$, and $\lceil 0.1 \rceil = 1$.

(1)   Given $-1 < x < -0.1$, it follows that $-1 < x \le 0$, since $-1 < x \le 0$ represents all numbers x that satisfy $-1 < x < -0.1$ along with all numbers x that satisfy $-0.1 \le x \le 0$; SUFFICIENT.

(2)   Given $\lceil x + 0.5 \rceil = 1$, it follows from the same reasoning used just before (1) above that this equality is equivalent to $0 < x + 0.5 \le 1$, which in turn is equivalent to $-0.5 < x \le 0.5$. Since from among these values of x it is possible for $-1 < x \le 0$ to be true (for example, $x = -0.1$) and it is possible for $-1 < x \le 0$ to be false (for example, $x = 0.1$), it cannot be determined if $\lceil x \rceil = 0$; NOT sufficient.

The correct answer is A; statement 1 alone is sufficient.

97.   If Aaron, Lee, and Tony have a total of $36, how much money does Tony have?

(1)   Tony has twice as much money as Lee and $\frac{1}{3}$ as much as Aaron.
(2)   The sum of the amounts of money that Tony and Lee have is half the amount that Aaron has.

Algebra Applied problems; Equations

(1)   From this, it can be determined that if Lee has x dollars, then Tony has $2x$ dollars, Aaron has $6x$ dollars, and together they have $9x = 36$ dollars. The last equation has a unique solution, $x = 4$, and hence the amount that Tony has can be determined: $(2)(4) = 8$ dollars; SUFFICIENT.

(2)   If the sum of the amounts that Tony and Lee have is y dollars, then Aaron has $2y$ dollars, and y can be determined ($3y = 36$, or $y = 12$). However, the individual amounts for Tony and Lee cannot be determined; NOT sufficient.

The correct answer is A; statement 1 alone is sufficient.

98.   Is z less than 0?

(1) $xy > 0$ and $yz < 0$.
(2) $x > 0$

Arithmetic Properties of numbers

When multiplying positive and negative numbers, that is, numbers greater than 0 and numbers less than 0, the products must always be (positive)(positive) = positive, (negative)(negative) = positive, and (negative)(positive) = negative.

(1)   Many sets of values consistent with this statement can be found when using values of z that are greater than or less than 0. For example, for the set of values $x = 1$, $y = 1$, $z = -1$, $z < 0$ and for the set of values $x = -1$, $y = -1$, $z = 1$, $z > 0$; NOT sufficient.

(2)   This gives no information about z or y, and the information about x is not useful in determining the positive or negative value of the other variables; NOT sufficient.

Taken together, since from (1) $xy > 0$, and from (2) $x > 0$, y must also be greater than 0, that is, positive. Then, since $y > 0$ and from (1) $yz < 0$, it can be concluded that z must be negative, or less than 0, since the product of yz is negative.

**The correct answer is C;
both statements together are sufficient.**

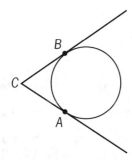

99.   The circular base of an above-ground swimming pool lies in a level yard and just touches two straight sides of a fence at points A and B, as shown in the figure above. Point C is on the ground where the two sides of the fence meet. How far from the center of the pool's base is point A?

(1)   The base has area 250 square feet.
(2)   The center of the base is 20 feet from point C.

Geometry Circles

Let Q be the center of the pool's base and r be the distance from Q to A, as shown in the figure below.

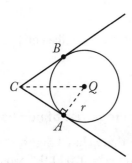

Since A is a point on the circular base, QA is a radius (r) of the base.

(1)   Since the formula for the area of a circle is Area $= \pi r^2$, this information can be stated as $250 = \pi r^2$ or $\sqrt{\dfrac{250}{\pi}} = r$; SUFFICIENT.

(2)   Since $\overline{CA}$ is tangent to the base, ΔQAC is a right triangle. It is given that $QC = 20$, but there is not enough information to use the Pythagorean theorem to determine the length of $\overline{QA}$; NOT sufficient.

**The correct answer is A;
statement 1 alone is sufficient.**

100.   If $xy = -6$, what is the value of $xy(x+y)$?

(1) $x - y = 5$
(2) $xy^2 = 18$

Algebra First- and second-degree equations

By substituting -6 as the value of xy, the question can be simplified to "What is the value of $-6(x+y)$?"

(1)   Adding y to both sides of $x - y = 5$ gives $x = y + 5$. When $y + 5$ is substituted for x in the equation $xy = -6$, the equation yields $(y+5)y = -6$, or $y^2 + 5y + 6 = 0$. Factoring the left side of this equation gives $(y+2)(y+3) = 0$. Thus, y may have a value of -2 or -3. Since a unique value of y is not determined, neither the value of x nor the value of xy can be determined; NOT sufficient.

(2)   Since $xy^2 = (xy)y$ and $xy^2 = 18$, it follows that $(xy)y = 18$. When -6 is substituted for xy, this equation yields $-6y = 18$, and hence $y = -3$. Since $y = -3$ and $xy = -6$, it follows that $-3x = -6$, or $x = 2$. Therefore, the value of $x + y$, and hence the value of $xy(x+y) = -6(x+y)$ can be determined; SUFFICIENT.

**The correct answer is B;
statement 2 alone is sufficient.**

101. If the average (arithmetic mean) of 4 numbers is 50, how many of the numbers are greater than 50 ?

    (1) None of the four numbers is equal to 50.
    (2) Two of the numbers are equal to 25.

Arithmetic Statistics

Let w, x, y, and z be the four numbers. The average of these 4 numbers can be represented by the following equation:

$$\frac{w + x + y + z}{4} = 50.$$

(1) The only information about the 4 numbers is that none of the numbers is equal to 50. The 4 numbers could be 25, 25, 26, and 124, which have an average of 50, and only 1 of the numbers would be greater than 50. The 4 numbers could also be 25, 25, 75, and 75, which have an average of 50, and 2 of the numbers would be greater than 50; NOT sufficient.

(2) Each of the examples in (1) has exactly 2 numbers equal to 25; NOT sufficient.

Taking (1) and (2) together, the examples in (1) also illustrate the insufficiency of (2). Thus, there is more than one possibility for how many numbers are greater than 50.

The correct answer is E; both statements together are still not sufficient.

102. $[y]$ denotes the greatest integer less than or equal to y. Is $d < 1$?

    (1) $d = y - [y]$
    (2) $[d] = 0$

Algebra Operations with real numbers

(1) It is given $d = y - [y]$. If y is an integer, then $y = [y]$, and thus $y - [y] = 0$, which is less than 1. If y is not an integer, then y lies between two consecutive integers, the smaller of which is equal to $[y]$. Since each of these two consecutive integers is at a distance of less than 1 from y, it follows that $[y]$ is at a distance of less than 1 from y, or $y - [y] < 1$. Thus, regardless of whether y is an integer or y is not an integer, it can be determined that $d < 1$; SUFFICIENT.

(2) It is given that $[d] = 0$, which is equivalent to $0 \le d < 1$. This can be inferred by examining a few representative examples, such as $[-0.1] = -1$, $[0] = 0$, $[0.1] = 0$, $[0.9] = 0$, and $[1.1] = 1$. From $0 \le d < 1$, it follows that $d < 1$; SUFFICIENT.

The correct answer is D; each statement alone is sufficient.

103. If x is a positive number less than 10, is z greater than the average (arithmetic mean) of x and 10 ?

    (1) On the number line, z is closer to 10 than it is to x.
    (2) $z = 5x$

Arithmetic; Algebra Statistics; Inequalities

(1) The average of x and 10, which is $\frac{x + 10}{2}$, is the number (or point) midway between x and 10 on the number line. Since z is closer to 10 than to x, z must lie between $\frac{x + 10}{2}$ and 10, be equal to 10, or be greater than 10. In each of these cases z is greater than the average of x and 10; SUFFICIENT.

(2) If, for example, $x = 1$, then $z = 5$. The average of x and 10 is $\frac{1 + 10}{2} = 5.5$, which is greater than z. If, however, $x = 1.6$, then $z = 8$, and the average of 1.6 and 10 is $\frac{1.6 + 10}{2} = 5.8$, which is less than z; NOT sufficient.

The correct answer is A; statement 1 alone is sufficient.

104. If m is a positive integer, then m^3 has how many digits?

    (1) m has 3 digits.
    (2) m^2 has 5 digits.

Arithmetic Properties of numbers

(1) Given that m has 3 digits, then m could be 100 and $m^3 = 1,000,000$ would have 7 digits, or m could be 300 and $m^3 = 27,000,000$ would have 8 digits; NOT sufficient.

(2) Given that m^2 has 5 digits, then m could be 100 (because $100^2 = 10,000$ has 5 digits) or m could be 300 (because $300^2 = 90,000$ has 5 digits). In the former case, $m^3 = 1,000,000$ has 7 digits and in the latter case, $m^3 = 27,000,000$ has 8 digits; NOT sufficient.

Given (1) and (2), it is still possible for m to be 100 or for m to be 300, and thus m^3 could have 7 digits or m^3 could have 8 digits.

**The correct answer is E;
both statements together are still not sufficient.**

105. If $t \neq 0$, is r greater than zero?

(1) $rt = 12$

(2) $r + t = 7$

Arithmetic; Algebra Arithmetic operations;
Properties of numbers; Simultaneous equations

(1) If $r = 3$ and $t = 4$, then $rt = 12$ and r is greater than zero. However, if $r = -3$ and $t = -4$, then $rt = 12$ and r is not greater than zero; NOT sufficient.

(2) If $r = 3$ and $t = 4$, then $r + t = 7$ and r is greater than zero. However, if $r = -3$ and $t = 10$, then $r + t = 7$ and r is not greater than zero; NOT sufficient.

If (1) and (2) are considered together, the system of equations can be solved to show that r must be positive. From (2), since $r + t = 7$, then $t = 7 - r$. Substituting $7 - r$ for t in the equation of (1) gives

$$rt = 12$$
$$r(7 - r) = 12$$
$$7r - r^2 = 12$$
$$r^2 - 7r + 12 = 0$$
$$(r - 3)(r - 4) = 0$$

Thus, $r = 3$ or $r = 4$. Therefore, 3 and 4 are the only possible values of r, each of which is positive.

**The correct answer is C;
both statements together are sufficient.**

106. If $kmn \neq 0$, is $\frac{x}{m}(m^2 + n^2 + k^2) = xm + yn + zk$?

(1) $\frac{z}{k} = \frac{x}{m}$

(2) $\frac{x}{m} = \frac{y}{n}$

Algebra First- and second-degree equations

The equation $\frac{x}{m}(m^2 + n^2 + k^2) = xm + yn + zk$ can be manipulated to obtain the following equivalent equations:

$x(m^2 + n^2 + k^2) = m(xm + yn + zk)$	multiply both sides by m
$xm^2 + xn^2 + xk^2 = m^2x + myn + mzk$	remove parentheses
$xn^2 + xk^2 = myn + mzk$	subtract xm^2

(1) When cross multiplied, $\frac{z}{k} = \frac{x}{m}$ becomes $xk = mz$, or $xk^2 = mzk$ when both sides are then multiplied by k. Thus, the equation $xn^2 + xk^2 = myn + mzk$ is equivalent to the equation $xn^2 = myn$, and hence equivalent to the equation $xn = my$, which can be true or false, depending on the values of x, n, m, and y; NOT sufficient.

(2) When cross multiplied, $\frac{x}{m} = \frac{y}{n}$ becomes $xn = my$, or $xn^2 = myn$ when both sides are then multiplied by n. Thus, the equation $xn^2 + xk^2 = myn + mzk$ is equivalent to the equation $xk^2 = mzk$, and hence equivalent to the equation $xk = mz$, which can be true or false, depending on the values of x, k, m, and z; NOT sufficient.

Combining the information in both (1) and (2), it follows from (1) that $xn^2 + xk^2 = myn + mzk$ is equivalent to $xn = my$, which is true by (2).

**The correct answer is C;
both statements together are sufficient.**

107. The sequence $s_1, s_2, s_3, \ldots, s_n, \ldots$ is such that $s_n = \dfrac{1}{n} - \dfrac{1}{n+1}$ for all integers $n \geq 1$. If k is a positive integer, is the sum of the first k terms of the sequence greater than $\dfrac{9}{10}$?

    (1) $k > 10$
    (2) $k < 19$

Arithmetic Sequences

The sum of the first k terms can be written as

$$\left(\frac{1}{1} - \frac{1}{2}\right) + \left(\frac{1}{2} - \frac{1}{3}\right) + \ldots + \left(\frac{1}{k-1} - \frac{1}{k}\right) + \left(\frac{1}{k} - \frac{1}{k+1}\right)$$

$$= 1 + \left(-\frac{1}{2} + \frac{1}{2}\right) + \left(-\frac{1}{3} + \frac{1}{3}\right) + \ldots + \left(-\frac{1}{k} + \frac{1}{k}\right) - \frac{1}{k+1}$$

$$= 1 - \frac{1}{k+1}.$$

Therefore, the sum of the first k terms is greater than $\dfrac{9}{10}$ if and only if $1 - \dfrac{1}{k+1} > \dfrac{9}{10}$, or $1 - \dfrac{9}{10} > \dfrac{1}{k+1}$, or $\dfrac{1}{10} > \dfrac{1}{k+1}$. Multiplying both sides of the last inequality by $10(k+1)$ gives the equivalent condition $k + 1 > 10$, or $k > 9$.

    (1) Given that $k > 10$, then it follows that $k > 9$; SUFFICIENT.

    (2) Given that $k < 19$, it is possible to have $k > 9$ (for example, $k = 15$) and it is possible to not have $k > 9$ (for example, $k = 5$); NOT sufficient.

**The correct answer is A;
statement 1 alone is sufficient.**

108. A bookstore that sells used books sells each of its paperback books for a certain price and each of its hardcover books for a certain price. If Joe, Maria, and Paul bought books in this store, how much did Maria pay for 1 paperback book and 1 hardcover book?

    (1) Joe bought 2 paperback books and 3 hardcover books for $12.50.
    (2) Paul bought 4 paperback books and 6 hardcover books for $25.00.

Algebra Applied problems

Let p be the price, in dollars, for each paperback book and let h be the price, in dollars, for each hardcover book. Determine the value of $p + h$.

    (1) From this, Joe's purchase can be expressed as $2p + 3h = 12.50$, or $2(p + h) + h = 12.50$. Therefore, $p + h = \dfrac{12.50 - h}{2}$, whose value can vary. For example, if $p = 1.75$ and $h = 3$, then $2p + 3h = 12.50$ and $p + h = 4.75$. On the other hand, if $p = 1.00$ and $h = 3.5$, then $2p + 3h = 12.50$ and $p + h = 4.50$; NOT sufficient.

    (2) From this, Paul's purchase can be expressed as $4p + 6h = 25.00$. If both sides of this equation are divided by 2, it gives exactly the same equation as in (1); NOT sufficient.

Since (1) and (2) yield equivalent equations that do not determine the value of $p + h$, taken together they do not determine the total cost of 1 paperback book and 1 hardcover book.

**The correct answer is E;
both statements together are still not sufficient.**

109. If x, y, and z are positive, is $x = \dfrac{y}{z^2}$?

    (1) $z = \dfrac{y}{xz}$
    (2) $z = \sqrt{\dfrac{y}{x}}$

Algebra First- and second-degree equations

Since $z \neq 0$, determining if $x = \dfrac{y}{z^2}$ is true is equivalent to determining if $xz^2 = y$ is true.

    (1) Since $xz \neq 0$, an equivalent equation can be obtained by multiplying both sides of $z = \dfrac{y}{xz}$ by xz. The resulting equation is $xz^2 = y$; SUFFICIENT.

(2) Since $z > 0$, an equivalent equation can be obtained by squaring both sides of $z = \sqrt{\dfrac{y}{x}}$. This gives $z^2 = \dfrac{y}{x}$. Since $x \neq 0$, an equivalent equation can be obtained by multiplying both sides of $z^2 = \dfrac{y}{x}$ by x. The resulting equation is $xz^2 = y$; SUFFICIENT.

The correct answer is D; each statement alone is sufficient.

110. If n is an integer between 2 and 100 and if n is also the square of an integer, what is the value of n?

(1) n is even.
(2) The cube root of n is an integer.

Arithmetic Properties of numbers

(1) If n is even, there are several possible even values of n that are squares of integers and are between 2 and 100, namely, 4, 16, 36, and 64; NOT sufficient.

(2) If the cube root of n is an integer, it means that n must not only be the square of an integer but also the cube of an integer. There is only one such value of n between 2 and 100, which is 64; SUFFICIENT.

The correct answer is B; statement 2 alone is sufficient.

111. In the sequence S of numbers, each term after the first two terms is the sum of the two immediately preceding terms. What is the 5th term of S?

(1) The 6th term of S minus the 4th term equals 5.
(2) The 6th term of S plus the 7th term equals 21.

Arithmetic Sequences

If the first two terms of sequence S are a and b, then the remaining terms of sequence S can be expressed in terms of a and b as follows.

n	nth term of sequence S
1	a
2	b
3	$a + b$
4	$a + 2b$
5	$2a + 3b$
6	$3a + 5b$
7	$5a + 8b$

For example, the 6th term of sequence S is $3a + 5b$ because $(a + 2b) + (2a + 3b) = 3a + 5b$. Determine the value of the 5th term of sequence S, that is, the value of $2a + 3b$.

(1) Given that the 6th term of S minus the 4th term of S is 5, it follows that $(3a + 5b) - (a + 2b) = 5$. Combining like terms, this equation can be rewritten as $2a + 3b = 5$, and thus the 5th term of sequence S is 5; SUFFICIENT.

(2) Given that the 6th term of S plus the 7th term of S is 21, it follows that $(3a + 5b) + (5a + 8b) = 21$. Combining like terms, this equation can be rewritten as $8a + 13b = 21$. Letting e represent the 5th term of sequence S, this last equation is equivalent to $4(2a + 3b) + b = 21$, or $4e + b = 21$, which gives a direct correspondence between the 5th term of sequence S and the 2nd term of sequence S. Therefore, the 5th term of sequence S can be determined if and only if the 2nd term of sequence S can be determined. Since the 2nd term of sequence S cannot be determined, the 5th term of sequence S cannot be determined. For example, if $a = 1$ and $b = 1$, then $8a + 13b = 8(1) + 13(1) = 21$ and the 5th term of sequence S is $2a + 3b = 2(1) + 3(1) = 5$. However, if $a = 0$ and $b = \dfrac{21}{13}$, then $8a + 13b = 8(0) + 13\left(\dfrac{21}{13}\right) = 21$ and the 5th term of sequence S is $2a + 3b = 2(0) + 3\left(\dfrac{21}{13}\right) = \dfrac{63}{13}$; NOT sufficient.

**The correct answer is A;
statement 1 alone is sufficient.**

112. For a certain set of n numbers, where $n > 1$, is the average (arithmetic mean) equal to the median?

    (1)   If the n numbers in the set are listed in increasing order, then the difference between any pair of successive numbers in the set is 2.

    (2)   The range of the n numbers in the set is $2(n-1)$.

Arithmetic Statistics

Let b be the least of the n numbers and B be the greatest of the n numbers.

(1)   If n is odd, then the median is the middle number. Thus, when arranged in increasing order and letting m be the median, the set of n numbers can be represented by $b, \ldots,$ $m - 4, m - 2, m, m + 2, m + 4, \ldots, B$. Notice that this set consists of the number m and $\dfrac{n-1}{2}$ pairs of numbers of the form $m - 2a$ and $m + 2a$, where $a = 1, 2, \ldots, \dfrac{n-1}{2}$, $b = m - (n - 1)$, and $B = m + (n - 1)$. The sum of each pair is $(m - 2a) + (m + 2a) = 2m$ and the sum of all $\left(\dfrac{n-1}{2}\right)$ pairs is $\left(\dfrac{n-1}{2}\right)(2m) = m(n - 1) = mn - m$. Then, the sum of all n numbers is $(mn - m) + m = mn$. Thus, the average of the n numbers is $\dfrac{mn}{n} = m$, which is the median of the n numbers.

If n is even, the median is the average of the two middle numbers. Letting m and $m + 2$ be the two middle numbers, the median is $\dfrac{m + (m + 2)}{2} = \dfrac{2m + 2}{2} = \dfrac{2(m + 1)}{2} = m + 1.$

Then, when arranged in increasing order, the set of n numbers can be represented by $b,$ $b + 2, \ldots, m - 4, m - 2, m, m + 2, m + 4,$ $m + 6, \ldots, B - 2, B$. Notice that this set consists of $\dfrac{n}{2}$ pairs of numbers of the form

$m - 2(a - 1)$ and $m + 2a$, where $a = 1,$ $2, \ldots, \dfrac{n}{2}, b = m - (n - 2),$ and $B = m + n.$

The sum of each pair is $\left[m - 2(a - 1)\right] + \left[m + 2a\right] = 2m + 2 = 2(m + 1)$ and the sum of all $\dfrac{n}{2}$ pairs is $\dfrac{n}{2}\left[2(m + 1)\right] = n(m + 1)$. Thus, the average of the n numbers is $\dfrac{n(m + 1)}{n} = m + 1$, which is the median of the n numbers; SUFFICIENT.

(2)   The range is the difference between the least and greatest numbers. Knowing the range, however, does not give information about the rest of the numbers affecting the average and the median. For example, if $n = 3$, then the range of the three numbers is 4, since $2(3 - 1) = 4$. However, the numbers could be 2, 4, 6, for which the average and median are both equal to 4, or the numbers could be 2, 3, 6, for which the average is $3\dfrac{2}{3}$ and the median is 3; NOT sufficient.

**The correct answer is A;
statement 1 alone is sufficient.**

113. If d is a positive integer, is $\sqrt{d}$ an integer?

    (1) d is the square of an integer.

    (2) $\sqrt{d}$ is the square of an integer.

Arithmetic Properties of numbers

The square of an integer must also be an integer.

(1)   This can be expressed as $d = x^2$, where x is a nonzero integer. Then, $\sqrt{d} = \sqrt{x^2}$ which in turn equals x or $-x$, depending on whether x is a positive integer or a negative integer, respectively. In either case, $\sqrt{d}$ is also an integer; SUFFICIENT.

(2)   This can be expressed as $\sqrt{d} = x^2$, where x is a nonzero integer. The square of an integer (x^2) must always be an integer; therefore, $\sqrt{d}$ must also be an integer; SUFFICIENT.

The correct answer is D; each statement alone is sufficient.

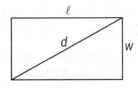

114.   What is the area of the rectangular region above?

(1) $\ell + w = 6$

(2) $d^2 = 20$

Geometry Area

The area of the rectangular region is ℓw and the Pythagorean theorem states that $d^2 = \ell^2 + w^2$.

(1)   Subtracting w from both sides of $\ell + w = 6$ gives $\ell = 6 - w$. If this value for ℓ is substituted in the equation $A = \ell w$, the area can be expressed in terms of w by $A = (6 - w)w$. However, more than one possible value for the area can be obtained by using different values of w between 0 and 6, and thus the value of the area cannot be determined; NOT sufficient.

(2)   It is given that $d^2 = 20$, or $\ell^2 + w^2 = 20$. However, this restriction on the values of ℓ and w is not sufficient to determine the value of ℓw. For example, if $\ell = 1$ and $w = \sqrt{19}$, then $\ell^2 + w^2 = 1^2 + \left(\sqrt{19}\right)^2 = 1 + 19 = 20$ and $\ell w = \sqrt{19}$. However, if $\ell = 2$ and $w = 4$, then $\ell^2 + w^2 = 2^2 + 4^2 = 4 + 16 = 20$ and $\ell w = 8$; NOT sufficient.

Given (1) and (2) together, it follows that $\ell + w = 6$ and $\ell^2 + w^2 = 20$. One way to find the value of ℓw is to solve this system of equations for both ℓ and w and then compute their product. Substitute $6 - w$ for ℓ in $\ell^2 + w^2 = 20$ to obtain $(6 - w)^2 + w^2 = 20$, or $36 - 12w + w^2 + w^2 = 20$, or $w^2 - 6w + 8 = 0$. Factoring the left side of the last equation gives $(w - 2)(w - 4) = 0$, and so w can have a value of 2 or a value of 4. Hence, using $\ell = 6 - w$, two solutions for ℓ and w are possible: $\ell = 4$, $w = 2$ and $\ell = 2$, $w = 4$. In each case, $\ell w = 8$, so the value of the area can be determined. Another way to find the value of ℓw is to first square both sides of $\ell + w = 6$, which gives $\ell^2 + w^2 + 2\ell w = 36$. Next, using $\ell^2 + w^2 = 20$, this last equation becomes $20 + 2\ell w = 36$, from which it follows that $\ell w = 8$.

The correct answer is C; both statements together are sufficient.

115.   Is the positive integer n a multiple of 24 ?

(1) n is a multiple of 4.

(2) n is a multiple of 6.

Arithmetic Properties of numbers

(1)   This says only that n is a multiple of 4 (i.e., n could be 8 or 24), some of which would be multiples of 24 and some would not; NOT sufficient.

(2)   This says only that n is a multiple of 6 (i.e., n could be 12 or 48), some of which would be multiples of 24 and some would not; NOT sufficient.

Both statements together imply only that n is a multiple of the least common multiple of 4 and 6. The smallest integer that is divisible by both 4 and 6 is 12. Some of the multiples of 12 (e.g., n could be 48 or 36) are also multiples of 24, but some are not.

The correct answer is E; both statements together are still not sufficient.

116. If 75 percent of the guests at a certain banquet ordered dessert, what percent of the guests ordered coffee?

    (1) 60 percent of the guests who ordered dessert also ordered coffee.
    (2) 90 percent of the guests who ordered coffee also ordered dessert.

Arithmetic Statistics

Consider the Venn diagram below that displays the various percentages of 4 groups of the guests. Thus, x percent of the guests ordered both dessert and coffee and y percent of the guests ordered coffee only. Since 75 percent of the guests ordered dessert, $(75 - x)\%$ of the guests ordered dessert only. Also, because the 4 percentages represented in the Venn diagram have a total sum of 100 percent, the percentage of guests who did not order either dessert or coffee is $100 - \left[(75 - x) + x + y\right] = 25 - y$. Determine the percentage of guests who ordered coffee, or equivalently, the value of $x + y$.

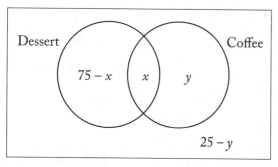

    (1) Given that x is equal to 60 percent of 75, or 45, the value of $x + y$ cannot be determined; NOT sufficient.

    (2) Given that 90 percent of $x + y$ is equal to x, it follows that $0.9(x + y) = x$, or $9(x + y) = 10x$. Therefore, $9x + 9y = 10x$, or $9y = x$. From this the value of $x + y$ cannot be determined. For example, if $x = 9$ and $y = 1$, then all 4 percentages in the Venn diagram are between 0 and 100, $9y = x$, and $x + y = 10$. However, if $x = 18$ and $y = 2$, then all 4 percentages in the Venn diagram are between 0 and 100, $9y = x$, and $x + y = 20$; NOT sufficient.

Given both (1) and (2), it follows that $x = 45$ and $9y = x$. Therefore, $9y = 45$, or $y = 5$, and hence $x + y = 45 + 5 = 50$.

The correct answer is C;
both statements together are sufficient.

117. A tank containing water started to leak. Did the tank contain more than 30 gallons of water when it started to leak? (Note: 1 gallon = 128 ounces)

    (1) The water leaked from the tank at a constant rate of 6.4 ounces per minute.
    (2) The tank became empty less than 12 hours after it started to leak.

Arithmetic Rate problems

    (1) Given that the water leaked from the tank at a constant rate of 6.4 ounces per minute, it is not possible to determine if the tank leaked more than 30 gallons of water. In fact, any nonzero amount of water leaking from the tank is consistent with a leakage rate of 6.4 ounces per minute, since nothing can be determined about the amount of time the water was leaking from the tank; NOT sufficient.

    (2) Given that the tank became empty in less than 12 hours, it is not possible to determine if the tank leaked more than 30 gallons of water because the rate at which water leaked from the tank is unknown. For example, the tank could have originally contained 1 gallon of water that emptied in exactly 10 hours or the tank could have originally contained 31 gallons of water that emptied in exactly 10 hours; NOT sufficient.

Given (1) and (2) together, the tank emptied at a constant rate of

$$\left(6.4\frac{oz}{min}\right)\left(60\frac{min}{hr}\right)\left(\frac{1}{128}\frac{gal}{oz}\right)=\frac{(64)(6)}{128}\frac{gal}{hr}=$$

$$\frac{(64)(6)}{(64)(2)}\frac{gal}{hr}=3\frac{gal}{hr}\text{ for less than 12 hours.}$$

If t is the total number of hours the water leaked from the tank, then the total amount of water emptied from the tank, in gallons, is $3t$, which is therefore less than $(3)(12)=36$. From this it is not possible to determine if the tank originally contained more than 30 gallons of water. For example, if the tank leaked water for a total of 11 hours, then the tank originally contained $(3)(11)$ gallons of water, which is more than 30 gallons of water. However, if the tank leaked water for a total of 2 hours, then the tank originally contained $(3)(2)$ gallons of water, which is not more than 30 gallons of water.

**The correct answer is E;
both statements together are still not sufficient.**

118. If x is an integer, is y an integer?

(1) The average (arithmetic mean) of x, y, and $y-2$ is x.
(2) The average (arithmetic mean) of x and y is <u>not</u> an integer.

Arithmetic Statistics; Properties of numbers

(1) From this, it is known that

$$\frac{x+y+(y-2)}{3}=x\text{, or:}$$

$x+y+y-2=3x$ multiply both sides by 3

$2y-2=2x$ combine like terms; subtract x from both sides

$y-1=x$ divide both sides by 2

This simplifies to $y=x+1$. Since x is an integer, this equation shows that x and y are consecutive integers; SUFFICIENT.

(2) According to this, y might be an integer (e.g., $x=5$ and $y=6$, with an average of 5.5), or y might not be an integer (e.g., $x=5$ and $y=6.2$, with an average of 5.6); NOT sufficient.

**The correct answer is A;
statement 1 alone is sufficient.**

119. In the fraction $\frac{x}{y}$, where x and y are positive integers, what is the value of y?

(1) The least common denominator of $\frac{x}{y}$ and $\frac{1}{3}$ is 6.
(2) $x=1$

Arithmetic Properties of numbers

(1) From this, $\frac{x}{y}$ can be $\frac{x}{2}$ or $\frac{x}{6}$, but there is no way to know whether $y=2$ or $y=6$; NOT sufficient.

(2) From this, y could be any positive integer; NOT sufficient.

If both (1) and (2) are taken together, $\frac{x}{y}=\frac{1}{2}$ or $\frac{1}{6}$, and again y is either 2 or 6.

**The correct answer is E;
both statements together are still not sufficient.**

120. Is $\frac{1}{a-b}<b-a$?

(1) $a<b$
(2) $1<|a-b|$

Arithmetic; Algebra Arithmetic operations; Inequalities

(1) From this, it is known that $\frac{1}{a-b}$ is negative and $b-a$ is positive. Therefore, $\frac{1}{a-b}<b-a$; SUFFICIENT.

(2) From this statement that the absolute value of $a-b$ is greater than 1, $a-b$ could be either positive or negative. If $a-b$ is positive, then $b-a$ is negative and $\frac{1}{a-b}>b-a$. However, if $a-b$ is negative, then $b-a$ is positive and $\frac{1}{a-b}<b-a$. For example, if $a=7$ and $b=4$, then $\frac{1}{3}>-3$, but if $a=4$ and $b=7$, then $-\frac{1}{3}<3$; NOT sufficient.

**The correct answer is A;
statement 1 alone is sufficient.**

121. If x and y are nonzero integers, is $x^y < y^x$?

(1) $x = y^2$

(2) $y > 2$

Arithmetic; Algebra Arithmetic operations; Inequalities

It is helpful to note that $\left(x^r\right)^s = x^{rs}$.

(1) Given $x = y^2$, then $x^y = \left(y^2\right)^y = y^{2y}$ and $y^x = y^{y^2}$. Compare x^y to y^x by comparing y^{2y} to y^{y^2} or, when the base y is greater than 1, by comparing the exponents $2y$ and y^2. If $y = 3$, then $2y = 6$ is less than $y^2 = 9$, and hence x^y would be less than y^x. However, if $y = 2$, then $2y = 4$ is not less than $y^2 = 4$, and hence x^y would not be less than y^x; NOT sufficient.

(2) It is known that $y > 2$, but no information about x is given. For example, let $y = 3$. If $x = 1$, then $x^y = 1^3 = 1$ is less than $y^x = 3^1 = 3$, but if $x = 3$, then $x^y = 3^3$ is not less than $y^x = 3^3$; NOT sufficient.

If both (1) and (2) are taken together, then from (1) $2y$ is compared to y^2 and from (2) it is known that $y > 2$. Since $2y < y^2$ when $y > 2$, it follows that $x^y < y^x$.

The correct answer is C; both statements together are sufficient.

122. If 2 different representatives are to be selected at random from a group of 10 employees and if p is the probability that both representatives selected will be women, is $p > \frac{1}{2}$?

(1) More than $\frac{1}{2}$ of the 10 employees are women.

(2) The probability that both representatives selected will be men is less than $\frac{1}{10}$.

Arithmetic Probability

Let m and w be the numbers of men and women in the group, respectively. Then $m + w = 10$ and the probability that both representatives selected will be a woman is $p =$

$$\left(\frac{\text{\# of women}}{\text{\# of people}}\right)\left(\frac{\text{\# of women after 1 woman is removed}}{\text{\# of people after 1 woman is removed}}\right)$$

$= \left(\frac{w}{10}\right)\left(\frac{w-1}{9}\right)$. Therefore, determining if $p > \frac{1}{2}$ is equivalent to determining if $\left(\frac{w}{10}\right)\left(\frac{w-1}{9}\right) > \frac{1}{2}$. Multiplying both sides by $(10)(9)(2)$ gives the equivalent condition $2w(w-1) > 90$, or $w(w-1) > 45$. By considering the values of $(2)(1)$, $(3)(2)$, ..., $(10)(9)$, it follows that $p > \frac{1}{2}$ if and only if w is equal to 8, 9, or 10.

(1) Given that $w > 5$, it is possible that w is equal to 8, 9, or 10 (for example, $w = 8$) and it is possible that w is not equal to 8, 9, or 10 (for example, $w = 7$); NOT sufficient.

(2) Given the probability that both selections will be men is less than $\frac{1}{10}$, it follows that $\left(\frac{m}{10}\right)\left(\frac{m-1}{9}\right) < \frac{1}{10}$. Multiplying both sides by $(9)(10)$ gives $m(m-1) < 9$. Thus, by numerical evaluation, the only possibilities for m are 0, 1, 2, and 3. Therefore, the only possibilities for w are 10, 9, 8, or 7. However, it is still possible that w is equal to 8, 9, or 10 (for example, $w = 8$) and it is still possible that w is not equal to 8, 9, or 10 (for example, $w = 7$); NOT sufficient.

Given (1) and (2), it is not possible to determine if w is equal to 8, 9, or 10. For example, if $w = 8$, then both (1) and (2) are true and w is equal to 8, 9, or 10. However, if $w = 7$, then both (1) and (2) are true and w is not equal to 8, 9, or 10.

The correct answer is E; both statements together are still not sufficient.

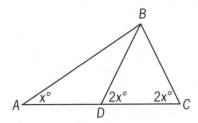

123. In triangle *ABC* above, what is the length of side *BC* ?

    (1)   Line segment *AD* has length 6.
    (2) $x = 36$

Geometry Triangles

The degree measure of an exterior angle of a triangle is equal to the sum of the remote interior angles. Note that angle *BDC* (with an angle measure of $2x$) is an exterior angle of triangle *ADB* and has an angle measure equal to the sum of the remote interior angles *ABD* and *DAB*. Thus, if angle *ABD* has measure $y°$, then $x + y = 2x$, or when simplified, $y = x$. Since two angles of triangle *ABD* are equal, then the sides opposite these angles have the same length and $AD = DB$. For the same reason $DB = BC$. If $AD = DB$ and $DB = BC$, then $AD = BC$.

    (1)   If $AD = 6$, then BC must also equal 6; SUFFICIENT.

    (2)   Since this gives no information about the length of any line segments, the length of side *BC* cannot be determined; NOT sufficient.

**The correct answer is A;
statement 1 alone is sufficient.**

124. If $rs \neq 0$, is $\dfrac{1}{r} + \dfrac{1}{s} = 4$?

    (1) $r + s = 4rs$
    (2) $r = s$

Algebra First- and second-degree equations

    (1)   Dividing each side of the equation $r + s = 4rs$ by rs gives $\dfrac{r+s}{rs} = \dfrac{4rs}{rs}$, or $\dfrac{r}{rs} + \dfrac{s}{rs} = \dfrac{4rs}{rs}$, or $\dfrac{1}{s} + \dfrac{1}{r} = 4$; SUFFICIENT.

    (2)   If $r = s = \dfrac{1}{2}$, then $\dfrac{1}{r} + \dfrac{1}{s} = 4$, but if $r = s = 1$, then $\dfrac{1}{s} + \dfrac{1}{r} = 2$; NOT sufficient.

**The correct answer is A;
statement 1 alone is sufficient.**

Appendix A   Percentile Ranking Tables

Verbal and Quantitative scores range from 0 to 60. Verbal scores below 9 and above 44 and Quantitative scores below 7 and above 50 are rare. Verbal and Quantitative scores measure different skills and cannot be compared with one another.

Your Total score is based on your performance in the Verbal and Quantitative sections and ranges from 200 to 800. About two-thirds of test-takers score between 400 and 600.

VERBAL SCORE

Percentage Ranking*	Score
99%	45–51
98%	44
96%	42
93%	41
90%	40
88%	39
84%	38
82%	37
80%	36
75%	35
70%	34
68%	33
65%	32
60%	31
57%	30
55%	29
50%	28
45%	27 — 27.3 Mean Score
42%	26
37%	25
35%	24
31%	23
29%	22
25%	21
21%	20
18%	19
17%	18
14%	17
11%	16
9%	15
8%	14
7%	13
4%	12
3%	11
2%	9–10
1%	7–8
0%	0–6

Sample Size: 794,601
Standard Deviation: 9.12

QUANTITATIVE SCORE

Percentage Ranking*	Score
97%	51–60
89%	50
81%	49
76%	48
70%	47
68%	46
66%	45
61%	44
58%	43
54%	42
52%	41
50%	40
46%	39
44%	38 — 37.5 Mean Score
42%	37
38%	36
35%	35
33%	34
31%	33
28%	32
25%	31
24%	30
22%	29
21%	29
19%	28
17%	27
16%	26
13%	25
12%	24
11%	23
9%	21–22
8%	20
7%	19
6%	18
5%	17
4%	14–16
3%	13
2%	10–12
1%	7–9
0%	0–6

Sample Size: 794,601
Standard Deviation: 11.00

TOTAL SCORE

Percentage Ranking*	Score
99%	760–800
98%	750
97%	740
96%	730
94%	720
92%	710
89%	700
87%	690
85%	680
83%	670
80%	660
77%	650
73%	640
71%	630
68%	620
65%	610
62%	600
58%	590
55%	580
52%	570
49%	560
46%	550 — 545.6 Mean Score
43%	540
39%	530
37%	520
35%	510
32%	500
30%	490
27%	480
25%	470
22%	460
20%	450
18%	440
17%	430
15%	420
14%	410
12%	400
11%	390
10%	380
9%	370
8%	360
6%	340–350
5%	330
4%	310–320
3%	280–300
2%	250–270
1%	220–240
0%	200–210

Sample Size: 794,601
Standard Deviation: 121.07

* **Percentage Ranking** indicates the percentage of the test-taking population that scored below a given numerical score.

Analytical Writing Assessment scores range from 0 to 6 and represent the average of the rating from the two independent scores. Because the essay is scored so differently from the Verbal and Quantitative sections, essay scores are not included in your Total score.

Integrated Reasoning (IR) scores range from 1-8, in single-digit intervals. The IR section was introduced on June 5, 2012, and is not an adaptive test. Results are based on the number of questions answered correctly. IR Percentile rankings are updated more frequently to reflect the increasing pool of IR scores.

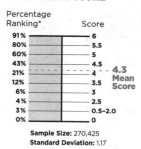

ANALYTICAL WRITING ASSESSMENT SCORE

Percentage Ranking*	Score	
91%	6	
80%	5.5	
60%	5	
43%	4.5	
21%	4	4.3 Mean Score
12%	3.5	
6%	3	
4%	2.5	
3%	0.5-2.0	
0%	0	

Sample Size: 270,425
Standard Deviation: 1.17

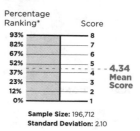

INTEGRATED REASONING SCORE

Percentage Ranking*	Score	
93%	8	
82%	7	
67%	6	
52%	5	4.34 Mean Score
37%	4	
23%	3	
12%	2	
0%	1	

Sample Size: 196,712
Standard Deviation: 2.10

Your Analytical Writing Assessment and Integrated Reasoning scores are computed and reported separately from the other sections of the test and have no effect on your Verbal, Quantitative, or Total scores.

Appendix B   Answer Sheets

Problem Solving Answer Sheet

1.	37.	73.	109.	145.
2.	38.	74.	110.	146.
3.	39.	75.	111.	147.
4.	40.	76.	112.	148.
5.	41.	77.	113.	149.
6.	42.	78.	114.	150.
7.	43.	79.	115.	151.
8.	44.	80.	116.	152.
9.	45.	81.	117.	153.
10.	46.	82.	118.	154.
11.	47.	83.	119.	155.
12.	48.	84.	120.	156.
13.	49.	85.	121.	157.
14.	50.	86.	122.	158.
15.	51.	87.	123.	159.
16.	52.	88.	124.	160.
17.	53.	89.	125.	161.
18.	54.	90.	126.	162.
19.	55.	91.	127.	163.
20.	56.	92.	128.	164.
21.	57.	93.	129.	165.
22.	58.	94.	130.	166.
23.	59.	95.	131.	167.
24.	60.	96.	132.	168.
25.	61.	97.	133.	169.
26.	62.	98.	134.	170.
27.	63.	99.	135.	171.
28.	64.	100.	136.	172.
29.	65.	101.	137.	173.
30.	66.	102.	138.	174.
31.	67.	103.	139.	175.
32.	68.	104.	140.	176.
33.	69.	105.	141.	
34.	70.	106.	142.	
35.	71.	107.	143.	
36.	72.	108.	144.	

Data Sufficiency Answer Sheet

1.	32.	63.	94.
2.	33.	64.	95.
3.	34.	65.	96.
4.	35.	66.	97.
5.	36.	67.	98.
6.	37.	68.	99.
7.	38.	69.	100.
8.	39.	70.	101.
9.	40.	71.	102.
10.	41.	72.	103.
11.	42.	73.	104.
12.	43.	74.	105.
13.	44.	75.	106.
14.	45.	76.	107.
15.	46.	77.	108.
16.	47.	78.	109.
17.	48.	79.	110.
18.	49.	80.	111.
19.	50.	81.	112.
20.	51.	82.	113.
21.	52.	83.	114.
22.	53.	84.	115.
23.	54.	85.	116.
24.	55.	86.	117.
25.	56.	87.	118.
26.	57.	88.	119.
27.	58.	89.	120.
28.	59.	90.	121.
29.	60.	91.	122.
30.	61.	92.	123.
31.	62.	93.	124.